SCOUSE REPUBLIC

SCOUSE REPUBLIC

David Swift

CONSTABLE

CONSTABLE

First published in Great Britain in 2025 by Constable

1 3 5 7 9 10 8 6 4 2

Copyright © David Swift, 2025

A CIP catalogue record for this book
is available from the British Library.

ISBN: 978-1-40871-970-1 (hardback)

Typeset in Minion Pro by SX Composing DTP, Rayleigh, Essex
Printed and bound in Great Britain by Clays Ltd, Elcograf S.p.A.

Papers used by Constable are from well-managed forests
and other responsible sources.

Constable
An imprint of
Little, Brown Book Group
Carmelite House
50 Victoria Embankment
London EC4Y 0DZ

The authorised representative
in the EEA is
Hachette Ireland
8 Castlecourt Centre, Dublin 15,
D15 XTP3, Ireland
(email: info@hbgi.ie)

An Hachette UK Company
www.hachette.co.uk

www.littlebrown.co.uk

For my parents, Marie and Gary Swift

CONTENTS

PROLOGUE

When I got married a few years ago, I gave a tour of Liverpool to relatives and friends from outside the city. Armed with a sports umbrella to signal my authority, I started off at the Philharmonic pub, with the obligatory trip to the men's toilets (to see their Grade I-listed marble magnificence, not for any nefarious reasons).

After walking to the far end of Hope Street, we went down into St James' Gardens, a small park in the shadow of the Anglican cathedral. Gazing up at that vast edifice, it's a fit spot for the contemplation of the sublime, though occasionally interrupted by a smackheads' brawl.

We then went down Duke Street, past the Chinese arch – the largest in the world outside of China – and past the bombed-out church, where I dispensed tales of late nights waiting for taxis and pointed out the cars of drug dealers idling in Bold Place.

Down to Matthew Street, which in the early afternoon on a Friday was perhaps not the best place to take my wife's Israeli relatives: the sight of middle-aged men and women blackout drunk by 3 p.m. is unusual in Israel, even on Purim.

We finally arrived at the Pier Head, where I pointed out the UK's largest clock faces and explained the lore of the Liver Birds.

Three years later, a thousand far-right protestors took to the same spot, where their protest turned into a riot, with bricks, bottles and flares thrown at the police. Later on, another mob attacked immigrant or minority-owned businesses on Walton's County Road, and even set fire to a library and community centre. In one particularly depressing video, widely circulated on social media, a man stood in the middle of the road, preventing a fire engine from reaching the scene to extinguish the blaze.

Those Merseyside riots – the one at the Pier Head came four days after a mosque was attacked in the nearby town of Southport – triggered a week of violent disorder, which spread to towns and cities across England and Northern Ireland. Mosques were besieged, immigrant neighbourhoods attacked and hotels set alight. There were over a thousand arrests, and at least 130 police officers injured, many of them seriously.

But just three weeks earlier, Southport had elected its first ever Labour MP. For the first time, every single Merseyside seat was held by Labour. And since those constituencies are so demographically different to the other Labour strongholds – much whiter and older, with fewer graduates and private renters – it seemed proof that Scousers did things differently, that here was a 'white working class' that rejected the nationalism and anti-migrant politics that was flourishing elsewhere in the country.

But we shouldn't have been surprised; only sixteen months earlier, a smaller-scale riot kicked off in the Knowsley area of the city, outside a hotel housing asylum seekers, which again saw a police van set on fire.

In those two disturbances, Liverpool proved not only that it is not immune to the kinds of ugly paranoia and ethno-nationalism affecting broad sections of the British public, but that it was a trendsetter; a place where the first two anti-immigrant riots of the twenty-first century took place.

Of course, this is only part of the story. After the Southport riot, hundreds of Scousers took to the streets of Liverpool to protect the city's Quilliam Mosque – the first mosque in the UK, established in 1887 – from anti-Islam protestors. The imam, Adam Kelwick, garnered international media attention for engaging with the protestors, speaking with them, offering food, and physically embracing some individuals. A week after the riot took place, over a thousand people marched in solidarity with refugees and asylum seekers. The coverage of the attack on the Spellow Hub library in Walton brought in over £250,000 in donations, and within months of the fire it had been repaired and renewed with thousands of additional books, donated from far and wide.

Liverpool, therefore, is a city that contains many contradictions, but which is often simplified in the eyes of outsiders. For some people, Scousers are all left-wing, anti-Tory, anti-nationalist, counter-cultural and community-minded; for others, we are impoverished thieves with an insufferable sense of grievance.

This is nothing new. Throughout its long and varied history, the city has consistently been reduced to simplistic images: the slave trade, Irish immigrants, sectarian strife, the Beatles, poverty, football hooligans, victims.

It certainly punches well above its weight in terms of fame and infamy within modern Britain. There are over 67 million people in the UK, and only about half a million in Liverpool (plus another couple of hundred thousand in the Merseyside area). Therefore, if things were proportionate, Liverpool and its citizens would occupy only about one hundredth of the stories in the media. You may have noticed that this isn't the case.

Whether it's trade-union barons, cage fighters, drag queens (two of the five winners of *Ru Paul's Drag Race UK* have been from Liverpool) or the plethora of professional football players and managers the city churns out, you might be forgiven for thinking we hear about Liverpool more often that we should.

Why is this? And why is it that we don't hear so much about the numerous Tory MPs and business executives that hail from the city?

The current identity of the city of Liverpool is, after all, a very recent creation. In 1925, an unlikely group of men gathered for the inaugural meeting of the Society of Lovers of Old Liverpool. Dedicated to 'the study of the history, traditions and development of Liverpool', this diverse crew included a journalist, an Irish Nationalist MP, an ex-policeman, and a docker. This society was founded during a time of change in the city. Sensing that their town's pre-eminence might be on the point of epochal change, their founding manifesto proclaimed that 'Liverpool's story is the world's glory':

> For over a century Liverpool has been the advance agent of Civilization; our record as a pioneer of thought, of national, nay of world-service, is so splendid that any cultivated man who knows the history of the great cities of Old Time – Athens, Rome, Bagdad, Constantinople, Paris and London, and measures our efforts against theirs, then this city, the pioneer of railways, nursing, lending libraries, blind asylums, ocean liners, cold storage, the city through which the virile life of the old world has flowed to fertilise the new, this, the chief city of New Time can inspire its sons and daughters to be worthy of the nobility, sacrifice, and endeavour of their fathers, and our Society can play its part by keeping alive the story of our city's past glories, of the wonders of the present, and so prepare the way for the wonders of the future.

The elites who dominated Liverpool at this time, during the height of its commercial and municipal power, had visions of 'Liverpolis', the Florence of northern England, a separate city state, free from the filth and industry of the rest of the North, a wealthy trading fiefdom, where profits were selflessly reinvested into scholarship and civic works.

The legacy of this vision can be seen today in the Athenian panorama of William Brown Street, spanning from St George's Hall to the Walker Art Gallery, the Central Library and World Museum.

But exactly sixty years after the Lovers of Old Liverpool first met, when the then Prime Minister Margaret Thatcher arrived at a dusty airport in Indonesia, she was met with chants of 'Liverpool! Liverpool!' from waiting students. By now the city had a different kind of fame – the chants were in reference to the Thatcher government's dispute with the left-wing city council.

This reflected the transformation of the city from the physical manifestation of the free trade ideas set out in Adam Smith's *The Wealth of Nations*, based on enterprise and innovation, to something entirely different, focused on the NHS and the public sector.

This transformation was summed up in a recent tweet by *Fans Supporting Foodbanks*, ahead of a Liverpool FC football match, which noted that Scousers are: 'caring, thoughtful, loyal, generous, compassionate, community-spirited, humanitarian'.

This book – a history of the creation of the modern city of Liverpool, and the modern 'Scouse' identity - is partly the story of this transformation. It's a tale of the shift from slavers to Scousers, from commerce to comedy, from Virgil, a favoured poet of the Lovers of Old Liverpool, to Virgil van Dijk.

In 2025, the private sector in the city is roaring back, creating jobs and wealth, and in the past ten years what remains of the Liverpool docks – based around the modern container port at Seaforth – have become more profitable than ever before.

Yet the current identity of the city that was forged in the last decades of the twentieth century and its current reputation seem to owe little to anything that went before that time, or to the prolonged and continued importance of capitalism, conservatism and the middle class to the city.

Today, the Scouse identity seems specific and exclusive: Scousers are left-wing, funny, warm and welcoming: they are not conservative, business-minded, or to be taken too seriously.

The city has many paradoxes: it has the oldest Chinese community in Europe and one of the UK's oldest black communities. And yet much of Liverpool is notably whiter than other large cities in the North and Midlands. Even now, the neighbourhoods bear the imprint of historic 'ghettoisation', with the city's black community concentrated in and around the Liverpool 8 district. And it is this unique history that has led to the contradictions of Liverpool today.

In the chapters that follow, I give an honest account of the complexity of the city, one that takes in all aspects of its past. Because, despite all the attention the city gets, there is no one book that really captures the history of the place in the round, nor honestly appraises its conflicted identity.

There's plenty of stuff about politics, or football, or music, but it's harder to find something that takes in every facet of the city's history. In general, books about Liverpool tell you about John Gladstone *or* John Lennon, the slave trade or the drugs trade, about White Star Lines but not about white lines. Other books might give you a great understanding of the economic and political history of the city, but give no mention to local characters such as Pete Price or 'Purple' Aki.

If you are looking to read something about how Scousers are all left-wing and communal; how we are all basically Irish; how black GIs in the Second World War couldn't believe how friendly the place was, then you are going to be disappointed. There are already plenty of places where you can read that stuff, and there's a bore in every pub in Liverpool who will tell you it for free.

Since you've invested your hard in cash in this book, or at least borrowed it from someone who has, I owe it to you to be honest.

1

'LIVERPOOL'S STORY IS
THE WORLD'S GLORY'

Down by the River Mersey, where the global measurement of 'Sea Level' would later be officially fixed, the sky itself is a kind of dirty pink-brown.

You can see this palette reflected in many of the buildings – the Town Hall, the university's Victoria Building (origin of the term 'redbrick university') and most notably the Anglican cathedral. The sandstone that provides so much of this built environment was hewn from Woolton quarry, the same area that produced John Lennon, and the name of his first band.

Of the splendid Edwardian architecture alongside the river, the Royal Liver Building, completed in 1911, has become the most famous edifice in the city. Its four clock faces are larger than those of Ben Big, and each of its two towers is crowned with a stone rendering of a mythical liver bird: Bella, looking out to sea, and Bertie, looking inland.

The origins of the liver bird itself are obscure: although later described as a cormorant, the bird was almost certainly intended to be an eagle, as this was the symbol of John the Evangelist, who was both the namesake and the patron saint of King John, the granter of the city's charter.

It's appropriate that the symbol of Liverpool comes from the medieval equivalent of those modern statues that look nothing like their subject – which make Cristiano Ronaldo look like Niall Quinn or Princess Diana resemble the Child Catcher – but we took it to heart anyway.

Nine hundred years ago, on the other side of the river, monks would trudge down grass slopes from their monastery in what is now Birkenhead. In the black robes of their Benedictine order, they escorted small groups of pilgrims who paid the friars to row them across the Mersey; it would take up to two hours to cross, struggling all the way against fierce and unpredictable currents.

At this time, there was nothing waiting for them on the opposite bank, apart from a few fishermen's cottages, and so it remained for several hundred years. Even after Liverpool gained its royal charter in 1207, it remained a hamlet made up of a hundred or so wattle-and-daub cottages, with mud walls and thatched roofs. It would be over four centuries before the town began to develop into something more substantial. At this time, the ancient Roman city of Chester was the major town, and port, of the north-west of England. A 1571 petition to Elizabeth I referred to 'Her majesty's poor decayed town of Liverpool'.

As late as 1650, not much had changed: the city consisted of thirty-six narrow streets, and it was still insignificant compared to other port towns in England, with only around one thousand residents, compared to six thousand in Hull, twelve thousand in Newcastle and twenty thousand in Bristol. It was only in the last decades of the seventeenth century that things began to change, and this is when our history really begins.

In 1698, the travel writer Celia Fiennes reported that a town which was once 'a few fishermens' houses' had grown to 'a very rich trading town, the houses of brick and stone built high and even . . . there are an abundance of persons you see very well dress'd . . . it is London in miniature as much as ever I saw anything'.

This comparison to London was a notable theme of the time, as Liverpool's growth was often measured in terms of how it compared to the capital. In some ways, its growing competition with the Port of London led to the birth of the modern city – via a very unusual case involving cheesemakers.

The London cheesemakers had claimed that if they unloaded their ships slightly upriver in Frodsham or Ince, they should be exempt from paying duties or taxes to the port of Liverpool. In response, the city seized their cheese, and the cheesemakers sued, resulting in a long and expensive legal case. The town council lost and the costs of the court case would be a burden on the city's finances for many years to come. Nonetheless, Parliament passed a Dock Act in 1709, which specifically authorised the levying of fees on boats and ships unloaded elsewhere on the Mersey and banned the cheesemakers' practice.

Victory over the cheesemakers came at a crucial time for the ambitious city, which opened its innovative 'wet dock' in 1715. With huge underwater gates to maintain water levels, it allowed ships to stay afloat after the tide had gone out, and for goods to be loaded and unloaded around the clock. At the time, it was the only port infrastructure in the world to be built by a local council.

It soon paid off. The wet dock was crucial to the take-off in the size and prosperity of the city. Prior to this, ships had to dock in 'the Pool', a small inlet running into the Mersey from which the city gets its name. It has long since been filled in and is today underneath the Liverpool One shopping centre.

The new Customs House, built by architect Sylvester Morecroft, was completed in 1722, and the dock layout and infrastructure served as inspiration for new docks in Bristol, Hull, Leith and London.

By the time novelist Daniel Defoe journeyed over the Mersey in 1723, being ferried from the Wirral to Liverpool, things had changed. By this time, England had been transformed from a small economy on the periphery of Europe to the centre of Atlantic commerce – and Liverpool was fundamental to this shift. Defoe reported that Liverpool was:

> The third town in England for trade, especially to the plantations . . . it is a large fine built town. Some merchants having houses that in Italy would pass for palaces. The new church is one of the finest in England; the streets neat, and those about that called 'the new town', are very handsome and well built. They have made a fine dock here for the security of their shipping, where fourscore sail of ships may lie in the greatest storms secure as a man in his bed.

There had been an 'extraordinary' increase in inhabitants and new buildings, and a 'very pretty Exchange, standing upon 12 free-stone columns', which was already too small for the ever-increasing business in the town.

Defoe concluded that 'this Town is now become so great, so populous, and so rich, that it may be call'd the Bristol of this Part of the England', which was high praise at the time, if not at any time since, unless you rate your cities according to the number of white people with dreadlocks.

During the eighteenth century, there were already a recorded 646 streets in the city, but the population density varied widely, with the majority of the town's inhabitants concentrated into the riverside areas. A quarter of sailors based in the city lived on just twenty-three streets, such as Strand, Pitt, Frederick, Cable, Chorley and Chapel. Although still relatively humble, it was beginning to build connections across the world; Williamson's *Liverpool Memorandum* of 1753 praised the flourishing port and described the inhabitants as 'universal merchants [who] trade to all foreign parts'.

Defoe had predicted that the city 'may become one of the first of the finest towns in England', and his prophecy soon came true. By 1796, Moss's *Guide* acknowledged Liverpool as 'the first town in the kingdom in point of size and importance, the Metropolis [London] excepted'.

In 1790, almost half a million tons of goods moved through the city's docks, an increase of 632 per cent in just four decades – by this point, Liverpool had left its provincial competitors in the dust and was even starting to bear comparison with London, a city many times its size.

In 1807, Parliament abolished the British slave trade – although it would be another thirty-one years before existing slaves in British territories were freed. By this point, the city was of such importance to international commerce that the abolition of the trade it had come to dominate had no effect on its upward trajectory.

If anything, abolition helped Liverpool go on to even greater strengths, hastening the move away from exporting the manufactures of the north-west in exchange for slaves, and towards becoming a global hub for international business. Trade with both the Eastern and Western hemispheres continued to grow, and the city became the primary departure point for paying, willing customers journeying across the Atlantic. At the same time, the newly created United States of America was becoming a key destination for legitimate cargo.

In Sefton Park – a bucolic legacy of the city's former wealth, complete with a boating lake – there is a statue of Christopher Columbus with the inscription: 'The discoverer of America was the maker of Liverpool'.

With the construction of the Erie Canal, New York City began growing in population and wealth. At the start of the nineteenth century, the population of New York stood at around 30,000; by 1860, it had already reached 813,000, becoming by far the largest city in the USA. Over the same time, New York's contribution to US imports and exports rose from 25 per cent and 20 per cent to 68 per cent and 40 per cent.

The connections between that city and Liverpool were developing quickly. On 5 January 1818, the *James Monroe* carried the first eight passengers from New York to Liverpool, at a cost of 40 guineas each, establishing a regular passenger service between the two towns.

In 1836, an American visitor recorded that he 'stopped at the Adelphi Hotel, then, and possibly now, the best inn for travellers in England' (just in case you didn't know this was written nearly 200 years ago). After reading in a tourist pamphlet that the 'American packet ships' moored in the docks were recommended as local items of interest, he confessed that he felt 'a glow of patriotic pride' on reading of 'this striking acknowledgement of the superiority of our passenger ships' in 'the most important seaport of the greatest maritime nation of the world'.

In addition to its better-known connections with New York, Liverpool also has lesser-reported links with the southern United States. The cannons at Fort Sumter that fired the first shots of the US Civil War were forged in Liverpool's Duke Street. During that war, the Confederacy signed a contract with Merseyside shipbuilder Macgregor Laird for the construction of two prototype ships, the *Alabama* and the *Florida*, to be followed by another thirty warships – the *Alabama* went on to sink sixty-eight Union ships, including the entire American whaling fleet. Overall, thirty-six blockade-running ships, designed to elude the US Navy boats besieging Southern ports, were built in the city and many of them were manned by Liverpool crews.

Improbably, the last official action of the war took place in the middle of the Mersey, when Confederate captain James Waddell surrendered his vessel to the Royal Navy on 6 November 1865.

Today, you can walk past 19 Abercromby Square, once the home of American cotton merchant Charles Kuhn Prioleau, which still has the eight rebel stars of the Confederacy on the columns of its portico, and the grave of the Confederate agent James Bulloch lies in nearby Toxteth cemetery.

Apart from the Atlantic trade, Liverpool helped itself to some of the vast fortunes being generated through trade with India, benefitting from its position next to the world's largest cotton manufacturer to export tons of the stuff to the captive markets of South Asia.

While this period was also a golden age for Manchester, the eastern neighbour couldn't compete with the amount of wealth being generated in Liverpool, which produced twice as many millionaires as Manchester during the nineteenth century, and more than any urban area apart from London.

In 1846, Prince Albert – husband of Queen Victoria – arrived in the city to open the historic dock that bears his name, which has since handled millions of tons of goods and seen a weatherman fall off an inflatable island. He remarked that while he had 'heard of the greatness of Liverpool the reality far surpasses my expectation'.

At this time, the city's fortunes seemed secure. One hundred and fifty years after the wet docks, Liverpool was still innovating: the new Albert Dock featured a hydraulic hoist system to handle cargo, the first of its kind in the world. Its warehouses were the first in Britain to be built from cast iron, brick and stone, with no wood in their structure, making them fire resistant. The port carried one third of Britain's exports, a quarter of its imports, and Liverpool-based companies controlled one seventh of the world's shipping.

At this point, Thomas Baine's *History of the Commerce and Town of Liverpool* could boast that 'the commerce of Liverpool extends to every port of any importance in every quarter of the globe . . . it far surpasses [that of] any city of which we have a record from past times, as Tyre, Venice, Genoa, Amsterdam, or Antwerp, and fully equals, if it does not surpass, that of London and New York'.

This desire to be seen as a competitor of London was reflected in the claims of another Liverpool patriot from the time, who conceded that 'while Liverpool yields to London in the extent of its trade with the continent of Europe, it surpasses the capital in its trade with America, and already rivals it in the trade with the East' – and this despite the city being barred from any commerce with India until the London-based East India Company's monopoly was ended in 1813, and from trade with China until 1833.

The Mersey Docks and Harbour Board was set up in 1858, and by the end of the century the Liverpool and Birkenhead docks constituted the largest port system in the world controlled by a single company. This led to efficiencies in integrating loading, storage and transport that were copied by ports around the world, from Baltimore to Rotterdam to Singapore and everywhere in between. During its pomp, the city's Martins Bank (eventually bought by Barclays in 1969) was the only national bank to be headquartered outside of London.

While British manufacturing was beginning to decline in the face of competition from the USA, Germany and other rapidly industrialising countries, British trade remained dominant until after the First World War, and Liverpool in the late nineteenth century showed no signs of slowing down. The Overhead Railway (known as the Dockers' Umbrella) opened in 1886, running from the Alexandra Dock in Bootle to the Herculaneum Dock in Dingle, and it transported thousands of dockers to and from work each day. By 1900, there were forty different docks drawn out along 35 miles of the Mersey, and the city's ships moved one sixth of all the world's cargo. As well as the dockers themselves, the port provided jobs for tens of thousands of clerks, secretaries, typists, insurers, brokers and various other administrative workers. When the Stanley Dock Tobacco Warehouse opened in 1901 it was the largest building in the world, with a floor space of 1.6 million square feet – and it is still the world's largest brick building in terms of surface area.

In 1911, at the peak of its population, the census revealed that almost 750,000 people were living in the city. In that year, the docks accounted for over a third of the UK's exports and a quarter of its imports. It was one of the very few truly global cities in the era before the First World War, its warehouses stuffed with everything from steel and coal to train engines, food, beer and pottery. At this point, as Liverpool-born author Andrew Lees has written, the Ganges and the St Lawrence were the Mersey's tributaries. As well as giving its name to towns in Australia and the United States, there is also a Liverpool in Liberia and one in Guinea.

Yet, although it was not appreciated at the time, in reality the wealth and influence of the town had already begun to decline. Soon enough, the docks that Prince Albert opened that day would become outdated; designed to process 1,000-ton sailing ships, they were effectively obsolete by 1900. Eventually, those docks would become more famous for a prancing weatherman than a place of commerce.

But it was only after the First World War that the exceptional wealth and affluence of the city seriously began to decline – and become noticeable to Liverpudlians.

INTERLUDE 1

'In Your Liverpool Slums'

There was always terrible poverty in Liverpool, worse even than that of other British cities during the Industrial Revolution. The historian Kingsley Davis has found that in 1841, average life expectancy was forty-one in England, thirty-six in London, but just twenty-six in Liverpool – the lowest in the UK. At that time, fully 75 per cent of the Liverpool lads who volunteered for the army were rejected as unfit for service.

Even before the Victorian age, when the town had a population of only a few thousand, a priest in Walton observed that 'the people around here, so far as I can see, are but little better than Hottentots; immoral untamed creates'. The massive population growth between 1750 and 1900 was to make matters worse.

Already by 1841, before the Irish famine influx, Liverpool had a population density of up to 1,210 people per acre in the most crowded areas; the worst for any large town in England.

The rapid development of the city meant that houses were built in a quick and shoddy manner; a strong wind in 1822 had blown down many of the houses in the city. The working poor were crammed into thousands of courts that housed around a fifth of the town's population.

Underneath each house were the cellars, where the poorest families stayed. There were 3,000 courts by 1847, housing 110,000 people, with 39,000 people living in some 7,800 cellars.

With many new residents being recent arrivals from the countryside, some kept livestock in their cellars, and in 1827 a baby died after having its ear chewed off by a pig. Outsiders spoke of these slum dwellers as if they were from another civilisation, with the *Daily Post* writing that 'the older and more densely-populated districts of the town are to a great majority of the people as much unknown and as little understood as the hut of the Esquimaux is to the African savage'.

In the mid-Victorian era, between Great Crosshall Street and Addison Street, a distance you can cross today in four minutes, eight thousand people crammed into 811 houses, with a density of 658,000 people per square mile. This was double that of London's East End – another notoriously overcrowded area. By way of comparison, today London as a whole – one of the most densely populated areas of the UK – has 9,654 people per square mile, and Manhattan Island has 72,918 residents per square mile. In this period, a woman in Vauxhall was discovered sharing a bed with her husband's stiff and stinking corpse, because of a lack of anywhere else to put the body.

Looking at this area today, you simply cannot imagine how 8,000 people could live there, nor what the filth and shit they produced would have looked and smelt like. American novelist Nathanial Hawthorne reported of the neighbourhood that 'the people are as numerous as maggots in cheese . . . you behold them, disgusting, and all moving about, as when you raise a plank or log that has long lain on the ground, and find many vivacious bugs and insects beneath it'.

The floors of courtyards and streets were festooned with animal and vegetable refuse in various states of decay, into which drained the overflowing toilets and sewers, to create a toxic sludge of such foulness modern minds are incapable of imagining. With back-to-back houses, the air could not circulate; one Irishman who lived in Spencer Court, off North Street, said the smell was 'bad enough to raise the roof off his skull'.

In one cellar, a family slept on a bed over a small four-foot-deep well, into which entered the contents of the neighbourhood outhouses. In 1842, 3,000 of these cellars were condemned as unfit for human habitation and were filled in, with the eviction of some 20,000 people. But this just increased the housing crisis, already at desperate levels; in one case, a family moved into an old boiler that they found on some waste ground.

For those without a home of their own, they could try to scrape together enough for a berth in a lodging house, where individuals and families could pay by the night to sleep in a filthy dorm. These places flourished in the city to accommodate the sailors, long-term vagrants and temporarily homeless. Ben Jonson Street alone contained nineteen lodging houses (and eight brothels) within just 200 yards. There were reckoned to be around a thousand men who called the street home, and only six were reported as able or willing to hold down jobs.

One businessman, describing the stench of a lodging house, reported that 'when the doors were open a dense vapour, palpable to the touch, so heavy was it and so dank, came out upon me, almost turning me sick'.

For those who couldn't afford a night in a lodging house, they could always try to get arrested, and many did just this, preferring shackles and hard labour to nights on the Liverpool streets. Begging itself was illegal, but most police officers turned a blind eye, given that, as one magistrate protested, if he had to send all the beggars in Liverpool to prison, it would need to hold 10,000 inmates.

A final option was the workhouse, and the Liverpool workhouse on Brownlow Hill, established in 1769, soon became the largest in Britain. In 1842, it was rebuilt to an increased capacity of 1,400; by the end of the 1860s, it held over 5,000 people.

In response to the dire housing situation, the city authorities came up with many innovations. In 1847, Liverpool became the first UK city to appoint a medical officer, Dr William Henry Duncan, who oversaw public health, and he pioneered the construction of council housing, with the creation of St Martin's Cottages in 1869. Nonetheless, by 1880, it was estimated that more than 70,000 people lived in dwellings unfit for human habitation. Despite the tremendous wealth of the city, there would be little done to rectify the parlous state of housing during this time. These conditions were only finally ended by a massive slum clearance programme and the resettlement of tens of thousands of families; by the end of the 1950s almost 150,000 Liverpudlians had been moved to new sites on the edge of the city.

2

DECLINE OF LIVERPOOL . . .

In the twentieth century, as shipping was declining, investment and employment in manufacturing began to increase – by 1939, the sector contributed more to the city's wealth than did trade for the first time. But even at this point, only 35 per cent of people worked in manufacturing – compared to half of the British workforce as a whole.

This meant that the city was particularly badly exposed to the Great Depression, which saw international trade decline more rapidly than industrial production; throughout the 1930s, the city's unemployment rate never fell below 18 per cent – double the national average for the period. To make matters worse, the schemes devised by the government to help depressed areas were focused on boosting manufacturing, rather than trade, and so Liverpool was excluded.

Things were about to get worse. Given the physical damage wreaked on the city by the Second World War, and the number of its citizens who died on ships or battlefields during the conflict, it is tempting to date Liverpool's material decline from this point. Around 2,500 were killed in the city during the conflict, with hundreds of buildings destroyed. The remnants of them, bomb-sites and demolished houses, remained for many decades after the war was over.

Post-war, there were over 20,000 unsafe buildings just in the centre of Liverpool, and as many as 30,000 people in need of homes. Reports on the extent of the destruction were censored to keep up morale.

But the economy had been on a downward trajectory since its glorious peak a hundred years earlier, and this simply continued through the post-war years.

The city's limited manufacturing base began to decline before it had really got started. After 1945, businesses including Dunlop, GEC and Kodak set up factories in the city, providing jobs for 27,000 workers, most of them recently let go by the contracting port. Ford Motors then set up a 346-acre plant outside of Halewood, at a cost of about £40 million.

Soon this provided 9,000 skilled and well-paid jobs. It seemed as though Liverpool could survive the decline of the docks, if it could get a share of the manufacturing jobs that sustained much of the rest of the country. Unfortunately, although it wasn't yet apparent in the 1960s, the manufacturing jobs were soon to go the way of the docks.

And the Liverpool docks suffered as great a fall from grace as has ever been recorded in the history of capitalism: in 1966, when the Beatles released *Revolver*, Liverpool was still the second biggest port in the UK; twenty years later it was the sixth.

The city's position roughly halfway up the west coast of Britain had made it ideally placed to prosper from Britain's expanding Atlantic empire. But after 1945, the share of British trade with the Americas and Asia declined and trade with Europe grew steadily more significant, especially after the UK's entry into the European Economic Community (EEC) in 1973. The city found itself on the wrong side of the country; in the post-war decades the number of ships docking in the Mersey declined by half, while those using the south-east port of Dover increased 4.5 times.

This decline spread to elsewhere in the city: from 1966 to 1977, 350 factories in Liverpool closed or relocated; by 1980, only one of the twenty largest manufacturing companies was owned locally. At the end of 1978, during the 'Winter of Discontent', 57,000 Ford workers went out on strike, and in recent decades, when companies have opened large-scale manufacturing plants, such as the Nissan factory in Sunderland or the Toyota plant in North Wales, they have tended, for whatever reason, to avoid Liverpool.

This decline was reflected in the population, which had stood at around 700,000 in 1945, but by the time of Thatcher's second election win in 1983 had declined to little more than 300,000.

This led to dark prophecies, from local as well as national voices; after 17,000 jobs were lost in the year 1978, the council feared that Liverpool might become the Jarrow of the 1980s – a reference to the north-east shipbuilding town which had been devastated by the Great Depression during the 1930s. The City Planning department predicted that by 1986, somewhere between 32 per cent and 41 per cent of people would be unemployed. By the mid-1980s, the *Liverpool Echo* was predicting that in 1990 the city would have no industrial base left.

This economic transformation had powerful social effects. Between 1973 and 1983, male employment on Merseyside fell by 53 per cent and female employment by 62 per cent. These losses were worse in some parts than others; in Kirkby, for example, 13,000 people – well over half the population – lost their jobs during this period. From tens of thousands at the start of the century, as of November 1984, the Mersey Docks and Harbour Company employed just 1,300 dockers.

By 1983, there were eighteen candidates for every managerial vacancy – and over 1,700 for every labourer's job. On the Youth Training Schemes set up by the Conservative government, there could be as many as 300 applicants for each apprenticeship.

In an infamous memo from 1981, the then Chancellor of the Exchequer, Geoffrey Howe, writing in the aftermath of the Toxteth riots three months earlier, questioned whether trying to stabilise and rebuild inner-city areas like Liverpool 8 was like trying to 'pump water uphill', and wondered whether instead it was better to 'go for "managed decline"?', adding that 'this is not a term for use, even privately'.

Howe's words remained private until the memo was made public in 2011, when they caused outrage, the assumption being that Howe was calling for the government to allow, or even to oversee, the economic and demographic demise of cities like Liverpool.

This memo is often brought up whenever Liverpool, the Conservative party and Margaret Thatcher are discussed. I think what rankles most about the phrase is the implied lack of agency and control; somewhere that was for so long one of the key generators of British wealth was now dependent on the whims of the government, waiting to see which way the thumb of Thatcher would turn.

In the end, Michael Heseltine won the day over Howe, the managed decline did not take place and Liverpool has now recovered to a degree unimaginable in the 1980s.

But this period of powerlessness, of failure and seemingly irreversible decline, combined with the growing hostility and piss-taking from their fellow citizens, led to an active packaging of 'Scouserness', with a radicalism that wasn't present in the post-war image of the Scouser.

A 2012 article from *Cherwell*, the Oxford University student newspaper – not necessarily the place you'd expect to see perceptive writing on Liverpool – contains a couple of lines that I think are useful for understanding the city today, and how it is perceived by outsiders. The article concerns what author Tom Goulding calls 'football hipsterism'. A football hipster, he writes:

> will tell you how he has rated Sergio Aguero ever since his days at Independiente. He will not care to talk of the brilliance of Lionel Messi – he is busy blogging about how inverted winger Isaac Cuenca is Barcelona's real prodigy. The football hipster

will scoff at you reading BBC Live Text, instead following the *Guardian*'s 'minute-by-minute', busy sending in an email explaining how Kierkegaard's anti-federalism is much like Juan Mata's style of play . . . The football hipster will be busy finding the new opinion to hold, the new tactical trend to blog about. Vincent Kompany used to be like The xx – then everyone bought the album, and the opinion that the Belgian is the best centre-back in Europe isn't worth expressing any more, given how many people have realised it. 'Mario Gomez? Please, Mario Götze' . . . Like real hipsterism, football hipsterism is essentially an attempt to subvert the mainstream, while simultaneously rarely being serious about anything. After all, if you take yourself or some pursuit too seriously, you are yourself vulnerable and open to ridicule. Thus a football hipster is rarely a passionate supporter of any club. Tribalism is to be laughed at, and the most evocative form of tribalism – Liverpool fans – are to be laughed at the most.

Even though he was talking about Liverpool FC fans, rather than Liverpudlians in general, this paragraph gets to the heart of why a lot of people don't like Scousers. We're just too overt, too credulous, too cheesy. In contrast, British conservatives prize stoicism, a stiff upper lip and emotional repression, and the Left values irony, understatement and a raised eyebrow above all else.

In 2004, when the Liverpool-born hostage Ken Bigley was executed by his Iraqi captors, leading to a minute's silence being observed at Anfield, Anthony Daniels wrote in the *Daily Telegraph* that:

the whole panoply of public mourning will be employed in Liverpool in Mr Bigley's case. Flags will be lowered, flowers sent, black armbands worn, including by those most sensitive of souls, professional footballers, which is a strange way to respond to an old man having his head cut off.

Daniels concluded that 'there are several words to describe such a politics: immature, dishonest and decadent would do'.

The then *Spectator* editor Boris Johnson penned an infamous editorial complaining about Liverpudlian 'mawkish sentimentality' and proclivity to 'wallow in a sense of vicarious victimhood'. When Johnson defended his *Spectator* piece on the death of Ken Bigley, he argued that he wanted to criticise the new vogue for histrionics in response to public tragedy.

As early as 2011, an article in *The Economist* complained that it felt 'as if every fixture was preceded by players standing around the centre circle, heads bowed, remembering the death of ever more obscure players'.

Meanwhile, it considered a minute's applause as a 'ghastly attempt at forced positivity that does not sit easily with the British psyche'. There is an element of classism to this, similar to complaints about flowers or teddy bears left at a site of a murder or car crash.

When Sky Sports appointed former Manchester United captain Gary Neville as a pundit in 2011, *Sunday Times* columnist Rod Liddle noted that Sky were at risk of 'estrange[ing] Britain's second most voluble and victimised minority, the Scousers' and joked that if Neville got the job 'the very least you might expect is a minute's silence at Anfield'.

As music journalist Paul Du Noyer said of England in the 1980s, 'it was a land where reserve was valued over exhibitionism, where enthusiasm was suspect and quiet irony the favoured means of subversion'. The English attitude is repressed apart from when drink is taken, and then feeling embarrassed afterwards. Scousers are different. Today, in a culture where subtlety, erudition, counter-intuitiveness, understatement and the eyebrow raised in irony are the standard modes, the open cheesiness of Scousers seems out of step.

Du Noyer drew a contrast between Thatcher's 'corner shop' mentality – 'thrifty, snobbish, respectable, narrow – and the personality of Liverpool – sloppy, generous, improvident, grand of gesture and sentiment'.

When irony is the highest virtue, and giving a shit the greatest crime, then Scousers are likely to come in for criticism. Scousers are very sarcastic, but not ironic; we tend to very much give a shit: about politics, about music, about football, about dead kids. We tend to be very ingenuous, open and honest, in a national culture that is broadly uncomfortable with overt displays of emotion.

Many people look at the banners and displays in response to a recent tragic death and cringe. Usually – with a few infamous exceptions – they will not make their distaste public, and so it festers.

To some extent this frosty dyke broke – and prompted a revealing response from certain quarters of the media – in response to the death of Princess Diana in 1997. Then, millions of ordinary people engaged in a form of public grieving that was undoubtedly gauche, cheesy and apparently very un-British. Maybe if this trend continues, and the broader British culture becomes more accepting of this kind of public emoting, then anti-Scouse prejudice will dissipate.

In 1992, the year of the James Bulger murder, the left-wing journalist Ian Jack wrote that Liverpool's 'last function in British life' was to provide theatre for the rest of the country. This transformation, from trading floor to theatre stage, is essential to understand the creation of modern Liverpool.

3

. . . RISE OF 'THE SCOUSER'

In his book *English Journey*, the writer J. B. Priestley begins his chapter on Lancashire with a visit to Liverpool. He mused on the contrasts of the city, from the poverty of the dockside districts to the splendour of his rooms in the Adelphi Hotel. But he never considered the city as anything other than a part of Lancashire, and of England.

By the time that the archivist George Chandler wrote his history of Liverpool a couple of decades later, he could describe it as 'the provincial metropolis of the United Kingdom: it is not English, like London, nor Lancashire, like Manchester'.

How did this come about?

When I first met my Israeli wife, she asked me if I knew what it was like to come from a place roundly despised by outsiders, but where the inhabitants genuinely couldn't care less and even derived some kind of weird pleasure from being so hated. Where the greater the opprobrium poured by outsiders, the more people were convinced of their own righteousness. I told her I had some idea.[1]

---

1 She knew very little of the city at this point. When we first went to the airport, I said it was named after probably the most famous person from Liverpool. She paused for a moment and then guessed: 'The fat man from *The Royle Family*?'

But the idea that Liverpool and Scousers were notably distinct in any way is itself a fairly recent invention. And until well into the eighteenth century, Liverpool was not especially prominent in the north of England.

At the end of the English Civil War period, around the year 1660, Liverpool had fewer than a thousand inhabitants – compared to about 2,000 in Preston and Wigan, and 1,600 in Warrington.

Until 1760, there was no direct stagecoach route between the city and London. Before then, you had to change to the main north–south road at Warrington – and, to this day, Liverpool is a terminus of the West Coast mainline railway; if you want to take a train northwards into Cumbria and on up to Glasgow, you still have to change at Warrington or Wigan.

The surrounding towns and villages of Lancashire were hugely important to the city's development, especially from the late 1770s, when the Leeds and Liverpool Canal allowed coal and textiles from wool country to be shipped into the city. In the year 1788, the canal network transported 465,000 tons to and from Liverpool – almost as much as the 479,000 tons imported and exported through the docks during the same period.

In the following decades, the massive expansion in US cotton production – picked by the descendants of slaves transported on Liverpool ships – and the continuing Industrial Revolution both transformed the economy of the north of England in general, and of one formerly no-account town in particular.

For it was in Manchester that the world's first steam-driven textile mill was opened by Richard Arkwright in 1781. At the beginning of the eighteenth century there were around 30,000 spinners and weavers operating in the Manchester area, most of them small cottage-based producers. In 1838, it finally received its charter – over 600 years after its more famous rival 30 miles to the west. By 1853, there were 108 industrial mills in the city, and by 1871 Manchester's mills and those of the surrounding towns made up a third of global cotton production. From 90,000 people in 1800, its population had risen to 700,000 a century later. And the bulk of both the raw cotton processed in Mancunian mills and the finished product then exported around the world came through the Liverpool docks. These two cities powered the transformation of the north-west: in 1693, Lancashire was thirty-fifth out of thirty-nine English counties in terms of wealth; by 1843, it was second.

As recently as the 1960s, there was no special antipathy between the two cities, and more of a friendly rivalry, encouraged by their parallel development and heightened by the opening of the Manchester Ship Canal in 1894, which allowed large seagoing vessels to bypass Liverpool entirely and load and unload goods at the Salford Quays.

A mocking Mancunian ditty from that time prophesied the effect the waterway would have on Liverpool:

> Alas then for poor Liverpool, she'd surely
> go to pot, Sir
>
> For want of trade her folks would starve,
> her Customs House would rot, Sir
>
> I'm wrong they'd not exactly starve or want,
> for it is true, Sir
>
> They might come down to Manchester,
> and we could find them work to do, Sir

Just before the canal opened, the footballing rivalry began, with the formation of Everton FC (1878), Manchester United FC (1878), Liverpool FC (1892), and Manchester City FC (1894). In the case of both places, their economic 'golden age' ended in the early twentieth century – at the same time their reputation for football and music was beginning, putting into sharp contrast their decline as places of trade and commerce.

The essayist William Hazlitt said he preferred Manchester to Liverpool, as in the latter you felt oppressed by both 'the aristocracy of wealth and letters . . . you could not help feeling that some of their great men were authors among merchants and some merchants among authors . . . the Manchester cotton-spinners, on the contrary, had no pretensions beyond their looms'.

The distinction at the time was made between 'Liverpool gentlemen' (who were cosmopolitan sophisticates) and 'Manchester men' (who were hard-headed men of commerce and industry) – with the nature of business in Liverpool being better suited to speculation and venture capital than the more stolid, sober manufacturing interests further east.

Recently, the Liverpudlian musician Pete Wylie told the journalist Simon Hughes that 'even though [Liverpool and Manchester] are thirty miles apart':

> the way people talk and think are very different. What I am goes way before me, with the docks. A mate of mine wrote a book which discussed seafaring, the way every night in Liverpool people were either coming home or going away. There was either a sense of celebration because you've just arrived or despondency because you were departing; you could never get too attached but when you did, your loyalty was intense. It has always been far more emotional than other English cities as well as more creative because of the uncertainty.

Certainly, there is a pessimistic pragmatism and love of hard graft in Manchester (and elsewhere in the North) that doesn't translate to Liverpool. The bee is one of the symbols of Manchester, reflecting their commitment to hard work – in Manchester they value 'grafters'; in Liverpool 'grafter' is slang for a drug dealer.

In the opinion of the Liverpudlian writer and broadcaster Spencer Leigh, 'Manchester is an airport, a shopping centre and not much else. It does not seem to have the character. It has no great buildings that come to mind. It's a sprawling city. It doesn't have the kind of waterfront skyline that Liverpool possesses.'

This is a fair point. My friend John – himself from the anonymous wastelands of west London – once sent me a piss-taking postcard bearing the legend: 'Manchester: Capital of the North'. For some reason this was emblazed on a Union Jack flag – I pointed out to him that they used the flag because Manchester didn't have any recognisable vistas.

If Manchester has a distinct identity and rivalry compared to its more famous western neighbour, for the wool country in between this identity is a bit more complicated. Does anyone actually see themselves as a wool? It's hard to know. Not least because exactly who or what is a wool is hard to define.

Stuart Maconie, in his brilliant *Pies and Prejudice*, reckons that while many of his attributes make him a wool, since he was born in Whiston Hospital he might, technically, be considered a Scouser.

No offence, Stuart, but you couldn't be more of a wool if you were eating a pie with one hand, holding a rugby league ball with t'other and playing the tuba with your arse.

The argument that being born in Liverpool means you can't be a wool reflects a key part of the nature of being a wool or indeed a Scouser: it can't be defined by legal or political boundaries.

For example, some would argue that to truly be from Liverpool you have to come from the Liverpool city council area, rather than from areas within Sefton or Knowsley council. Therefore, to be a Scouser you have to have a purple wheely bin, instead of whatever colours they use in Sefton and Knowsley.

But can you call someone from Bootle or Huyton a wool? I wouldn't advise it.

It's also complicated by the lack of defined physical boundaries. With the Wirral, the very large and obvious physical barrier of the River Mersey means that no one would seriously argue that people from the Wirral can be considered Scousers. (Apart from Wirralite students/tourists away from home, who chance it and hope that they are not overheard by an actual Scouser.)

But with Liverpool's northern and eastern boundaries, who's to say where Liverpool ends and wooldom begins?

I've even seen the argument that Liverpool extends as far east as a boat can sail up the Mersey – but this would mean that people such as the Stone Roses singer Ian Brown (who was born in Warrington) are Scousers, which is clearly ridiculous.

It's complicated by most Liverpudlians not knowing where most of these places are, and suspecting that many of them don't even exist. Through grim circumstance, I have actually been to both Rainhill and even Thatto Heath, so I know that they are real. But the other day I had to look up the exact locations of Maghull, Ormskirk and Skelmersdale, because I realised that, despite repeatedly hearing of them, I had no idea where they actually were.

As with 'Geordies', even the origins of the term 'wool' are disputed. One version has it that during one dock strike, shipping companies brought in workers from nearby Lancashire who apparently wore distinctive woollen coats. Another is that coal delivery men from mines in the nearby areas would use sheep fleeces as padding for their backs when carrying bags of coal. The term might have an even longer history, as it may have been used to denote non-resident Welsh and English people attempting to avoid the entrance fee into Chester on market day by sneaking through the livestock entrances with a sheep on their back.

Irrespective of the origins of the term, there is a clear sense that wools are not Scousers – culturally, linguistically, socially and economically. The *Echo and the Bunnymen* guitarist Will Sergeant grew up in Melling, only eight miles away from Liverpool, and recalls that his neighbours 'were the scum, the ruffians from the council estate ... [and] to be fair, there was a high proportion of nutjobs, criminals, wife beaters, drunkards and thugs'. But in Liverpool, he remembers, 'the perception of Melling was that it was posh'.

(This image might have been more powerful in determining outcomes and life chances than socio-economic reality. Paul Du Noyer tells me that after his family moved from Anfield to Maghull, he attended secondary school in Bootle, and though his parents were slightly worse off than many of the Bootle kids, the lads from Maghull and Ormskirk consistently did much better at school, for whatever reason.)

Today, of course, the most notable way to distinguish a Scouser from a wool is through their accent. But not so long ago, there was no distinctive Liverpool accent. In fact, until the twentieth century there was so much variety among English dialects and accents that people from different parts of the country would have difficulty understanding each other, even though they were technically speaking the same language.

Over the past two hundred years, the growth of newspapers, radio, cinema, television and more recently the internet and social media have all led to what linguists call 'convergence', whereby different dialects and accents of the same language become more similar over time. This means that English regional accents today sound less distinct now than they did a hundred years ago. All except one.

For some reason, over the past 150 years the Liverpool accent, almost unique among English language accents across the globe, has grown more distinctive.

As late as the 1880s, phonetic studies (the study of sounds made by human accents and dialects) made no distinction between Liverpool and the surrounding areas; the accent was considered no different to that of the rest of south Lancashire.

Some Liverpudlians argued differently; in 1888, Sir James Picton (of the clock and baths fame) claimed that that Scousers spoke 'without the mincing word-clipping of the cockney, and [are] equally distant from the rough Tim Bobbin Lancashire dialect', even arguing that former prime minister William Gladstone's 'tones and modes of utterance' are 'decidedly of Liverpool origin'.

By the mid-twentieth century, things were beginning to change, with the Liverpool accent becoming recognised as distinctive, and attracting praise from unexpected quarters. In 1978, the playwright Tennessee Williams sat down in the BBC studios in Broadcasting House to record his episode of *Desert Island Discs*, the long-running radio series which invites celebrities to pick the eight tracks they would want to listen to if they were stuck on the eponymous sandy atoll.

Thanks to the wonder of the BBC archives, you can listen to it today and hear Williams – his voice sounding like a William Faulkner character, smooth and syrupy like molasses, languid like an iced tea sipped on a porch at sunset – talk about his life and his favourite songs.

Williams' selected songs include numbers by Elvis Presley, Sarah Vaughan, Harry Belafonte and the Ink Spots – and 'A Day in the Life' by the Beatles. Explaining his choice for the final track, he said: 'I've always loved the Beatles. I was very sad when they broke up. I thought they had the most beautiful diction.'

Today, interviews with the Beatles act as a kind of time capsule for the south Liverpool accent of the 1960s, but even this was exaggerated. John Lennon's Aunt Mimi gave an interview to the *Sunday People* where she alleged that, originally, 'John spoke what I call the King's English without a trace of Liverpool accent. One day I complained when he lapsed into broad Liverpudlian. He turned on me, saying he felt embarrassed by his accent and suddenly ran upstairs in a fit of temper.' Lennon might be the world's most famous person from Liverpool (sorry Ricky), but even he was doing an impersonation of a Scouser.

Lennon himself gave a different impression, telling an interviewer that when the band first became successful they 'were looked down upon as animals by the Southerners, the Londoners'.

This tension within Lennon – a middle-class, south Liverpool Scouser ill at ease with his own identity, but still seen as irredeemably Liverpudlian by outsiders – even informed debates about him in the House of Commons, where he was described as both 'highly articulate' and in a state of 'pathetic near-literacy'.

As historian John Belchem has argued, 'the [Liverpool] accent is the essential medium for the projection and representation of the local micro-culture, the "Scouse" blend of truculent defiance, collective security, scallywaggery and fatalist humour which sets Liverpool and its inhabitants apart'.

Lacking the long history and evolution of Cockney, Scouse is, in the words of Belchem, 'a recently invented tradition, a cultural response to the city's decline'. The journalist Dixon Scot called it 'a bastard brogue: a shambling degenerate speech of slipshod vowels and muddled consonants – a cast-off clout of a tongue, more debased even than the Whitechapel Cockney, because so much less positive and acute'.

Scouse is, nonetheless, an accent rather than a dialect; even though there are some words that seem to be used exclusively on Merseyside, it mostly uses the same vocabulary and grammatical rules as standard English. Instead, its distinctiveness is 'phonological' due to the sound it makes. This is powered by, according to Belchem, the 'preferred position of speech organs, the way plosives and nasals are produced, and the distribution of prominence in diphthongs and pitch patterns . . . Velarization, the accompaniment of other articulations by the raising of the back of the tongue towards the soft palate . . . Scousers articulate a constant stream of prosodic patterns and segmental features which distinguish them unmistakably as Liverpudlians'. In more accessible language, the literary critic John Kerrigan described Scouse as 'a mixture of Welsh, Irish and catarrh'.

Exactly why it should be so distinctive today is a mystery. Whereas people in Salford-Manchester and Leeds-Bradford speak differently from people in the surrounding areas, their accent is still of a similar type.

One theory behind the development of the Lancastrian and Yorkshire accents is that the dust-strewn air of textile mills made it hazardous to open your mouth, and so people developed a tight-lipped way of speaking.

On the Liverpool docks, however, and on ships, people barely kept their mouths shut for more than a few seconds – whether it was exchanging warnings, or partaking in banter and work songs. John Belchem reckons that the distinctiveness of Scouse came about as a form of 'linguistic bonding' among the different nationalities and classes who met along the Liverpool waterfront.

Today, there are broad variations in the Scouse accent. Middle-class Scousers with a 'softer' accent, who find themselves working outside the city (as with their contemporaries from Glasgow, Newcastle and elsewhere), face a double bind of having the piss taken out of their accents by their colleagues and friends (or, even worse, being told that they 'don't really sound' like they're from Liverpool), and being ridiculed for sounding 'posh' when they're back home.

But there are important commonalities across the whole of the city: for example, there is no 'th' sound in Gaelic, and so Scousers pronounce 'th' either with a d – as in der, deir, dem, dose, etc – or an f: fink, finking, fursday, first (as in thirsty) and so on.

As Cilla Black pointed out, her heavy 'ur' sound – 'Clur with the fur' – was actually her putting on a posh accent; a true Scousewife of her time would pronounce it 'Cleer with the feer', but that would probably have sounded too ridiculous for Saturday night primetime television.

Liverpool vocabulary is also ever changing, with new words coming in and old ones going out of fashion. Not so long ago, 'wacker' was one of the most frequently heard words in the city, used in the same way that 'la', 'lad', or 'mate' might be used today, but also as a sort of generic term for someone from Liverpool. But I have never heard anyone use this term in my life, and I suspect that neither has anyone else under forty.

Around ten years ago, 'What are you saying?' became popular as a greeting, but now seems to have faded without a trace. Today, the word 'tory' seems to have become an all-purpose insult, a sort of combination of 'grass', 'victim' and 'meff'.

My mate Paddy somehow seamlessly adopts all the latest phrases, which is strange because he's lived in Barcelona for the last thirteen years. Maybe he's just so Scouse that he telepathically picks up on these things.

Some terms that originated in Liverpool have become popular and fallen into common usage around the UK: 'Y'know', 'no-mark' (for a scumbag), 'made-up' (for happy), 'fit' (for attractive) and so on.

Today, Liverpudlian vocabulary not only contains words otherwise unknown in English slang, but also words that have a different meaning to how they might be understood by someone from outside the city.

The gangster Curtis Warren's accent and use of slang gave the Dutch police eavesdropping on him no end of trouble. For weeks they were trying to work out where the 'House Byarse' was or what it referred to, until they eventually realised that Warren was saying the 'house by ours'.

I remember when I was a student, around 2007, a girl from north London said to me that, whatever she thought of his politics, there was no denying David Miliband was an 'absolute beaut'. I told her I couldn't agree more.

The word beaut is one of dozens of Liverpudlian terms for 'disagreeable person', some of them used elsewhere in the north-west or Ireland, and some of them seemingly unique to the city. A non-exhaustive list of Scouse insults includes beaut, bell whiff, biff, blert, fruit, jarg, melt, ming, mong, meff gone wrong, scrote, Taig (originally used as a slur for a Catholic but now denuded of its sectarian origins), Tory, ted, a bad ted, Texan, whinnet, whopper, wool, victim, quim, quilt and queg.

These feature alongside standard British English insults such as arsehole, bell end, cunt, dickhead, shit(e)house, twat, etc. In Liverpool, someone who was cross-eyed might be told they had 'one eye in Huyton, one in New Brighton'. It may be said of a tight-fisted person that they 'wouldn't give you the steam off their piss'. A miserable individual could be said to have a 'face like a smacked arse'. A meathead could be described as a 'grock' – which, when pronounced with a rolling 'r' and plenty of phlegm on the 'ck', is probably the most Scouse word ever.

There is also an extensive use of nicknames, so that – among young men at least – few people are referred to by their actual names. Off the top of my head, I know of or knew people called Cheers Driver, Paddy Big-nose (who ironically died of a cocaine overdose), Fat Paul, Adam Bighead, Sean the Shark, Ste the Goat, Jason the Jamaican and Igor Wobbly Jaw.

So why is Liverpool so different?

Unusually for a large English (or European) city, Liverpool has no Roman or medieval heritage; its history as an important settlement dates from the eighteenth century, like 'New World' cities such as New York, Toronto, Boston or Sydney.

In Herman Melville's novel *Redburn*, an American visitor exclaims: 'And this is England? But where are the old Abbeys, and the York Minsters, and the Lord Mayors, and coronations, and the May-poles, and fox-hunters, and Derby races, and the dukes and duchesses?'

One publication from 1907, celebrating the 700th anniversary of the city's royal charter, described Liverpool as 'a city without ancestors':

> Its people are people who have been precipitately gathered together from north, from south, from overseas by a sudden impetuous call. Its houses are houses, not merely of recent birth, but pioneer houses, planted instantly upon what, so brief a while ago, was unflawed meadow-land and marsh.

Possibly the huge influx of outside immigrants – from Ireland most notably, but also from Wales, Scotland and the far-flung reaches of the world – limited the room for inward migration from the nearby countryside, ensuring Scouse separateness from the rest of Lancashire.

This idea is seen in the words of the twentieth-century historian Ramsay Muir, who as early as the 1920s was writing that the city could stand as an 'example for all the world that the descendants of the Normans, Anglo-Saxons, Irish, Welsh, Scots and Vikings who have peopled Liverpool are now united in a common pride in being Liverpolitans'.

If Scouse separatism is a relatively new phenomenon, then the designation 'Scouser' is even more recent. With historical figures – real or fictional – who hail from the city, often the fact they were from Liverpool was irrelevant. William Gladstone, for example, or Heathcliff in *Wuthering Heights*, were from Liverpool – but they were not 'Scousers'.

About two hundred years ago, people from Liverpool would add a male first name (usually Dick, for whatever reason) to Liver (as in the liver bird), and so might describe a fellow Liverpudlian as 'Dick Liver'.

For reasons which remain obscure, possibly due to the increasing American influences in the town, Dick Liver was replaced by Dick(e) y Sam, which became the preferred local description of someone from Liverpool during the nineteenth century. James Picton described himself as 'a Liverpool man, or Dicky Sam, as we love to call our native-born inhabitants'.

This fell out of fashion in the early decades of the last century, and by the time of the Second World War, 'wack' or 'wacker' became the standard term to denote a Liverpudlian.

For some time, as people from Liverpool became known as 'Scousers' to outsiders, those in the city refused to use the term and continued to refer to themselves as 'wackers'. By the '70s, however, wacker's time was done, and 'Scouser' was universally used within the city.

Now, very few people have chosen to name themselves after food, and its particularly unusual for people to call themselves after a cheap and humble dish that they don't even eat that often.

Deriving from the Norwegian word *lapskaus*, the first known use of the term in English came in 1837 when the surgeon of the Liverpool workhouse wrote about his successful 'evaporation' of 'Meat Scouse'. Over the course of the Victorian Era, the simple lamb and potato stew became the favourite staple of the city; by the 1890s, middle-class socialist women volunteering in a city soup kitchen were confused and dismayed when the poor children they were catering to rejected offers of 'cocoa and cake' and insisted instead of being treated to a dish of scouse.

One common suggestion is that the legacy of Irish immigration changed Liverpool from a Lancastrian town to something different and distinctive. But it is easy to exaggerate the influence of Irish immigration to the modern identity and politics of Liverpool. After all, various other UK cities – such as London, Birmingham, Glasgow, Edinburgh, Newcastle and Manchester – have all welcomed (if that's the right word) large numbers of immigrants from Ireland over the past two hundred years, and do not have the same kind of distinctiveness as Liverpool.

Paul Du Noyer doesn't get much wrong in his magisterial history of Liverpool, but it's a bit of an overstatement to say that when the

Irish arrived 'it became a Celtic Catholic enclave in a Protestant Anglo Saxon kingdom'. This would have been news to Liverpool's protestant majority, who feared and fought against exactly that outcome well into the twentieth century.

Centuries before Liverpool became the key centre for Irish migration into Britain, the city had played a central role in the history of its western neighbour. It is well known that Liverpool was granted a royal charter by King John in 1207 – what is less well known is that he wanted to build a new port for dispatching troops to Ireland.

Three hundred and fifty years later, the city was the key port supplying the armies of Elizabeth I as she attempted to counter various Irish rebellions and began the Plantation of Ulster, when English and Scottish Protestants were given land in the province – at that point the least Anglicised part of Ireland – to suppress the continuous rebellions against English rule that erupted in the area. And in 1689, William III (King Billy) used Liverpool to ship troops to Ireland to defeat James II at the Battle of the Boyne.

Long before the Irish came to Liverpool, Liverpool was integral to the development of Ireland: from 1650 to 1800 Dublin was the fastest-growing city in Europe, its population increasing from a meagre 17,000 to a whopping 168,000 – Liverpool was central to this growth, serving as the main port for exporting necessities such as salt and coal to the Irish city.

Even after the massive influx of Irish people into Liverpool, it was only fairly recently that this aspect of the city became prominent to its identity. Although all of the Beatles had Irish ancestry, it was not something they spoke about, and nor was it assumed that being from Liverpool they were not symbols of Englishness; in the documentary footage of the Beatles' arrival at John F. Kennedy airport in 1964, among the crowd of screaming teenagers are a small group of protestors holding a sign: 'England Get Out Of Ireland'.

A better explanation than the Irish influence is the unusual history of the Liverpool economy. Given its late development from windblown riverbank to prosperous metropolis, Liverpool did not have the medieval guilds that influenced the economic and business life of more established cities. Instead, occupations related to the sea always dominated the economy of the city. In the mid-1760s, about a quarter of the workforce were sailors – an extremely high proportion for a major British town at this point. In comparison, in London at this time, although it was also a major seaport, fewer than 5 per cent of its working population were employed as sailors.

When you add jobs such as shipbuilding and maintenance, dock administration, customs work and so on, probably somewhere between a third and half of all jobs in the city were dependent on shipping. Though – in comparison to other major ports such as Newcastle and Bristol – there was little actual shipbuilding in Liverpool itself, so from its very conception the city was dependent on trade and services rather than manufacturing.

This importance of the sea to the city did provide opportunities to young men (and some women) in Liverpool that were not available to the factory- and millhands elsewhere in Lancashire. There are plenty of examples of humble sailors surviving and prospering long enough to become merchants, captains and shipowners themselves. These included David Tuohy, a poor immigrant from Ireland who used his profits from fourteen years as captain of a slave ship to set himself up as a prosperous legitimate merchant.

As historians Diana Ascott, Michael Power and Fiona Lewis have argued, 'the Liverpool merchants of 1695 were new men, in trade and politics. They shared the same commercial interests, and, in the absence of a previous entrenched generation, could work together without challenge.'

But there were many men engaged in dangerous and uncertain occupations, and plenty of those who made it to be merchants would later become bankrupt. Historically, merchant seafaring was the most dangerous occupation in Britain: in the mid-nineteenth century a thousand sailors died every year around the coasts of Britain alone, and the risk for crew and passengers on longer journeys was even more hazardous.

In 1865, 8 per cent of British ships reported the death of at least one person on board. In 88 per cent of cases this was a sailor; 11 per cent of the deaths were of passengers; and in 5 per cent of cases the captain himself died. (There were also regular births on board ships, with just under 1 per cent of vessels reporting a birth in 1865.)

Diseases such as typhoid, dysentery, cholera, yellow fever and malaria were the main cause of death, especially for ships visiting tropical climates. After that, falls from the rigging onto the deck or into the sea were the next most common killer, while occasionally a crew member was swept straight overboard during a storm, although this was rare.

In addition to the high mortality rate for individual sailors, ships would very often sink with the loss of all crew and passengers, in some cases disappearing without trace. In the years around 1850, several such disasters befell ships leaving Liverpool.

In 1848, the *Ocean Monarch* caught fire and sank in the mouth of the Mersey, killing 178 of the 398 on board. In 1854, the *City of Glasgow* disappeared en route from Liverpool to Philadelphia with 480 passengers and crew aboard. In 1856, the *Driver* was lost with 344 passengers and 28 crew members on their way to New York. That same year the *Pacific* disappeared with all 186 people on board. In 1859, the emigrant ship *Pomona*, carrying mainly Irish emigrants from Liverpool to New York, sank after hitting a sandbank off the coast of Ballyconnigar, with 389 deaths.

Furthermore, dock work was beset with chronic insecurity, dependent on whether a ship came in, and whether you got to work on it. There was also a complex hierarchy among dockers. Those who worked on the water – stevedores, watermen and lightermen – were considered an elite, and those who worked on land were deemed inferior. Then, on the land, there were interminable levels of skilled workers – including corn porters, riggers, tallymen, warehousemen and baulkers – and men who only handled one kind of good might refuse to socialise with those who didn't specialise. The Edwardian trade-union activist James Sexton said that the Liverpool docks had 'a caste system quite as powerful as India's'.

In 1900, 20,000 men sought work each day on the docks of Liverpool and Birkenhead, uncertain if they would get anything. They would often fight each other for jobs – similar to the fights you might see today between delivery drivers outside popular takeaway restaurants.

Life was tough for the working men, and even worse for their wives, who had to make their meagre, irregular and sometimes non-existent pay cover a week's rent, food and other essentials. One money lender exploited the desperation of his customers in ingenious ways, for example, insisting that anyone wanting to borrow money from them also had to take 2 shillings worth of rancid fish for every 4 shillings that was loaned, so that they would have to pay 6 shillings back the next Saturday.

It was these economic factors, more than anything else, that would create a Liverpudlian identity distinct not only from the other great metropolis of the north-west that sat thirty miles east, but also from the towns and villages of its Lancastrian hinterland.

The 1921 census found that there were twelve times as many men without a fixed address or workplace in Bootle as in St Helens, just 12 miles away inland. This did not necessarily mean that unemployment or homelessness was much worse in Bootle, but instead that an unusually high number of men were employed in seafaring or casual employment on the docks – whereas employment in St Helens was dominated by stable, predictable, long-term jobs in glass, coal and manufacturing.

This unusual dominance of irregular labour had a massive effect not just on the workforce at the time, but for many generations to come – as well as on the broader culture and politics of the city.

Speaking of seafarers, L8 community activist Jimi Jagne, himself part-Gambian, told the journalist Simon Hughes that wherever people come from in the world, by the time they get to Liverpool the sea has changed them:

> Seamen – wherever they are from – develop an easy set of values, they don't necessarily have a home. They set down in a port, they make acquaintances then they move on. The lifestyle involves casual relationships; drink and music. There's a distinction between Africans who came here through the port and Caribbeans who came as part of the Windrush generation.

For Liverpool men, over a large part of its history, running away to sea, leaving your family and troubles and debts behind, was a realistic and commonly taken opportunity that didn't apply for most men in the mill towns and villages of the north of England. Among many others, John Lennon's own father did exactly this.

For those who didn't abscond there were still lots of local men, like my Grandad Stan, who'd been to Buenos Aires and Montevideo, but not to London. As Ringo Starr once recalled, as noted in Paul Du Noyer's *Liverpool – Wondrous Place*: 'Everyone in Liverpool had a camel saddle or something in the corner, because in every other house someone went to sea and would bring all this crap back.'

The culture of coal-mining communities, such as in South Wales and north-east England, sprang from the need to look after each other, above and below ground. Self-motivation was hugely important in pits; the discipline and surveillance common to factories did not apply. For the more casualised labour force of Liverpool things were different again; the main thing that mattered on the docks was could you get the shit on and off fast enough. And then could you handle your drink and keep up with the chat. At sea it was even more fundamental: were you going to make it more likely that they would all get back safe and alive, or more likely that they'd drown?

The idea of 'the Scouser' as friendly, welcoming, funny, etc, is mostly down to a juxtaposition between Scousers and outsiders, particularly southerners. In fact, in this respect our self-image is not that different to other northerners, who loudly talk about how unfriendly London is and how their kind are different.

And even as a distinct Liverpool – as opposed to northern or Lancastrian – identity was developing, this never excluded a sense of English or British patriotism.

At first, brute force provided what natural patriotism could not; in 1795, for example, Liverpool was told to provide over 1,700 sailors for the Royal Navy, and no ships were allowed to leave until the quota was filled. As well as from pubs and brothels, men would also be seized from their own homes; one man taken from a house on Pool Lane disappeared for four years. When he returned, he found his wife about to be married for the third time. Naturally, Scousers fought back, and from 1739 to 1805 there were sixty-six violent incidents recorded against press-gangers in the city.

But by the twentieth century, Liverpool had become a steady source of men for both the Royal Navy and the British Army. The Kop stand at Anfield (as with all the other 'Kops' at football grounds across the country) is named after the Battle of Spion Kop during the Boer War.

A decade after that conflict, around 7,000 Merseyside dockers volunteered to fight in the First World War, with around 13,500 Liverpudlians dying in the conflict. While this may have been motivated by the desire for a regular wage, three meals a day and a taste of adventure, material concerns were not the only motivation: plenty of these men genuinely thought it an honour to die for 'King and Country', just like those from elsewhere in Britain.

In its early days, the ranks of the SAS were dominated by Geordies, Scots and Scousers. Whatever their motivation for joining, Scousers

– just like Scots and Irish soldiers at different times – were an integral part of the British military and its actions over the past 200 years.

(In fact, the 1707 political union of Scotland with England and Wales was a key reason for the economic development of Liverpool in the early eighteenth century from standard, nondescript village to the richest city in the north-west. Maybe this is why Liverpool is more a 'British' city than it is English; it has a modern and outward-looking identity rather than one focused on Alfred and the Cakes or whatever, much in the same way that many black and brown people whose families were immigrants to England feel more comfortable describing themselves as British rather than English.)

There are those who argue that the long history of Scousers, Geordies, Cockneys and Scots within the British military was just down to poverty or desperation, but this is an anachronistic view, usually expounded by people who find the idea of volunteering to fight and die for 'King and Country' incomprehensible and distasteful, and who assume that there must always have been economic pressures forcing men to do so.

In reality, this was not the case. Bill Shankly, an honorary Scouser well known for expounding on his socialist politics, volunteered to join the Royal Air Force at the start of the Second World War, even though – as a former miner and riveter – he could have avoided military service since both of those jobs were 'protected' occupations, immune from conscription. He rose to the rank of corporal and proudly recalled in his autobiography that he was 'a better example to the men than some of the sergeants were'. Derek Hatton's dad was in the Coldstream Guards, one of the most elite regiments in the British Army. Will Sergeant remembers that he and his mates used to play war games with a tattered swastika flag, captured by his father at the battle of Monte Cassino; his dad later became a Labour councillor, and went out knocking on doors for Huyton MP and Labour prime minister Harold Wilson.

Paul McCartney recalls that in his street, 'everyone got television sets for the Coronation [of Queen Elizabeth II] in 1953. Literally the whole street got them', and it was his parents' desire to watch the coronation that led to him seeing Bill Haley and the Comets, thus changing his life. When McCartney was knighted by Queen Elizabeth in 1996, he was joined in Buckingham Palace by Cilla Black and the poet Roger McGough, who were accepting OBEs on the same day. The idea of people from Liverpool being more left-wing and anti-monarchy than the rest of the country is younger than I am.

Even today, all the evidence shows that most people in Liverpool easily hold both an English and a Scouse identity together. The political scientist David Jeffery has found that just 18 per cent of Liverpudlians feel 'only Scouse', merely 5 percentage points higher than the 13 per cent who feel 'only English', with the rest feeling some mixture of Scouse and English. Although the six safest Labour seats are all on Merseyside, and they feature in the bottom quarter nationwide for pro-monarchy sentiment, they are still 15 points more pro- than anti-monarchy

There are lots of people in the city who are closer to the Tories culturally, but they vote Labour nonetheless. And much of the support for someone like Jeremy Corbyn had an element of 'the enemy of my enemy is my friend'. Corbyn hated things that we hate, so we love him, even if the politics of Liverpool are very different to those of Islington North.

Much of the 'Scouse not English' attitude is generated by a few people who fly banners and flags at Anfield, which is assumed by outsiders to be indicative of some innate working-class Scouse sensibility and representative of the whole city. But this is notably absent from Goodison Park, and even denounced by some Gwladys Street regulars as 'Kopite behaviour'.

It also has a big element of 'Scousers on tour'. Middle-class fans don't have anything like this – other than getting behind the England team in the Euros or World Cup. Probably one of the reasons why Liverpool has been more resistant to the working-class shift to the right over the past few years is that people from Liverpool have something that other heterosexual white people don't have. In the identitarian top trumps that has pervaded so much of Anglosphere culture over the past decade or so, being a Scouser is not as valuable as being black, or trans, or Muslim, but it's still *something*. White straight men from, say, Southampton, or Sunderland or wherever don't even have that.

INTERLUDE 2

Middle-Class Scousers

Rodney Street in Liverpool city centre is a typical example of the city's glorious Georgian architecture. Walking along the road that connects the Liverpool Institute where Paul McCartney went to school at one end with a street named for the infamous slave-trading Hardman family at the other, a plaque at number 62 brings your attention to the significance of the house within. At this address in 1809, William Gladstone – future four-time prime minister of the United Kingdom – was born.

The Gladstones are perhaps the most famous example of the Liverpool gentry; prosperous families responsible for a great deal of the architecture and infrastructure of the city. When the 109-year-old Racquet Club was burned down during the riots of 1981, it was an appropriate signal of changing times, the dawn of a new era, in which the likes of the Gladstone family would have little place within the mythos of Liverpool.

There is a long and proud history of the Liverpool middle class, who have made a huge impact locally, within the UK and around the world, but who are usually obscured within the modern image of the city and most tellings of its history. Today, the middle-class Scouser has a peculiar place in the popular imagination because, just like a middle-class Geordie or Glaswegian, they are assumed not to exist.

But one analysis of early twentieth-century Liverpool housing department records concluded that 41 per cent of families in council housing could be classified as middle class by 1939 standards. And as the journalist Paul Du Noyer tells me, if you 'look at the Three Graces[2], look at those millions of tiny little windows, who do you think worked up there? It wasn't dockers.'

Many famous Scousers have decidedly middle-class origins. At the Liverpool Institute school, the future Militant leader Derek Hatton once played Gratiano in a production of *The Merchant of Venice*, alongside future Conservative minister Steve Norris as Portia and the future theatre impresario Bill Kenwright as Shylock ('Where's the Arteta pound of flesh, Bill?')

Because the public conception of the Scouser does not just mean 'person from Liverpool', middle-class Scousers face a precarious existence when outside the city; on the one hand, they might be told that they 'don't sound like they're from Liverpool', on the other hand, they might be told to 'calm down, calm down'.

But in mid-Victorian Britain, to think of Liverpool was to think of the Gladstones, Rathbones, Roscoes and other rich merchant families. It was to think of commerce, industry and self-reliance. Although the city was associated with immigration, and the living conditions of the famine-starved Irish were sensationalised in the press, these were not integral to the broader image of Liverpool any more than channel-crossing asylum seekers today are considered to be a natural feature of Dover.

Dale Street at the turn of the twentieth century was characterised by one local journalist as featuring 'wealth and ambition' and 'busy, happy

---

2 The three historic waterfront buildings on the Pier Head: the Royal Liver Building, the Cunard Building and the Port of Liverpool Building.

men, all bent on winning some prize in the world'. It was a place 'of ship windows, of gossiping politicians lounging on steps, of carriages rattling past the Conservative Club'.

Gladstone's father, John Gladstone, was born in Leith, the port of Edinburgh, was the second of sixteen children and left school at the age of thirteen. In 1785, attracted by the exponential growth of the town and the opportunities it offered, Gladstone senior moved to Liverpool. He initially lived on Bold Street until his marriage in 1790 to Jane Hall, daughter of a lesser Liverpool merchant, after which the couple settled into the new house in Rodney Street. He soon became involved in the slave trade and eventually acquired ownership of several slave plantations in Jamaica and Guiana. The Demerara rebellion of 1823, one of the most significant rebellions by enslaved people in the British Empire, began on one of Gladstone's plantations. The extent of his ownership of slaves was such that after slavery was abolished by Parliament in 1833, he received the largest of all of the payoffs given to slave owners by the British government under the Slave Compensation Act 1837. William Gladstone was named after a close friend of his father, William Ewart, another Liverpool merchant. Gladstone junior was educated from 1816 to 1821 at a preparatory school situated in the vicarage of St Thomas' Church at Seaforth, close to his family's residence of Seaforth House, and in 1821 he followed in the footsteps of his elder brothers and attended Eton College, before starting at Christ Church College, Oxford, in 1828.

The Rathbone family were nonconformist merchants and ship-owners who became prominent philanthropists in the city. The family origins trace back to Gawsworth, Cheshire, where the first William Rathbone was born in 1669; it was his son, William Rathbone II, who left Gawsworth for the growing port of Liverpool, where he worked initially as a sawyer and soon established his own timber business. Having arrived in Liverpool before 1730, the family subsequently became involved in the building and ownership of ships, as well as general trade. In 1788,

William Rathbone IV leased the family house and estate of Greenbank, then part of the Toxteth Park estate, to serve as a country retreat for his young family, and purchased the freehold of Greenbank House in 1809, the year of his death.

William Roscoe was born in 1753; his father was a market gardener and publican, owning the bowling green on Mount Pleasant. Roscoe junior left school at age twelve and, after a stint in bookkeeping, was apprenticed to a solicitor. He started working as a lawyer in 1774 and became increasingly outspoken in his opposition to the slave trade – at great professional and no little personal risk. Roscoe was elected Member of Parliament for Liverpool in 1806 but stood down the following year; during his brief stay, however, he was able to cast his vote in favour of the successful abolition of the slave trade in 1807.

Foster Cunliffe, whose family gives its name to one of the most prominent buildings on the Liverpool waterfront, was a tobacco baron, originally from rural Lancashire, who had left to make his fortunes in the big city. By buying damaged or second-rate tobacco he was able to pay about 25 per cent less in customs duties. His business paid for about three or four ships a year in the triangular trade. He became a founder of the Blue Coat School and eventually a three-time Lord Mayor of Liverpool. His son Ellis became an MP for the town.

One of the most successful Liverpool entrepreneurs was Henry Tate, originally from Chorley, Lancashire, and the last of eleven children of a Unitarian minister. He was apprenticed to a grocer, and by the age of twenty he had his own grocer's shop in Old Haymarket. In 1847, he opened a second shop in Old Hall Street. Eager to modernise the traditional methods of getting white gold from cane syrup, he brought in a new centrifuge that had been developed in Scotland and, in partnership with John Wright, opened his factory on Love Lane. In the first year, they processed 400 tons of cane from places as diverse as Peru, Mauritius and the Caribbean. Soon, the refinery was producing 1,319 tons a week and, by 1874, it employed 642 people. Tate then patented sugar cubes and opened a second factory on the banks of the Thames in 1878.

As well as these male merchants and politicians, many women from the upper reaches of the Liverpool middle class became national figures in Victorian Britain. After her husband was appointed headmaster of Liverpool College, Josephine Butler and her family moved to the city in January1866. Butler had recently lost her five-year-old daughter, Eva, who died after falling forty feet from a banister onto the stone floor of their hallway. She later wrote of this period that she 'became possessed with an irresistible urge to go forth and find some pain keener than my own, to meet with people more unhappy than myself' and 'it was not difficult to find misery in Liverpool'.

She began to make regular visits to the workhouse at Brownlow Hill, and sat with the women in the cellars, picking oakum with them, praying or discussing Bible passages. She also opened up her own home as a shelter for some of the women, often prostitutes in the final stages of venereal disease, before setting up a hostel to provide accommodation for such women. By mid-1867, she opened a second, larger home, providing work for the women to support themselves, in embroidery and making envelopes. Butler's greatest achievements came in her campaigns against child prostitution, which resulted in the Criminal Law Amendment Act 1885 that raised the age of consent from thirteen to sixteen, and her successful campaign for the repeal of the Contagious Diseases Act in 1886, which had allowed for suspected prostitutes to be detained and forcibly examined for evidence of venereal diseases.

These people certainly did not consider themselves 'Scousers', or the nineteenth-century equivalent of that. Instead, just like their contemporaries in Manchester, Leeds, Newcastle and Dublin, they thought of themselves as enlightened philanthropists, doing what they could for the unfortunates of the cities that had given them so much. But at the same time, the Victorian provincial middle class were not 'citizens of nowhere', at their greatest comfort on ocean liners and deriding provincial pride as reactionary and chauvinistic. Instead, they were massively proud of their provincial origins and worked very hard to make Liverpool the equal of any city in the world.

It could be considered a cruel fate that these people have no place in the popular imagination of the city today. But given that they dedicated much of their lives and no little of their fortunes so that Liverpool would be considered a place of business, prosperity and sober self-improvement . . . they might see it as all for the best.

4

GOOD RIOTERS, BAD SOCIALISTS

It's fairly well known by now that Liverpool was once a hotbed of working-class Toryism. Even at the 1906 general election – a wipeout for the Tories and their worst result until 1945 – the Liberal Party only managed to win two of Liverpool's nine seats, with the Conservatives taking six out of the other seven.

That election was dominated by the issue of free trade – whether or not there should be tariffs on certain goods coming into the UK – and the main reason the Conservatives lost so badly was the fear that their proposed tariff reforms would damage trade and put up food prices.

Yet even in a town so totally dependent on trade as Liverpool – even in a *port* town, in an election dominated by debates over free trade, the city put two fingers up to the national trend and voted for the Tories anyway. The Liberals despaired.

Labour, at that stage, were not a serious force on Merseyside. In 1910 Ramsay MacDonald – later to become the first Labour prime minister – seemed to accept defeat in the city: 'Liverpool is rotten and we had better recognize it.' Why was this the case?

The fledgling Labour party had no luck in the city until 1923. At this point, the areas that voted Labour had either strong trade unions or high levels of nonconformist Protestants – Baptists, Methodists, Quakers, etc – or both. Places such as South Wales, West Yorkshire and the Durham coalfield. In contrast, Liverpool had neither: trade unions were either small, or weak, or both.

Over the centuries, the politics of the city's elected representatives have been notably inconsistent: from the Whig ascendency of the Restoration and Georgian England, through to the Fenian-baiting popular Toryism of the late Victorian Era, and from New Labour faithful, such as Luciana Berger and Stephen Twigg, to today's vestigial Corbynites in Kim Johnson, Paula Barker and Ian Byrne.

Before the so-called 'Glorious Revolution' of 1689, when the Catholic King James II was deposed by Parliament and replaced with the Protestant William of Orange, most of the MPs who represented Liverpool in the House of Commons were handpicked by the Earl of Derby, a local landowner.

In the decades afterwards, political corruption remained endemic, and only a few per cent of people had the right to vote. Sir Thomas Bootle, for example, smoothed his election first as an MP in 1724 and then as mayor of the town in 1726 by donating two fire engines to the city.

By 1750, an elite of around twenty families, made up mostly of nonconformist Protestants (Baptists, Quakers, Methodists, etc), controlled most of the trade in the city. But if the official politics of the time was dominated by a close-knit elite, the politics of the street was always more rambunctious and disorderly. Politically motivated mob violence was well established in Liverpool from the mid-eighteenth century, with one notorious riot occurring during the 1757 general election; there was also a rampage by sailors in 1775 and riots during the 1841 election so severe that 400 special constables were required to suppress the disturbances.

At this time, Liverpool was represented in Parliament by people like Banastre Tarleton, infamous for his butchery in the US War of

Independence (and later played by the Liverpudlian actor Jason Isaacs in Mel Gibson's *The Patriot*), and Isaac Gascoyne, a reactionary MP who among other things vigorously defended bull baiting and was known as 'Hopper-Arsed Isaac' by his constituents.

As the franchise began to expand after the Great Reform Act of 1832 and politics became more democratic, campaigns took on a more populist nature, trying to harness the prejudices and piss-taking of popular street politics. At the 1835 general election, one of the city's two MPs, the Whig/Liberal William Ewart, was challenged by James Morris, a director of the Bank of England. Local conservatives attacked Morris as a 'cockney', envious of his metropolitan connections and privileges. In a mock poster advertising two 'hacks' for sale, Ewart was dismissed as 'Lot 1: NONENTITY' and Morris was described as:

Lot 2: COCKNEY: a South Country Horse ... sent here with a *false pedigree*; Sire stated to be *Free Trade*, but though *quite unknown* here, he is ascertained to have been got by *Monopoly*, trained in Threadneedle-street, where he was been used by an *Old Lady*, who has got a Patent, for making Rags into Money, and who prosecutes with the utmost rigour anyone else that attempts to follow the same trade. Though not vicious in other respects, 'COCKNEY' like all *London-bred* Horses, is very *jealous* of those bred in the *North*, particularly *Liverpool*.

With the Second Reform Act of 1867, most men aged twenty-one or over in 'borough' constituencies such as Liverpool could now vote. Between then and 1885, the whole of the city was covered by one constituency, represented by three MPs. In most elections during this time the Tories won two of Liverpool's seats and the Liberals one. In this period the old Liberal elites – the Rathbones, Holts, Gladstones, etc – were replaced by Liberal Unionists and Conservatives, 'the party of the lesser Liverpool entrepreneur', according to the historian Murray Steele.

From 1885 onwards, to take account of the massive expansion of the city and the increasingly large electorate, Liverpool was divided into nine different constituencies, each represented by one MP. From then on, with a few exceptions, the Conservative candidate won in every general election and by-election until 1923.

The exceptions were the Liverpool Exchange constituency, which was won by the Liberals in 1886, 1887, 1906 and 1910; Liverpool Abercromby, which was won by the Liberals in 1906; and, most notably, Liverpool Scotland, which was held by Irish Nationalist T. P. O'Connor until his death in 1929 – the only constituency outside of Ireland to have been represented by an Irish nationalist MP.

During this time, Toxteth was represented by people such as Henry de Worms and Augustus Frederick Warr, while for fourteen years the MP for Kirkdale was a Baronet called De Fonblanque Pennefather.

To some extent the franchise – who got to vote, and how many votes they had – affected politics at this time. From 1867, men in 'borough' constituencies (usually towns and cities like Liverpool) were able to vote in general elections if they were a 'householder' (generally meaning a man living with his wife and children or by himself), and paid rent of £10 a year or more. This meant that most working-class men were in theory enfranchised, but an estimated 40 per cent of men nationwide could not vote as late as 1918.

Many men couldn't vote because they lived with their parents or in houses with multiple families, and this would have had a big impact in a port city like Liverpool, where much of the population worked away for long periods. And if a voter moved house, they only retained their right to vote if they stayed in the same constituency, which meant that people who moved more often were less likely to be able to vote.

Between August 1909 and 1910, for example, 26,000 people or 31 per cent of the electorate were taken off the electoral role in Liverpool. This one was of the highest rates in the country, even compared to other working-class areas with a mobile population, such as Leeds North and Wolverhampton West (both 30 per cent) and Tottenham (27 per cent), although not as high as Tyneside and Birmingham East, where removals in this period made up 39 per cent of the electorate.

As well as this, some men had more than one vote – and Liverpool was believed to have a relatively high proportion of 'plural voting', whereby someone who lived in one constituency but had a business in another could vote in both places. Given the tendency of such people to support the Conservatives, this also enhanced the Tory vote in the town.

And until the Secret Ballot Act of 1872, people's votes were public, so everyone knew how you voted. The potential of this for bribery and intimidation are obvious, and the Conservative party's long and productive relationship with the brewery industry came in very handy here, as brewers and publicans would 'treat' men who voted for the Conservative candidate with a free pint.

So there are good reasons to think that the franchise in the Victorian era went some way to making Liverpool a hotbed of Toryism. However, some historians have challenged the idea that the pre-1918 franchise disproportionately affected the working-class vote, noting that, on average, men from working-class backgrounds found work, left home and started families slightly earlier, and middle-class professionals were more likely to be lodgers, who often couldn't vote.

While it is a complicated picture, it's too easy to use the disenfranchisement of working-class voters to explain the Tory dominance in the city. And since all women were unable to vote in general elections until 1918, the selective franchise might have hurt the Tories, as for decades women as a whole tended to favour the Conservatives by wide margins. In fact, it's been estimated that if women could not vote, the Labour party would have won every election between 1945 and 1979.

In Glasgow, another town dependent on ships and seafaring, and which also had violent sectarian divides, the Conservatives were notably weaker – and had been for some time. Whereas Liverpool bucked the national trend and voted for the Tories in 1906, Glasgow had done the same for the Liberals at the 1886 election, when 'Home Rule' for Ireland was the dominant issue, and a divided Liberal party (led by Scouser William Gladstone) lost over 150 seats. Not in Glasgow, however, where the Liberals won four of the city's nine seats, and two of the rest were won by so-called 'Liberal Unionists' who all later returned to the Liberal party.

At the 1906 general election – only the second to be contested by the newly formed Labour party – the former shipyard worker George Barnes was elected for Glasgow Blackfriars and Hutchesontown, and he held the seat until he was elected for the new Gorbals constituency in 1918, alongside Neil Maclean, who won in Govan. Four years later, Labour won ten of the city's fifteen seats at the 1922 election. In contrast, no Liverpool constituency elected a Labour MP until after the party had already taken most of the seats in Glasgow.

One reason for this was that in Glasgow, although it was a major port itself, the dominant industry of shipbuilding provided an industrial base with skilled, secure jobs and well-organised trade unions. Even if we include the Cammel Laird shipyards in nearby Birkenhead, Liverpool never had a similar level of manufacturing jobs.

There was also little direct competition between Catholics and Protestants before the First World War in Glasgow due to the skilled economy: Protestants tended to work in the shipyards and Catholics on the docks. But in the casualised economy of Liverpool, with a lack of skilled jobs and competition for unskilled work, Catholics and Protestants had to sometimes literally fight to get access to jobs.

The historian Joan Smith argues that these differences, along with the influence of religious nonconformity and political liber-alism, meant that organised socialist groups took hold in Glasgow much earlier than in Liverpool. For example, in a 1909 May Day demonstration by labour and socialist groups, up to 30,000 took to the streets of Glasgow; in contrast, Liverpool had never held a successful May Day march.

Alongside competition for work and the religious divides on Merseyside, another issue made an important contribution to Tory dominance: drink.

Strange as it seems today, at the start of the twentieth century, alcohol licensing was a key political issue, behind only free trade and Irish Home Rule among the contentious issues of the time.

And while the liberal left was able to cultivate a popular culture in Glasgow through groups such as the Independent Labour Party, which served as a kind of conduit for working men to liberal and socialist politics, in Liverpool it was the Conservatives who cultivated a local political culture through emphasising anti-Catholicism and nationalism, alongside opposition to restrictions on pub licensing hours.

But despite Labour making inroads into the elite politics of Glasgow much earlier than in Liverpool, the Liverpudlian street was often more willing to turn out in support of some cause or other, and Glaswegians were less likely to get involved in spontaneous protests and riots.

In 1912, over 100,000 people attended a pro-Ulster Unionist demonstration in Liverpool's Sheil Park. Even if organised labour had difficulties in transferring practical solidarity into political results, as the Sheil Park demonstration and the previous year's transport strike show, plenty of people in Liverpool were willing to march and protest. As Smith concluded, if Glasgow men could be described as good social-ists but bad rioters, Liverpool men were exactly the opposite.

Smith argued this all led to a situation where 'Glasgow was a Liberal city which became the home of municipal socialism and communism; Liverpool was a Conservative city where the only hope for socialists appeared to be a mass strike that could destroy the influence of the dominant ideologies and organisations, hence syndicalism.'

Syndicalism – the idea that workers should control the industries they worked in – was collectivist and anti-statist; unlike nationalisation, where industries were publicly owned through the government, syndicalism did not require an over-mighty state.

Even at its height, syndicalism was a minority pursuit on the British left, most of which advocated a reformist, parliamentary approach, using the British state to bring about socialism – but it's probably not surprising that Liverpool was one of the areas were this brand of grassroots, anti-authoritarian politics had greater influence.

Fred Bower and Jim Larkin were two of the leading Liverpool syndicalists of this time. Bower wrote that earlier in their lives, in 'infantile ignorance', they had 'tried to kill each other over religion', but by 1904 they were labourers building the foundations of the Anglican cathedral, looking on slums 'not fit for swine . . . no more than a stone's throw away' from the cathedral site.

On 27 June 1904, they approached the place where the massive foundation stone was due to be laid three weeks later. Bowers carried a biscuit tin containing copies of two socialist newspapers, *The Clarion* and *Labour Leader*, and a 'letter addressed to a future socialist society' which contained their hopes and ambitions for a better tomorrow. They bent over the ends and edges to make it as airtight as possible and then placed it between two rows of bricks.

Two days later, Bower left Liverpool on a White Star liner bound for New York. On 19 July, King Edward VII, alongside the Queen and roughly 7,000 Liverpool dignitaries, laid the foundation stone where Bower and Larkin had hidden their time capsule. It remains there to this day.

As the examples of Bower and Larkin show, even though socialist political parties were weak on Merseyside, there is a long heritage of grassroots radical movements – they just didn't transfer into electoral success for left-wing parties. By 1891, the Trades Council had 121 delegates representing forty-seven trades and 46,000 members, making it the largest Trades Council outside London. In this period, the Conservative MP and former Lord Mayor Arthur Forwood warned that 'dangerous doctrines were being preached by the new school of trade unionists – the Burns, Mann and Tillett type of demagogue'.

He was talking about Joe Burns, Ben Tillett and Tom Mann – the latter two had founded the National Transport Workers' Federation in an attempt to organise the various smaller unions representing dockers, sailors and transport workers. This activism led to the events of 1911, which made it seem like Forwood's prophecy was coming true. For in that year, the city which had so consistently backed the Tories at the ballot box erupted into the most serious labour unrest seen in decades.

It was triggered by sailors on the ship *Baltic,* belonging to the White Star Line, who demanded a pay increase of one pound a month. They were refused, and five hundred sailors downed tools and went on strike. When the dockers walked out in sympathy, the 1911 transport strike was under way.

That year featured a combination of several strikes involving at one time or another every section of transport workers in the port, culminating in a general strike across the city. Unionised and non-unionised, Protestant and Catholic, specialists and general labourers all joined together. Men used to fighting each other on the streets now marched and fought as one.

The strike temporarily broke down the internecine craft divisions that characterised the waterfront: seamen, ships' stewards, catering staff, dock labourers, carters, tug-boatmen, coalheavers, cold storage men, boiler scalers, railwaymen, tramwaymen, electric power-station workers and scavengers all took part.

As well as this, female workers at Mayfield sugar works, and garment workers and women at the Walton rubber works all walked out, and the

National Union of Women Workers succeeded in organising increasing numbers of women throughout the year.

The syndicalist Tom Mann called for a huge demonstration outside St George's Hall. In response, extra police and soldiers were quickly brought into the city. On 'Bloody Sunday', 13 August 1911, over 90,000 people packed onto St George's Plateau – standing there now and trying to imagine such numbers, one and a half times the capacity of Anfield, packed into such a space, gives you an idea of the atmosphere.

It was a bright and sunny day in a very hot summer, and the drafting in of police from outside the city had ratcheted up the tension further. Eventually, baton-wielding police, on horse and on foot, charged the masses gathered on the plateau – over 200 people were injured and one policeman died. According to Fred Bower, afterwards 'the Plateau resembled a battlefield, disabled and wounded men, women and children, lying singly and in heaps over a vast area'.

Two days later, on Tuesday 15 August, a convoy of prison vans containing men who'd been arrested that day left St Anne's Street police station, aiming to get to Walton Gaol. The authorities were taking no chances, and it was accompanied by thirty-two soldiers from the 18th Hussars regiment, on horseback and armed with rifles, bayonets, pistols and swords, alongside a number of mounted police.

A confrontation occurred on Vauxhall Road and the troops opened fire, injuring three men and killing two others. The first was John Sutcliffe, a twenty-year-old Catholic who was shot twice in the head just outside his house on the corner of Hopwood Street. The second, Michael Prendergast, a twenty-nine-year-old Catholic docker, was shot twice in the chest on the corner of Lamb Street.

Their funerals were attended by hundreds of Protestants and even Orange Lodge men. Tom Mann pointed to the strike as evidence that the religious divisions that had plagued the city had been replaced by a new class consciousness, although this was based more on hope than fact.

During the rioting on the night of 13 August, there were still incidences of sectarian violence; on Great Homer Street and around Islington shops and pubs were looted and burned, and Catholics and Protestant mobs fought until the intervention of the armed troops finally restored order.

During the week-long general strike that followed, while strikers fought with the soldiers and police, there were still sectarian attacks on homes and businesses of both Catholics and Protestants. The warship HMS *Antrim* was sent to the Mersey, its cannons pointing at the docks, and another 2,000 troops were rushed into the city.

These measures were enough to calm the violence and return the city to order, but it had been a close-run thing. Speaking in Parliament on 22 August, the then Home Secretary Winston Churchill stated that if the strike had continued it 'would have produced a swift and certain degeneration of all the means, of all the structure, social and economic, on which the life of the people depends'. The journalist Phillip Gibbs reported in *The Times* that 'Liverpool [was] as near to a revolution as anything I had seen in England'.

But despite the drama, the 1911 strike did not represent a turning point in the city's politics. Three years later came the First World War, with high levels of enlistment across the Liverpool working class, both Catholic and Protestant. Eight thousand Merseyside dockers joined the military in the five months from August 1914 to January 1915.

Not that the war ended grassroots radical politics in the city; in March 1915, an unofficial weekend strike took place at both the Birkenhead and Liverpool docks, and, immediately after the war, the police themselves went on strike, with Liverpool again a centre of the action – in Bootle, all but one of its seventy officers joined the strike, the highest percentage in the country.

When Herbert Asquith commended female munitions workers' efforts in Liverpool, he was heckled by several female suffrage campaigners in the crowd who had tied themselves to seats so they could not easily be removed.

At the 1919 meeting of the Women's International League Council, a representative from Liverpool, Alice Ker, suggested 'that the W.I.L. show its appreciation of women's splendid work during the past five years by making a firm stand against the present practice of turning women from their posts in the Civil Service and other Public Departments'. The Liverpool branch also raised an objection to the 'British subject' clause of the association's membership, with Ker moving a motion to substitute the article for one that stated 'Membership shall be open to all women' who accepted the internationalist, pacifistic objectives of the League. Despite the actions of the Liverpool ladies, the Council voted in favour of keeping WIL's membership 'purely British'.

The importance of street politics, protest and direct action in Liverpool was reflected in the background of the city's first Labour MP, who was able to make the breakthrough in a by-election for the Edge Hill constituency in 1923. Jack Hayes was a former Irish Nationalist and Metropolitan policeman, who had played a role in organising the police strikes in Liverpool and London. This multifaceted identity of Hayes – policeman, Irish Nationalist, Labour MP – was no coincidence. As Jack Jones, the Liverpool docker who fought in the Spanish Civil War and became the General Secretary of the Transport and General Workers' Union, said of James Sexton, 'a man who came out of the Fenian stable but over the years became a pillar of society', much of the Liverpool Left at this time had complicated, conflicted politics.

Since the 1911 strike, the most notable industrial action in the city was the dock lockout of 1995–98. Although sometimes referred to as the dock strike, a lockout – when employers sack or refuse to admit workers – is much harder to resolve than a strike. In a strike, the workers can put pressure on the company due the amount of business lost each day. In a lockout, by contrast, the company willingly dismisses the workers and takes on new men. It does not want the sacked men to go back to work – in fact, it prevents them from doing so. In this case, the workers have far less leverage. It is even more important than during a strike to prevent 'scab' labour from taking over their jobs, and they are especially reliant on solidarity and support from elsewhere to put pressure on their employers.

In 1972, the Mersey Docks and Harbour Board, in existence since 1858, was relaunched as a limited company and floated on the stock exchange. The move brought in extra capital to fund a new dock at Seaforth, but despite various injections of cash in the next two decades – including £112 million of loans, £37 million of government investment and £13 million from the EEC, the Port of Liverpool's long-term decline seemed irreversible.

During the Margaret Thatcher premiership, the company funded the redundancy of 600 dock workers, enabling a 41 per cent saving in wages, so that the Port of Liverpool had the most productive workforce in Western Europe. But the Dock Work Act of 1989 enabled the reintroduction of casualised labour and undermined hard-won rights such as minimum wages, sick pay and holidays. Maximum working hours were gone: dockers would be on call twenty-four hours a day and had to finish jobs irrespective of the length of time they'd been working. Accidents soon increased.

In 1992, the MDHB placed adverts in the *Echo* to replace all of their staff. The threat of this allowed the company to force through the end of overtime payments and 12-hour shifts. Three years later, a subcontractor, Torside Limited, fired five of their workers in a dispute over overtime pay. The refusal of other dockers to work until the five were reinstated led the MDHB to dismiss 300 of the 380 remaining dockers for breach of contract, beginning a dispute that would last three years, and ultimately end in failure.

The experience of the dock dispute, alongside the Hillsborough Justice Campaign, and more recently grassroots initiatives such as Fans Supporting Foodbanks demonstrates the community-mindedness and solidarity of the city, but this has not translated into high membership of and engagement with the Labour party itself.

You don't often see Liverpool compared to Iran. And certainly, a stroll through the city centre on a Friday or Saturday night brings sights you probably wouldn't see in downtown Tehran. Or at least, not since 1979.

But the two places are more similar than you might think. In an essay comparing the politics of Iran and Egypt, the Asef Bayat noted that Iran never had much of a popular Islamist movement before the revolution, but due to the government of the Shah eliminating secular opposition – liberals, socialists, trade unionists, etc – the Mullahs were the only people able to take over.

Something similar has happened in the political transformation of Liverpool over the past hundred years. From a bastion of working-class Toryism, it became a city which not only provides the six safest Labour seats in the country, but where support for the Labour party has grown over the past twenty years, even as other areas with similar demographics have gone in the opposite direction.

But the politics of Liverpool have undergone a Labour revolution without ever having much of a Labour movement. Although Liverpool had elected its first Labour MP in 1923 (the former policeman and Irish nationalist Jack Hayes), and the party won eight of the eleven constituencies in its 1945 general election landslide, it slipped back to three out of nine by the mid-1950s. There were Tory MPs elected for Walton and West Derby until 1964, and Wavertree and Garston until 1983.

As late as the 1959 local elections, six of Liverpool's nine council wards were controlled by the Conservatives, and three of those were solidly working-class areas, including Toxteth and Walton. Labour only won the local elections for the first time in 1955, but the Tories regained control of the council for most of the 1960s. For the rest of the 1970s, the council swung between the Tories and the Liberals, so that when Militant took over in 1983, they succeeded a Conservative–Liberal coalition.

In these years, Liverpudlian politics tended to follow the national trend in stark contrast to 1906 and 2019. The political scientist David Jeffery, who studies electoral politics in Liverpool, told me that after the Second World War there was a 'nationalisation of politics whereby local politics and circumstances began to matter a lot less, and the Liverpool vote began to track the national vote share'.

Therefore, as elsewhere in the country, the party that was in power nationally would usually do badly in local elections. As Jeffery explains, the Tory landslides in council votes during the late 1960s were not driven by a surge in support for the Tories, but rather a collapse in the Labour vote due to the growing unpopularity of Harold Wilson's government in Westminster. And then in the early 1970s, when Ted Heath was unpopular, Labour and the Liberals did better in local elections. In 1998, a year after Tony Blair's Labour landslide, the Liberal Democrats once again took power on the Liverpool city council.

Nonetheless, the last decades of the twentieth century saw a change in the political culture of Liverpool, which meant that the city's time of tracking the national vote would be short-lived. For Jeffery, this was mostly due to the experience of the 1980s, in which the Trotskyist Militant Tendency came to dominate the local Labour party. Labour's victory in the 1983 council elections led left-wing demagogues like Derek Hatton to public office, and it was in this period that Liverpool – for the first time – became thought of as a particularly left-wing city. But even though the party owes its current dominance in the city to this period, the politics of that era were not down to the strength of the local labour movement – in fact, one of the reasons Militant were able to take over Liverpool Labour was because the local Labour parties had relatively few members.

It was only during the 1980s that a real change came about in terms of the political culture and identity of the city. The by-election in Liverpool Walton in 1991 gave an indication of the new politics of Liverpool; occasioned by the death of firebrand Eric Heffer, the Labour candidate Peter Kilfoyle won over 50 per cent of the vote, with the Liberal Democrats on 36 per cent and the independent 'Walton Real Labour' candidate – Militant activist Lesley Mahmood – receiving a respectable 2,613 votes, or 6.5 per cent of the total. The Tory candidate, Berkeley Greenwood, received just 2.9 per cent – and only just finished ahead of Screaming Lord Sutch, the candidate for the Monster Raving Loony party.

But even today, when the city's current political allegiances are not in doubt, the extent of progressive liberal internationalism in the city is easily (and frequently) overstated. At the 2024 election, Reform UK came second in most of the Liverpool seats, finishing in third place in the others. There are plenty of right-wing voters in Liverpool, David Jeffery tells me, they just don't vote. And as long as the first past the post system prevails for local and national elections, meaning that overall vote share is irrelevant, they will not bother to vote.

In many ways, this shouldn't be a surprise. Unlike other Labour strongholds, which typically have large numbers of graduates and recent immigrants, the Merseyside constituencies usually have very different demographics. Sefton Central, for example, has relatively few young people, is 98 per cent white and has one of the highest rates of home ownership in the country. Yet since 2010, in stark contrast to 'Red Wall' seats with similar demographics, Labour's Bill Esterton MP has increased his share of the vote from a marginal 3,862 to a comfortable 18,282.

In Liverpool, unlike the rest of the UK, overwhelming support for Labour can coincide with social or cultural conservatism; hence the three safest Labour seats in the whole country – Liverpool Walton, Knowsley and Bootle – all voted Leave in the 2016 referendum.

If the assumptions around Liverpool politics can be misleading, it's worth asking why we have these assumptions. It might be due in part to the Scouse diaspora, living outside the city, who loudly voice their politics in opposition to the people around them, as well as online 'professional Scousers' who pretend the city is some kind of *Guardian* readers' paradise – but they usually know deep down that there's a few things they don't mention.

People who are more liberally inclined are more likely to vote in local elections (which in Liverpool usually have about 30 per cent turnout), and this distorts the local picture, making the city seem more left wing than it actually is. If there was some form of proportional representation, where the number of seats in the council reflected the proportion of the vote won, then various smaller parties would be better represented.

Just as in the early twentieth century, Liverpool today has a large working-class population, but it doesn't have much of a labour *movement* – despite Labour consistently winning elections.

Historically, in areas without strong trade unions, there would be relatively few people in the local Labour parties. Once the unions lost their strength and influence, alongside a decline in local government, the traditional routes for working-class people into local politics dried up. Because, historically, working-class people who are not in trade unions have tended not to join the Labour party, this has led to the membership of Labour parties in working-class areas gradually declining. For example, the biggest constituency Labour parties today, such as Hornsey and Wood Green, have over 3,000 members, but Liverpool Walton has just over 1,000.

London, by comparison, has far higher levels of middle-class graduates – exactly the kind of people who have historically joined political parties – and therefore sees much more enthusiasm for and engagement with the Labour party.

This relative lack of enthusiasm and political engagement can be seen by comparing the turnouts of the last mayoral races in Liverpool and London; in both cases, everyone knew that the Labour candidate would win, yet in London the turnout was 40 per cent, whereas in Liverpool it was just 29 per cent.

For much of the twentieth century, left-wing politics in Liverpool was dominated by prominent men: the trade union leader Jack Jones, the prime ministers Harold Wilson and James Callaghan –who was born and raised in Portsmouth – and Derek Hatton. Speaking in a debate on wage councils, Conservative MP Angela Rumbold criticised Eddie Loyden, MP for Liverpool Garston, arguing that Loyden and his kind were:

> Not willing to show the decency of allowing that women of any origin have the ability to move forward for themselves. We do not need to be supported indefinitely by the opinions or views of the male sex. This is the first time in my life that I have ever been moved to make such a feminist and pro-feminist speech. But I find that increasingly in this place the number of times men wish to tell women what they are capable of doing and what they should do with their bodies and their lives is becoming quite intolerable.

Loyden went on to lose his seat in Margaret Thatcher's first general election win in 1979, as the Tories took Garston.

But women were to play an increasingly important role in Merseyside politics in the second half of the twentieth century. In 1972, a protest by young women, many of them pushing prams and carrying toddlers, forced Birds Eye to reinstate twenty-four men who had been dismissed after an informal strike. And probably the most famous female Scouse politician of the twentieth century was Bessy Braddock, who served as Member of Parliament for the Liverpool Exchange division from 1945 to 1970. She was never appointed as a minister in any of the Labour governments during this time, but achieved national recognition for her campaigning over issues such as public health and housing.

Braddock's mother, Mary Bamber – usually called Ma Bamber – was herself a key figure in the political transformation of the city during the twentieth century. She took Elizabeth to see the syndicalist Tom Mann speak during the 1911 strike. Eight years later, when she was a delegate at the 1919 Labour Party convention, Ma Bamber gave a speech to the conference floor:

> If the Labour Party . . . would stop trying to be statesmen, and get on with the work which the rank and file were doing outside, they would be surprised at the support they could get from the country . . . With one or two exceptions it has not been possible in most of the Labour speeches to draw a dividing line between the speeches of Labour Members and some of the advanced Liberals in the House of Commons . . . Speaking as a woman of the working class, but a woman who understood the whole international position, she declared that there was a mighty difference in being a Labour Member and understanding the international situation. If they were going to build up a Party to dominate the thinking of workers of this country, they would have to go on definite working-class lines.

This attitude sums up much of Liverpool's political identity in the middle decades of the twentieth century, when an aversion to ideas and issues considered to be wishy-washy liberalism transferred into a solid 'common sense' working-class identity.

Braddock was also one of the first members of Labour Friends of Israel, a patron of the Histadrut Committee and of the Rescue Committee active during the war years. She was a close friend of Louis

Caplan, the first and only Jewish Lord Mayor of Liverpool, and she was also connected to the Pioneer Women's group.

In July 1965, the Pioneer Women hosted a reception for Labour women MPs at the House of Commons, in honour of the wife of the new Israeli ambassador, which was attended by Harold Wilson's wife, Mary. Braddock welcomed the guests, after she had hosted the Pioneers in the Commons on a previous occasion.

On her death, Sidney Goldberg, general secretary of Poale Zion, a socialist Zionist movement, wrote that both she and her husband 'held staunch pro-Jewish and pro-Zionist views', and were often seen and spoke at Poale Zion functions in Liverpool: 'I have vivid memories of a crowded Picton Hall, about 28 years ago, being addressed by Professor Harold Laski and Berl Locker, with Bessie in the Chair.'

Eric Heffer – a committed socialist and MP for Liverpool Walton from 1964 until his death in 1991 – who came from another section of the party, was also a member of the LFI. An article in *The Times* from 1970 said that Heffer, who had just been elected deputy of the LFI, would 'concentrate on spreading the word among Labour MPs about Israel's development as a socialist state'. After explaining that 'Heffer is a keen internationalist who carries a great deal of weight with the Parliamentary left', the report continued:

> he believes not enough has been done to explain the socialist character of the Israeli state: 'There's no doubt that it's very democratic – every Israeli you meet thinks he's Foreign Secretary – the kibbutzim are probably the most socialistic institutions in the world, and a large sector of the economy is publicly owned.

In recent years, the Liverpool left has become more radical on cultural issues such as race and ethnicity, but it is doubtful that the people of the city are as liberal as their representatives on these issues.

The website Electoral Calculus breaks down the demographics and political culture of each of the UK's 650 constituencies, and ranks them according to their political opinion on economics (left vs right), internationalism (global vs national) and culture (liberal vs conservative), and designates them as one of various 'tribes' such as progressives, traditionalists and so on. It also has estimates for each seat's vote in the Brexit referendum.

Of the five safest Labour seats, Liverpool Walton is rated as 27 degrees left, 3 degrees globalist and 1 degree conservative, and 52 per cent voted Leave. Knowsley is 26 degrees left, 2 degrees globalist, 2 degrees conservative; 52 per cent voted Leave. Bootle is 25 degrees left, 3 degrees globalist, 0 degrees social; exactly half of Bootle residents voted Leave. West Derby is 26 degrees left, 6 degrees global, 1 degree liberal; 48 per cent voted Leave. All four of these constituencies are classed as 'traditionalists', according to the Electoral Calculus formula. The people in these seats have, on average, left-wing economic views but cultural and social views that are centrist or conservative.

(The notable exception is Liverpool Riverside, which is rated as 21 degrees left, 29 degrees globalist and 18 degrees liberal. Merely 27 per cent voted to leave the EU.)

Therefore, despite the victories of the Labour party in parliamentary and local elections, there is a large amount of conservative sentiment in the city. That is why up to three constituencies likely voted Leave, and why UKIP came third in the 2014 local elections – only 969 votes off the Greens in second place. They did especially well in working-class wards such as Club Moor, County, Fazakerley and Norris Green.

Just because the city has become more self-consciously left-wing, it does not mean that racism has been done away with. During the dockers' lockout, Peter Kilfoyle recalls telling his friend who was 'going on about the dockers' support for the oppressed blacks of South Africa':

'Hang on, you're the official for the docks, Jimmy; you've been through those periods when there were up to 28,000 workers on the docks. You tell me, how many black guys did you have in that work force?' He could think of two. And yet you had all of Liverpool 8, which is effectively a ghetto for black people, running alongside the southern docks when they were operative.

Wavertree, in particular, had a large National Front presence as late as the 1980s. Irene Affuel, who grew up in the area, remembers being chased down the street by dogs set on them by racist families. Today, the organised far right is no longer a presence in the city, and you can see on social media the welcoming such groups can expect, such as when National Action were held in the left luggage area at Lime Street station by the police to save them from the crowd outside. The founder of Quiggins – a famous incense-filled alternative boutique in Liverpool city centre – stood as a candidate for the National Front in the 2012 mayoral elections and won only 453 votes.

But Liverpool is not immune to crowd action in the opposite direction. In February 2023, there was a serious disturbance outside a centre housing refugees, and there were anti-immigration riots in Southport, Walton and the city centre in 2024.

Meanwhile, although Wavertree is free of the National Front, extreme views of a different nature are still likely to crop up in local politics; in 2015, the chair of Liverpool Wavertree Labour Party, Dr Alex Scott-Samuel, formerly a senior lecturer in public health at the University of Liverpool, lost his honorary position at the university over his appearance on a show broadcast by anti-Semitic conspiracist David Icke. Scott-Samuel, who is himself Jewish, said that, 'The Rothschild family are behind a lot of the neo-liberal influence in the UK and the US. You only have to google them to look at this.' Another local Labour member, Kenneth Campbell, who submitted his own no-confidence motion in Luciana

Berger, was earlier found to have described her as a 'disruptive Zionist'. In a social media post, one woman reportedly asked: 'Is it any wonder the Zionest [sic] are hated and despised [sic] throughout the world.' On 17 November 2018, she added: 'How can we not have empathy with Palestinians when they are not up against these murdering, Zionest [sic] bastards. Their NAZI masters have taught them well.'

When the MMA fighter Paddy 'the Baddy' Pimblett chants 'Fuck the Tories', he isn't making a political message. The same lad badmouthed Georgian fighter Ilia Topuria and the Dagestani-origin fighter Muhammad Mokaev as part of the prefight routine.

Likewise, when it comes to LGBT issues, Liverpool's rainbow colours are recently acquired, as poor old Pete Price can bitterly attest. Price, a well-known radio host and one of the most prominent gay Scousers, has faced decades of abuse ranging from the sinister to the obscene. There is one indestructible meme that he is in fact a lizard.

Paul Rutherford of Frankie Goes to Hollywood spoke candidly about this:

> Where you're from does make you who you are . . . but do you *owe* it to that place? . . . I personally had a really hard time there. I used to get kicked in the face at least twice a night for being a puff, and dressing weird, being a punk or whatever . . . But we are definitely leftists. That's socially inbred by being from Liverpool. You just don't dream of voting any other way.

The former football hooligan Andy Nicholls, in a rare moment of political commentary, mused of ticket touting that 'it needs sorting out at the source, not the scally end'. In the popular politics of Liverpool there is an implicit understanding that people making a few quid from illegal activities are the tip of the iceberg, and that there are individuals and organisations making vast sums through criminal activity – except it usually isn't labelled as such. If not many people say this explicitly, they understand it implicitly.

If you have genuine opportunities to advance and get ahead, then it makes sense to work hard, keep your head down and play by the rules. If you do not, and if there is a market for your hard work and talents elsewhere, then the sensible thing to do is to get into that sector quickly, the better to gain skills and experience.

In trying to sum up the politics of the city, it might simplistically be said that most Scousers today identify with a politics that is collectivist economically, but culturally liberal.

In reality, this is only half the picture. Independence is valued, but there is a powerful element of conformism. People are community-minded in terms of fairness and helping those worse off than themselves, but also entrepreneurial and appreciative of the finer things in life. There's an element of suspicion and hostility to outsiders, but a willingness to welcome different people and judge them by their character. It is definitely anti-authoritarian, and perhaps the most characteristic trait in Liverpool politics – a hundred years ago and today – is the instinct to go against prevailing trends and do the opposite of what people expect.

Given this history, and the fact we have a Labour government at a national level for the first time since 2010, what are the odds of the city's current loyalty to Labour waning? For now, there looks to be no chance of any party other than Labour winning one of the city's parliamentary seats, although now that Labour are back in government nationally, it is likely that the majorities of local MPs will dwindle back down to the levels seen under Tony Blair and Gordon Brown (by the time of the 2005 election, the then Liverpool Wavertree MP Jane Kennedy had a majority of 'only' 5,000), but things will probably change more notably in terms of local politics.

At a local level, David Jeffery tells me, though, there won't be a clear pattern, and he expects to see different trends in different places. He reckons the Liberal Democrats should be able to take back a lot of their middle-class heartlands in south Liverpool, although many voters still have not forgiven them for their national coalition with the Conservatives from 2010–15. In north Liverpool, Jeffery expects the Greens, Conservatives and independents to gain ground against Labour given the expected criticisms of a centrist Starmer government in Westminster, while the Liberal party should consolidate their stranglehold over the Tuebrook ward. But the variety of their opponents will help Labour at a local level – in the New Labour era, an unpopular Labour government in Westminster would have had a more positive impact on the Lib Dems in Liverpool as they were 'the only game in town'.

An independent candidate, Stephen Yip, did surprisingly well in the last city mayoral election in 2021, finishing second in the first round – about 5,000 votes ahead of the Liberal Democrat's Richard Kemp in third – and getting 40 per cent in the second round, only 14,000 votes behind the victorious Joanna Anderson.

This shows that there is broad-based opposition to Labour, and Jeffery can see a situation where, if the Lib Dems and the Greens cooperated, it would be possible for an independent to win a mayoral election held under a national Labour government.

If the contemporary politics of Liverpool were fused in a period of economic decline – for Liverpool in particular, if not the country as a whole – then they might provide a guide to the future politics of the UK, now that the economy of much of the country features low-paid, casualised work and underinvestment.

Scouse Capitalism

The city has elected politicians supporting free trade, protectionism, nationalisation, renationalisation, privatisation and deregulation – but among their voters, the instinct to make a few quid has remained.

Back in the days before artificial fertiliser, guano – bird and bat droppings – sold for £7 to £8 per tonne. Liverpool villains would ship in South American guano and mix it with things like sand and ammonia to make their own watered-down version in an uncanny pre-empting of later business practices.

From the eighteenth century onwards, wooden ships would have their hulls covered in copper sheets to protect them from barnacles and woodworm, and, at the city's south graving docks, ships would periodically come in to be re-sheathed. When the tide went out, enterprising Scousers would comb through the mud, searching for scraps of copper from the hulls. The council got onto this and started paying a contractor to collect and extract the copper from the mud – in one year, this netted the council £1,600.

Occasionally a shipwreck in the Mersey would supply an unexpected windfall. In 1866, when the *Elizabeth Buckam* was wrecked, looters drank so much rum that two of them died. When the *Grecian* sank in 1832, one woman chewed the earlobe off a female corpse to steal her earring.

In 1950s portside drinking dens, such as L8's All Nations Club – known as the Lucky Bar – prostitutes read the shipping forecasts to work out what ships would be in port and for how long, and thus try and predict business over the coming days.

This entrepreneurial instinct combines with black humour to lead to money-making opportunities in dire circumstances; at the hide market, where they dressed the skins of animals, workers would collect the slivers of meat, called 'scalps', and sell them to the poor. When one member of a Victorian betting ring shot dead an associate, the others instantly offered odds on the result of the trial.

As noted in Simon Hughes's *There She Goes*, during the Toxteth disturbances in 1981, one enterprising L8 resident sold drinks and snacks to the various hippies and students who had turned up to watch the violence and soak up the vibes. At the Heysel disaster – when Liverpool fans collapsed a wall in a Belgian stadium, resulting in the deaths of 39 people - Scouse 'doormen' tried to prevent ticketless fans from entering the stadium – without first giving them 100 francs. Then there's the legendary figure of the Scouser at Glastonbury selling cans of Red Stripe from a wheelbarrow.

Even some of the most successful criminals the city has produced were not above petty scams: Tommy 'Tacker' Commerford – who was technically unemployed and received a council flat and weekly DHSS payments – once took his wife on a £5,000 cruise to the Caribbean and New York, but still filed an £11,500 insurance claim for suitcases 'lost' at JFK airport.

The Liverpool crook turned supergrass Paul Grimes told the journalist Graham Johnson, as reported in his book *Powder Wars*, that during the post-war period, 'Even if me dad got £20,000 out of a safe, he'd be out tarmacking or whatever the following week.' Billy Grimwood's gang, who pretended to be steeplejacks, once accidentally won a contract to knock down the Overhead Railway, which they had to go through with to maintain their cover.

John Haase, even when rich, would still rob the pubs and clubs he was protecting, doing the heist himself with a balaclava and a cosh. Paul Grimes was impressed, telling Johnson: 'One of the country's top villains, with millions, doing blags, but he got a buzz out of it. I think it took him back to his youth, like a proper villain against instead of some fucking drug-dealing fucking organised crime king sat behind a desk'.

Back in the Victorian era, provincial cities such as Liverpool, Edinburgh and Newcastle, with their flourishing economics and burgeoning middle class, funded academic and cultural institutions. This provided another possible income for Liverpool crooks: graverobbing.

Mostly fuelled by the demand for corpses from doctors and medical students, people would bury their loved one, return to lay flowers the next day and find the grave already robbed. Mary Harrison was buried at Walton cemetery one day in October 1827, but her grave was found empty on the following day. This led to a raid on the house of a surgeon, William Gill, who had the body of a baby preserved in brine, the dissected body of a woman believed to have been an Irish migrant and the corpse of Mrs Harrison with the skin stripped from her face.

Such was the demand for cadavers that some gangs would occasionally sell a corpse to one surgeon, steal it back and then sell it to another. Sometimes they'd snatch a comatose drunk, put him in a sack and hope they got the money before the recipient realised.

This led to some heinous discoveries; on one occasion, three casks labelled 'bitter salts' bound for the Port of Leith in Scotland were intercepted at the docks. When opened they contained eleven bodies, pickled and salted. This led to a raid on an address in Hope Street, where detectives found twenty cadavers in a cellar. There was also a barrel, one-third full of brine, with the bodies of several babies inside.

The corpses had apparently been taken from the workhouse cemetery a few hundred feet away.

This has sinister parallels with the Alder Hey scandal of the late twentieth century, during which it was discovered that the Liverpool children's hospital – one of the largest in the country – had practised the widespread removal, retention and disposal of human tissue, including children's organs, throughout the period 1981 to 1996. In total, over 2,000 pots were discovered, containing body parts from around 850 infants. Alder Hey also stored without consent 1,500 foetuses that were miscarried, stillborn or aborted.

The pathologist Dick van Velzen was blamed for the practice, whereby every organ was removed from each child who had had a postmortem at the hospital during his time. This occurred even when the parents had specifically stated that they didn't want a full post-mortem for their child.

It later emerged that, along with Birmingham Children's Hospital, Alder Hey had given thymus glands, removed from live children during heart surgery, to a pharmaceutical company in return for financial donations.

5

RED OR BLUE?

In 1907, White Star Lines – the world's leading passenger shipping company – relocated from Liverpool to the south coast port of Southampton. Amid much handwringing and accusations of betrayal, the company insisted that the four daily tides of the Solent – the body of water in between Southampton and the Isle of Wight – allowed for more departures than the two tides of Liverpool, so it made no business sense to remain in the city. This was seen as a blow at the time, but a minor one. In retrospect, it signalled the start of almost a century of decline.

In recent decades, the city has had some measure of revenge, with Liverpool Football Club making regular raids on Southampton FC's best talent, poaching some wonderful world-class players such as Virgil van Dijk and Sadio Mane, as well as journeymen such as Dejan Lovren and Ricky Lambert. This reflects the broader change in Liverpool from an economic to a footballing powerhouse.

This was not something that could have been envisioned in 1878, when St Domingo's Football Club was founded to give the male congregation of St Domingo's Methodist Church – who already had a cricket team for the summer months – something to do in the winter.

Soon it was renamed Everton Football Club after the surrounding area, and ten years later the club became a founding member of the English Football League, taking part in the inaugural season of 1888–89, and winning its first League Championship title two years later in 1890–91.

At this time, Everton played their home matches on the Anfield pitch owned by their president, John Houlding. Due to a dispute with Holding over how much rent the club had to pay for use of the ground, they relocated to nearby Goodison Park in 1892, and Houlding founded Everton Athletic to play on his now tenant-less ground. The Football Association refused to recognise another club named Everton, so, in March 1892, they were renamed Liverpool Football Club.

Houlding's new team won the local Lancashire League in their debut season of 1892–93 and joined the national Football League's Second Division for the start of the next term. Three years later they were promoted to the First Division and they won their first league championship in 1901.

I wonder if any of these Victorian gents realised the significance of what they were doing; in the late nineteenth century, football clubs were an important pastime, but still paled in importance to other fixtures of life such as work, family, religion and, for some, the nascent trade unions.

It would have been hard for them to imagine a world where many of those other institutions had declined or been transformed, and football had assumed a whole new kind of significance. They could surely not have known that their newly founded clubs would have so much weight to bear in the Liverpool of the early twenty-first century.

In the past thirty years in particular, football clubs which had primarily been the focus and expression of community loyalties and passions have become commercial behemoths, and, at the same time, an expression of the identity of the cities they came from on the domestic and world stage.

As the domestic and then global audience of English top-flight football began to take off, an increasing number of the players were drawn from overseas, mostly Europe but increasingly South America and Africa. The commercial potential of football meant that teams like Manchester United and Liverpool could help make billions through overseas and domestic TV revenues.

Someone from Liverpool can now have a conversation based on the city's football clubs with a range of people in the UK and across the world in a way they couldn't as recently as forty or fifty years ago. For a Scouser today, meeting a Liverpool fan – or, less likely but still possible, an Everton fan – in far-flung climes means you have an instant source of conversation, and in some scenarios, such as in a pub full of American or Singaporean fans, you might be treated like minor royalty or an actual working-class person at a revolutionary communist meeting.

As football clubs have taken up this heavy burden and the stakes of the sport have increased, so too has animosity towards supporters of other teams, of both the online performative kind and the Stanley knife to the face kind.

As recently as the 1960s there was little violence between supporters of Liverpool and Manchester United. (In fact, fans were not even segregated at matches until 1975.) By the twenty-first century, this had decisively changed. During a game between Liverpool and Manchester United at Anfield in 2006, when the United player Alan Smith broke his leg and was taken to a waiting ambulance outside, the vehicle had to make it through a crowd of supporters leaving the game, who started throwing bottles and rocking the ambulance.

It is important to stress that by no means does everyone on Merseyside follow football. Many people, of both sexes, have no interest in the game. There's also a danger of working backwards by taking the sport's popularity in the city today and assuming this was always the case.

That was clearly not true as recently as the 1990s; in 1992–3, the first season of the new 'Premier League', an Everton game away against Wimbledon saw only 3,039 people attend, which is not only the lowest recorded attendance for a game involving Everton (at least at the time of writing), but the lowest attendance for any Premier League game ever. Across the whole season, Everton's average home attendance that year was 20,457, the lowest since the First World War.

Even many of those who used to attend matches would often be there for the fights or the fashion as much as the football. Echo and the Bunnymen's Will Sergeant notes how he 'was an avid watcher of the crowds at the match and often missed the goals because I was scanning the stands for interesting people or trouble'.

Until the '90s, there was also little crossover between football and the city's music scene; Paul McCartney famously said that he supported 'both' Liverpool and Everton. Pete Wylie remembers that 'football was working class, and although we were working class, we also had this thing of being classless and we weren't going to be categorised. To some extent we rebelled against that football culture.'

There is also a common generational problem, for Liverpool fans especially, in that older generations seem unremittingly negative. The novelist Anthony Quinn, himself now in his sixties, wrote of his father that 'in later years I couldn't talk to my dad about Liverpool, largely on account of his relentless negativity. "What about that lot on Saturday?" he would say, grimly, even if we had won 5–0.' One of our friend's dads, who I will only refer to here as 'MB', is a case in point. Watching Liverpool with him – even when we are playing well – is a traumatic experience for everyone around.

There's also the problem that as Liverpool have become so famous, the city and its inhabitants are associated with that team, irrespective of whether or not they support them, or have any interest in football. When my mate Rob, an Everton fan like all his family, got married in

Essex, the DJ, hearing that there were Scousers present, played 'You'll Never Walk Alone' and nearly caused a riot.

It's sometimes strange to think that Liverpool Football Club existed for fifty-eight years before 'You'll Never Walk Alone' was written, and for seventy-one years before the Gerry and the Pacemakers version was recorded in 1963.

That year was a pivotal moment for the city and the world, with the release of the first Beatles album, and the beginning of a period of triumph for the two football clubs – Liverpool in particular.

The TV series *Z-Cars* had debuted the previous year, and was acclaimed for its harsh, realist look at crime and crime fighting in Liverpool. Its theme tune, adapted from the Liverpool folk song 'Johnny Todd', became an unofficial anthem for Everton fans, who would sing the tune before kick-off.

Anfield had no equivalent at this stage, although the ground's sound system used to play the top ten bestselling singles of the week in the half-hour or so before matches began.

In October 1963, local band Gerry and the Pacemakers scored their third number one hit with a cover of 'You'll Never Walk Alone', a show tune from the musical and film *Carousel*. It stayed at number one for four weeks.

One version has it that when this dropped out of the top ten, and was no longer played before matches, supporters began chanting 'Where's our song?' and continued to sing it themselves.

Former Liverpool player Tommy Smith recalls it differently, writing in his autobiography that Gerry Marsden gave Bill Shankly a copy of the single during a pre-season coach trip in 1963, and that 'Shanks was in awe of what he heard . . . Football writers from the local newspapers were travelling with our party and, thirsty for a story of any kind between games, filed copy back to their editors to the effect that we had adopted Gerry Marsden's forthcoming single as the club song.' According to

Marsden himself, Shankly said to him: 'Gerry, my son, I have given you a football team and you have given us a song.'

That same season, 1963–4, Liverpool won the league championship for the first time under Shankly, their first league title since 1947. The following season they entered the European Cup for the first time (a competition they have won a record six times, to date, more than any other British club) and adopted their famous all-red kit.

Shankly chose the song as his eighth record when he was on *Desert Island Discs* in 1965; six days after the episode aired, Liverpool won the FA Cup for the first time. When fans sang the song at Wembley, commentator Kenneth Wolstenholme was already referring to it as 'Liverpool's signature tune'.

Ian Callaghan, who played for Liverpool between 1960 and 1978, notes that it was a singularly transformative time, for the club and the city: 'We were a Second Division club going nowhere, this great man arrives, and then everything changes and then the music as well. To be part of that as a local lad especially was just magic.'

After Liverpool played away at Glasgow Celtic in the semi-finals of the 1966 Cup Winners' Cup, the Scottish team adopted the song themselves, despite losing 2–1 on aggregate to the Reds. In that year's final, Liverpool lost to German side Borussia Dortmund, whose fans now also sing 'You'll Never Walk Alone', in their case ten minutes before kick-off at each home match.

Whatever the origins of the relationship between the song and the football club, it has become easily the most famous terrace song in world football. This probably owes something to the lyrics, which are at the same time thoughtful, stoic and deeply cheesy – just like the city itself. It also owes a great deal to Anfield, and particularly the Kop, and the acoustic resonance of over 25,000 fans packed in to a vast single-tiered stand.

There's also the lyricism and love of music of Scousers in general – YNWA is one of many terrace songs and chants originating in Liverpool that have been taken up elsewhere. Probably one of the reasons for this is the imperative for originality, and the disdain for so-called 'wool chants', such as asking the opposition 'Who are ya?', etc – at one game in the 1970s up to 150 different chants were counted.

In the words of legendary Dutch player Johan Cruyff: 'There's not one club in Europe with an anthem like "You'll Never Walk Alone". There's not one club in the world so united with the fans. I sat there watching the Liverpool fans and they sent shivers down my spine.'

Sixty years after the clashes between the police and strikers on St George's Plateau, Bill Shankly welcomed the team home after their defeat to Arsenal in the 1971 FA Cup final. The crowds that day demonstrated how the city had changed since its commercial heyday over a century earlier. Even though they lost that match, Shankly installed belief and loyalty in a people who had begun to lose their sense of purpose. But the final part of his life was pretty tragic.

After Liverpool won the 1974 FA Cup with a 3–0 victory over Newcastle, a fan ran onto the pitch and threw himself down to kiss Shankly's feet. Despite being at the peak of his powers, it would be the Scot's last game in charge at Anfield.

After he retired, he worked for the Liverpool radio station Radio City, presenting his own chat show, at one point interviewing Prime Minister (and local MP) Harold Wilson, as well as commenting on matches for its football coverage. He was briefly involved with advisory roles at North Wales club Wrexham and the Wirral's Tranmere Rovers. There was speculation that he would return to management in November 1976 at Derby County, but this didn't materialise. He offered advice to some of his former players who had gone into management, such as Ron Yeats at Tranmere and John Toshack at Swansea City. Well into his sixties he was taking part in five-a-side football, and occasionally joined in with young lads playing in Liverpool parks.

He had to do all this because Liverpool had banned him from their Melwood training ground, after the newly retired Shankly had kept appearing during coaching sessions. When the Liverpool players reported back to Melwood to train ahead of the 1974–5 season, Shankly was standing there to greet them, dressed in his training kit as if nothing had happened. The players continued to call him 'boss' or 'gaffer' instead of the new manager, Bob Paisley.

After he was told not to return to Melwood, Shankly became increasingly bitter. 'I have been received more warmly by Everton than I have been by Liverpool,' he complained. His former star striker Kevin Keegan later described this as 'the saddest, saddest thing that ever happened at Liverpool'.

His granddaughter Karen Gill would later recollect that when they were staying over in his house, they could hear the great man downstairs, playing 'You'll Never Walk Alone' to himself.

One of the notable features of football allegiances on Merseyside is that unlike other cities with two prominent clubs, such as Manchester, Sheffield or Bristol, there is no correlation between location and support for one club or the other. Neither is football loyalty determined by religious background, as in Glasgow or Edinburgh. In fact, until the 1980s, during quieter periods of matches, the supporters on the Kop used to chant 'Rangers' or 'Celtic' depending on their allegiance.

While talk of a friendly derby is overstated, you can see pictures from the 1980s of groups of fans mixed together at derby matches. Despite violence in town and on school playgrounds between Liverpool and Everton fans, there was surprisingly little history of violent confrontation between the two sets of fans, and on some occasions co-operation, as on one European excursion when casuals from both teams – finding themselves together in a foreign city – hijacked a bin lorry and filled it with the contents of a designer shop.

It used to be said that Everton, despite their being founded by Methodists, was 'the Catholic club', as a large proportion of Irish immigrants were drawn to Goodison, rather than Anfield. This may have always been something of a myth, and, today, any kind of ethnic or religious alignment has long since passed.

John Houlding – former president of Everton and founder of Liverpool – was a member of the Orange Lodge, while their first manager, John McKenna, was an Irish Freemason. In Liverpool's first game – against Everton – Liverpool fielded no fewer than nine Glaswegians, known as 'the Macs', from both sides of the sectarian divides. From these diverse origins came a resilient loyalty to something that was not a religion, or a nation, or a political movement, but something else that could inspire the loyalty – and violence – that had once been reserved for these other identities.

As Andy Nicholls is keen to point out, Everton 'had the tag of a racist, not sectarian, club' and 'if you came [to Goodison] singing either IRA or King Billy songs, you would get a slap and that was the end of it'.

In 1995, Everton hosted Glasgow Celtic in the testimonial match for longtime Everton goalkeeper Neville Southall. Nicholls claimed that it 'kicked off with Celtic when they put a huge IRA flag up outside the Oak and were playing Republican music on a ghetto blaster'. He thought it was no time to 'promote terrorism' as it was not long after the death of Tim Parry, a young Evertonian, in the Warrington bombings.

By the time you're reading this book, Everton should, in theory, have moved into a new stadium at the Bramley-Moore dock. The dock took its name from John Bramley-Moore, one-time Conservative Lord Mayor of Liverpool, as well as a notorious Catholic-baiter and sponsor of the Protestant street preacher George Wise.

You'd think that if Celtic moved their home stadium to a site named after a Glaswegian equivalent to Bramley-Moore then there would be uproar. It demonstrates just how little these old sectarian divisions matter in the modern city, and how little religion affects football allegiances.

Though sectarianism has not had much of a role in Merseyside football, the same cannot be said for race. The first black person *reported* as signing for a Liverpool team was, improbably, the American heavyweight boxing champion Joe Louis, who visited the city during the Second World War for an exhibition boxing match to entertain US troops, and was said to have signed for Liverpool FC as a publicity stunt.

The first black footballer to actually sign for either Merseyside club was Mike Trebilcock, who joined Everton from Plymouth Argyle on 31 December 1965, making his debut a few days later against Aston Villa. Everton reached the final of the FA Cup that year, and although injuries had limited Trebilcock's playing time to four appearances for the reserves, he was picked ahead of England international Fred Pickering for the final and became the first black player to score in an FA Cup final, netting twice in the 3–2 win over Sheffield Wednesday.

For whatever reason, in the next two years he played only eleven league games and scored just three goals, leaving for Portsmouth in January 1968.

The first black Scouser to join either club was Everton's Cliff Marshall in 1973. Born in Liverpool in 1955, he grew up supporting Everton and, despite interest from Liverpool and Manchester United, elected to go to Goodison under then manager Billy Bingham.

After starting off with the youth side, in the 1974–5 league season he was promoted to the first team squad and made his debut as a late substitute in a 3–0 home victory over Leicester City on 11 January 1975 – becoming the first black player after Trebilcock to play for either Everton or Liverpool. The next week he made his first start for the club in a 3–0 away win against Birmingham City. Despite this promising start, he only played twice more that season, once in the league and once in the FA Cup.

In the 1975–6 season, Marshall had only four league starts, leading to him requesting and being granted an exit at the end of that term. In Marshall's telling, race had nothing to do with his disappointing experience at Everton, instead citing differences over playing styles: 'What disillusioned me was some of the coaches at Everton [who] said, "your first priority is to defend", and I didn't like that. I'm an attacker; defending should be my second priority. I moved on.'

His subsequent career at Miami Toros and Southport suggests that cold-hearted footballing meritocracy was at work, and that Marshall just wasn't good enough.

The first black player to sign for Liverpool FC – boxing champions aside – was Howard Gayle in 1977. He was probably a better talent than Marshall and went on to have a successful playing career elsewhere, but he had a similar experience at Liverpool that Marshall had at Everton. He only made five appearances in total, the first away against Manchester City on 4 October 1980, when he came on as a second-half substitute for David Fairclough.

It was six months until his next appearance, against Bayern Munich in the second leg of the European Cup semi-final. In the first leg at Anfield neither team had scored, making Bayern the favourites given their home support in the return fixture. Before the game, several of the Liverpool first team players picked up injuries, leading to a rare appearance on the bench for Gayle, at a time when only one substitute was permitted per team.

When Kenny Dalglish came off injured, Gayle had his chance, and subsequently ran Bayern ragged. The German team had not prepared for the skilful and direct winger and had no idea how to handle him. He was fouled several times, some of them potential leg breakers that would result in a red card today, but none was forthcoming.

He was booked for retaliating, after lashing out at a Bayern defender. After that, with only one hour on the field, he was substituted off, replaced by Jimmy Case – becoming the first ever Liverpool substitute to himself be substituted.

Ten minutes later, Ray Kennedy scored for the Reds, and although Bayern managed a late equaliser, Liverpool went through on away goals to the final against Real Madrid.

The following Saturday, Gayle started in a League match, scoring his first Liverpool goal, and playing the whole 90 minutes in a 1–1 draw away against Tottenham Hotspur. Benefitting from injuries to key players Kenny Dalglish and David Johnson, Gayle was able to gain minutes at a key time in the season, with the league run-in and European Cup final looming.

Gayle made such an impression that some fans argued he should keep his place even when David Johnson recovered. One match report from the *Guardian* suggested that 'the impressive pace and timing of Gayle's runs, which bemused Bayern Munich, could well restore a dimension and width to Liverpool's attack missing since the dropping of [Steve] Heighway'.

In the end, Gayle played only two more games for Liverpool: a 0–1 home loss against Sunderland and 1–0 home win against Manchester City. Loan spells followed with Fulham and Newcastle, then a transfer to Birmingham City in 1983, followed by Sunderland, Dallas Sidekicks, Stoke City, Blackburn Rovers and finally Halifax Town. In 1984, while at Birmingham, he made three appearances for the England Under-21 side.

When Gayle first played for Liverpool, black people couldn't safely attend Anfield. Many of the black men in the city had never even been into the town centre despite living a mile or two away. As late as the 1980s, even the black Sunday league players had their own separate segregated league. Anonymous letters urged the board not to sign Gayle.

Addressing comparisons between himself and John Barnes, Gayle wrote in his autobiography that:

John and I had very different upbringings. While I was brought up in white Norris Green where there were very few black families and racism was a part of life, John lived in Jamaica around other black people. His family were reasonably wealthy and well respected in Kingston. John Barnes did not have to confront racism on a daily basis. For me, racism was the norm – the routine.

He remembers that the attitudes of his teammates and staff were 'mixed', although 'the majority did not have a problem with a young black male entering [what had been] an absolutely white environment'.

After recalling the words and jokes he had heard when people thought he was out of earshot, Gayle talks about the awkwardness of banter:

Phil Thompson had a big nose so people took the piss out of him for that. David Fairclough had bright red hair, so he became a target. Me? I was black. I wasn't accustomed to this type of humour. It was difficult to tell whether some of it was humour or whether it was really intended to offend. What is unacceptable language when it is passed off as banter?

The culture at Liverpool dictated that I was expected to just allow it to go over my head and not take things so seriously. But it wasn't in my make-up to let certain words get used without responding forcefully. So I came back at them. It contributed towards me getting the reputation as someone who had an attitude problem: someone who was reluctant to fit in.

This is a bind that many black people in majority white environments often report finding themselves in: either laugh along with the banter or be accused of playing the race card, not having a sense of humour, etc. It is also a situation many Scousers can find themselves in; laugh along with the 'calm down, calm down' jibes or get accused of being a typical whingeing Scouser.

The saddest part for Gayle was hearing comments from people he got on with and looked up to:

> The racism was easier to take from the terraces because you reasoned it was down to your performance; you liked to think you were doing something right. Maybe that's naive: I was abused frequently, whether I played well or badly. When it comes from the people that you work with, though, it hurts. Because you don't tolerate it and because you snap, the management perceives that as a weakness. How could they trust you to keep your calm in a pressure situation?

At a drunken team party shortly after Gayle joined the squad, a stripper hired by other players covered herself in talcum powder and rubbed Gayle's face between her breasts so that his face was covered in the white residue. The 'comedian' Roy Chubby Brown was compèring the party and joked, 'Try and walk through Toxteth now!', and people howled with laugher. Gayle later said that since the compère had taken the piss out of everyone else he was able to laugh along with the joke.

Eventually Gayle squared up to legendary midfielder and hardman Tommy Smith, who had been his lead tormentor among the Liverpool players, after yet another racist insult: 'I look back now and remember this moment as a real low point,' said Gayle. 'I'd grown up loving Tommy Smith.'

In both cases, Marshall and Gayle were local lads who came up through the clubs' academies. Although Everton signed Trebilcock in the '60s, they did not sign another black player until Daniel Amokachi in 1994.

In contrast, the first black player to play for Manchester United was Dennis Walker in 1963, and the first black player they signed from another club was Tony Whelan in 1968.

For Chelsea, Paul Canoville, who was signed from Hillingdon Borough in 1981, was both their first black signing and the first black player to feature for the club.

And even Millwall, historically characterised fairly or unfairly as a particularly racist club, had their first black player, Frank Peterson, as early as 1968.

Infamously, when Liverpool's John Barnes played at Goodison he was met with racist abuse and bananas. As Barnes' biographer Dave Hill pointed out, Evertonians would not have chanted 'N***erpool' and 'Everton is white' if they could not be sure that those taunts would hit their mark and wound the pride of Liverpool fans.

Some Everton fans wearing lapel badges saying 'Everton are White – Defend the Race' were caught trying to smuggle a monkey – an actual live monkey – into Goodison for one derby.

The abuse and bananas that greeted Barnes at Goodison were hurled by people who went to the same schools, lived in the same neighbourhoods and worked alongside the Liverpool fans. And the only reason the roles weren't reversed is that Barnes was playing in red, not blue.

Barnes' upbringing meant that he never considered himself anything less than anyone else, and the words of impoverished Scousers bounced off him, in much the same way anti-Scouse insults bounce off Scousers today. When the tea lady didn't bring a mug for Barnes, unlike the other players, he quipped: 'What's wrong, am I black or something?' One year, he turned up at the Christmas do in a KKK outfit.

Obviously, there were plenty of other places in England that had this attitude. But they seemed to evolve faster than Liverpool. And this is completely written out of a history which emphasises internationalism and anti-Toryism and solidarity, without ever conceding that that solidarity was racially exclusive until very recently.

In 1985, Liverpool FC – the reigning European champions, having won their fourth European Cup the previous year – made it through once again to the final, and were due to play Juventus, that year's Italian champions.

The setting for the match, the Heysel Stadium in Brussels, was antiquated and unusually small for such a high-profile event. Liverpool and Juventus had each been allocated 14,500 tickets – in addition to this, there was meant to be a 'neutral' area, something that had never featured before in a UEFA final. The purpose of this neutral area was never explained, and it was at the expense of the Liverpool supporters, since it halved the terrace space allotted to them at their end of the ground.

Before kick-off, some Liverpool fans charged at the end containing the Juventus fans, who tried to flee, resulting in the collapse of a stadium wall and the deaths of thirty-nine people, with another 600 injured. Although it was an era in which football violence had become commonplace, the number of casualties was unprecedented and condemnation was swift. In the aftermath, English club sides were banned indefinitely from European competitions.

As a result of this ban, that year's English First Division winners – Everton – were unable to compete in the following season's European Cup competition, and over the next five seasons Manchester United, Tottenham Hotspur, Southampton, West Ham, Sheffield Wednesday, Oxford United, Coventry, Arsenal, Nottingham Forest, Wimbledon, Luton Town and Derby County all missed out on the chance to play European football. In some cases, it was their first and only opportunity to play in European competitions, and their exclusion was due to the actions of Liverpool fans at Heysel.

Given the widespread hooliganism in the game at the time, there is no reason to think that fans following any other English club would have behaved differently. It could have been supporters of any club who caused the Heysel disaster. But it wasn't.

Events four years later were entirely different, although in both cases crumbling stadia and shoddy infrastructure played a crucial part.

There had already been a crushing incident at Sheffield Wednesday's Hillsborough stadium in 1981, also in the Leppings Lane terrace, when Tottenham played Wolverhampton in one of that year's FA cup semi-finals. On that occasion it grew so overcrowded that police let fans out of the terrace to sit on the side of the pitch – fortunately, no one died.

An expert assessment estimated that the stand's maximum capacity was 5,246 people, while the safety certificate permitted 7,200. But for the 1989 FA cup semi-final, nearly 10,000 tickets were sold to Liverpool fans. The recommended number of fans to be processed at each turnstile was 700, but in the Leppings Lane terrace, 1,453 people had to pass through each turnstile. There were sixty-two turnstiles for the Nottingham Forest fans at their end of the ground, but only twenty-three turnstiles in total for all the Liverpool fans.

By the time of the kick-off on 15 April 1989, the Leppings Lane terrace was already packed beyond capacity, and people were already beginning to die. Outside more fans were arriving, and a crush also began to develop at the turnstiles. Just before the 3 p.m. kick-off, David Duckenfield, the police officer overseeing crowd safety, ordered the gates to be opened, causing the fans outside to rush into the terrace, greatly exacerbating the situation inside.

The match was called off at 3.06, but by that time it was already too late. Ninety-five people were crushed to death, and 766 were injured, many severely. One of the latter, Tony Bland, died four years later after being in a persistent vegetative state and, thirty-two years later, Andrew Devine, who suffered severe and irreversible brain damage, passed away, with a coroner ruling that he should be considered the ninety-seventh fatality.

The then Liverpool manager Kenny Dalglish went to as many funerals as he could, and resigned as manager two years later, unable to carry on. For many others, the psychological damage was devastating; football had been one of their few sources of pride and optimism, and now even this was a source of tragedy and despair.

The broadcaster Nicky Campbell remembers how, in his first show following the disaster, the Radio 1 presenter and Liverpool fan John Peel played Aretha Franklin's version of 'You'll Never Walk Alone':

> The Monday evening show after the Hillsborough tragedy was a piece of broadcasting I'll never forget. He said nothing at the start of his show. He just played a record. A long slow record. It was Aretha Franklin's heart-breaking gospel version of 'You'll Never Walk Alone'. I looked through the glass from my adjacent studio and John was just weeping. Silently. So were all of us.

The events at Hillsborough and its aftermath, coming as it did at the nadir of Liverpool's social and economic fortunes, had a profound impact on the city and the development of its modern identity. Central to this was the press coverage of the tragedy, and that of one newspaper in particular.

A few years ago, in a taxi from Lime Street station to my mum's house, my wife pointed at a sticker on the window, depicting a stick figure putting *The Sun* newspaper in a bin. She thought it was notable that these kinds of stickers could be found in taxis, but I had long ago stopped noticing them. It's estimated that *The Sun* lost almost half a million readers in the five years between 1987 and 1992, with a large chunk of those coming from Liverpool, where the paper had previously been the bestselling daily newspaper.

Although it is often forgotten today, anger on Merseyside was initially directed at the *Daily Mirror*, which printed colour pictures of people being crushed, dying or receiving treatment on the pitch. Eight days after Hillsborough, an article by Edward Pearce in the *Sunday Times* proclaimed:

For the second time in a decade a large body of Liverpool supporters has killed people . . . The futile erection of football into a cult is the city's only modern acquaintance with excellence, matches elsewhere being the one chance to swagger and intimidate. There are soapy politicians to make a pet of Liverpool, and Liverpool is always standing by to make a pet of itself. 'Why us? Why are we treated like animals?' To which the plain answer is that a good and sufficient minority of you behave like animals.

In an early example of the trope that Scousers are overly gauche in grief, Pearce also complained about 'the shrine in the Anfield goalmouth', as well as 'the cursing of the police, all the theatricals, come sweetly to a city which is already the capital of self-pity', before concluding that if the South Yorkshire police were to be criticised, it was for not realising 'what brutes they had to handle'.

By that point, *The Sun*'s infamous 'The Truth' front page, published four days after the tragedy, had become the focus of Liverpudlian fury. Accusing Liverpool fans of 'scapegoating' the police, the paper claimed that the disaster only happened because 'thousands of fans, many without tickets, tried to get into the ground just before kick-off – either by forcing their way in or by blackmailing the police into opening the gates'.

In the immediate aftermath, South Yorkshire Police had started putting out their version of events via off-the-record briefings. They told reporters that fans were drunk, violent and had interfered with rescue efforts. They included gratuitous details, stating that people had robbed from the dying, urinated on the dead, that some fans said to officers trying to resuscitate a dying woman: 'Pass her up here, we'll shag her.'

Needless to say, there is no reason to believe that any of this happened. The Hillsborough Independent Panel found conclusively there was 'no evidence among the vast number of disclosed documents and many hours of video material to verify the serious allegations of exceptional levels of drunkenness, ticketlessness or violence among the Liverpool fans'. The slur of fans urinating or defecating on the dead was particularly cruel, given that in crushing deaths the contents of people's bowels are often forced out of them.

Prior to the publication of *The Sun*'s initial article, a number of local papers such as the *Sheffield Star* and the *Yorkshire Post* published very similar allegations.[3] It has since emerged that many national newspaper editors were offered the same story from the same sources a day before *The Sun* article was published, and though a few printed some of the allegations about Liverpool fans being responsible for the disaster, only *The Sun*'s Kelvin MacKenzie and his counterpart at the *Daily Star* newspaper were prepared to print the more outlandish allegations about theft and abuse of dead bodies, with many other editors feeling that the claims sounded too suspect.[4] Apparently, MacKenzie wanted the headline to read 'You Scum', but was talked out of it by other people in the newsroom.[5]

The front page elicited fury on Merseyside, not just because of its cruelty, but due to a genuine fear that people would believe the claims. After all, *The Sun* was the bestselling paper in the city. Many people in Liverpool had believed front-page reports about inner-city rioters, miners and immigrants, so what if the paper's millions of nationwide readers believed this? That Liverpudlians were guilty of the worst behaviour imaginable?

Because many people were all too willing to do that, and plenty still do. The sports journalist Tony Evans, who was in the stadium on that day, has written that in the years since, 'on countless occasions', people have 'sidled up' to him, sometimes after having had a couple of pints,

---

3 http://www.contrast.org/hillsborough/history/media.shtm
4 https://www.spectator.co.uk/article/hillsborough-and-me/
5 https://www.independent.co.uk/sport/football/hillsborough-the-sun-truth-headline-coronavirus-government-boris-johnson-a9472861.html

'and said something like, "Come on, you can tell me the truth, I used to go to games in the 1980s. I know what it was like. Your lot were drunk, knocked down the gates and that's why it happened. Admit it."' Over the years he developed a stock response, which was to say: 'Would you do it? If you were in the ground that day, would you have done it?' When they invariably say of course not, he asks them: 'Then why [do] you think I would?'

Appearing on BBC Radio Four's *The World at One* programme the day after the infamous front page, MacKenzie apologised, stating: 'It was my decision and my decision alone to do that front page in that way and I made a rather serious error.'

But during an after-dinner speech to Newcastle-based law firm Mincoffs Solicitors on 30 November 2006, MacKenzie is reported to have reneged on this apology:

All I did wrong there was tell the truth. There was a surge of Liverpool fans who had been drinking and that is what caused the disaster. The only thing different we did was put it under the headline 'The Truth'. I went on *The World at One* the next day and apologised. I only did that because Rupert Murdoch told me to. I wasn't sorry then and I'm not sorry now because we told the truth.

In the immediate aftermath of the disaster, there were attempts by the survivors and relatives of the dead to hold someone or somebody accountable. But early on the Director of Public Prosecutions ruled out bringing criminal charges against either Sheffield Wednesday Football Club, the local council or the company responsible for stadium safety.

In March 1991, the original inquests into the ninety-five deaths on the day of Hillsborough declined to consider evidence relating to fans who died after 3.15 p.m., as the coroner claimed 'the damage was done' by that time.

David Duckenfield, the police officer in charge of the ground on the day, was swiftly retired from South Yorkshire Police on medical grounds, two years after being suspended from duty. He was diagnosed with severe depression and post-traumatic stress and received a full pension.

For the next two decades, relatives and survivors staged a fruitless campaign for a fresh investigation. At the twentieth anniversary memorial event, the then Culture Secretary Andy Burnham was heckled over the Labour government's lack of action on the issue. Burnham himself was born in Leigh, on Merseyside, and is a lifelong Everton fan. He would later go on to be elected mayor of Greater Manchester, making a shrewd exit from Parliament during the Corbyn years, and positioning himself as a kind of King in the North during the Boris Johnson premiership. Before he left Parliament, he joined the calls for all information held by public bodies on Hillsborough to be released, as did 140,000 others in a petition to the House of Commons.

In January 2010, the outgoing Labour government convened the Hillsborough Independent Panel to review all previously unseen evidence, which two years later published a fresh report into the disaster. It was damning of the police, in particular of senior officers for authorising the opening of the gates.

At this point the national narrative changed. Kelvin MacKenzie gave his 'profuse apologies to the people of Liverpool', stating: 'I published in good faith, and I am sorry that it was so wrong.'

The independent report led to a legal inquest into the tragedy, which was held in Warrington for two years from 2014, becoming the longest such inquest in UK history. A year into the inquiry, David Duckenfield faced six days of questioning during which he admitted that his failure to close a tunnel before opening gate C 'was the direct cause of the deaths of 96 people'. He told the jury that he 'froze' under the pressure of the situation and gave the order to open the gate without thinking of what would happen to the thousands of fans on the already packed terraces.

The inquest concluded in April 2016, finding that the then ninety-six victims were 'unlawfully killed'. The jury concluded that fans played no part in the deaths and instead blamed police failures, stadium design faults and a delayed response by the ambulance service for the tragedy.

Just over a year later, the Crown Prosecution Service announced that David Duckenfield would be charged with manslaughter by gross negligence for ninety-five of the fatalities, the ninety-sixth victim, Tony Bland, having died outside the statute of limitations.

Alongside Duckenfield, the former Sheffield Wednesday club secretary Graham Mackrell was charged with safety offences; former South Yorkshire Police chief inspector Sir Norman Bettison was charged with four counts of misconduct in public office; and former police solicitor Peter Metcalf and officers Donald Denton and Alan Foster were charged with perverting the course of justice. (Charges against Bettison were later dropped due to insufficient evidence, while Metcalf, Denton and Foster were acquitted.)

In April 2019, thirty years after the tragedy, the jury failed to reach a verdict in the case against Duckenfield, although club secretary Mackrell was found guilty by a majority verdict on a health and safety charge relating to inadequate provision of turnstiles.

After a six-week retrial, Duckenfield was found not guilty of manslaughter.

After the Hillsborough Independent Panel reported its findings in 2012, *The Sun* covered the report under a front page headlined 'The Real Truth', adding that it was 'profoundly sorry' for their 'false reports' twenty-three years earlier. The then editor, Dominic Mohan, tried to shift the blame onto the police, stating: 'It's an appalling story and at the heart of it are the police's attempts to smear Liverpool fans. It's a version of events that 23 years ago *The Sun* went along with and for that we're deeply ashamed and profoundly sorry.' MacKenzie similarly added that he was 'part of a concerted plot by police officers to discredit the supporters'.

For some people, convinced that Liverpool fans were indeed to blame and that *The Sun* was unfairly traduced, this profuse apology just added to their anger, conspiracism and sense of grievance, and shows how deeply a kind of anti-Scouse prejudice has embedded itself in certain minds.

It's important to the modern-day identity of Liverpool that Heysel and Hillsborough occurred in a context where football was the city's last success story. At the time, the signs of a decaying, deindustrialising Britain – riots, strikes, football hooliganism – and a decline in working-class solidarity and political power contributed to a rise in media hostility towards an apparent underclass. Scousers were apt to be demonised by the national press anyway, but that they remained so proud, about football if nothing else, really rankled.

By the 1980s, it had become traditional for young lads from the streets around Anfield and Goodison to offer to 'mind' the cars of visiting fans, in exchange for a few quid. If the punters refused, they could expect to find on their return that their car had been keyed, denuded of its hubcaps or wheels, or even an empty space where their car used to be. There's a tale, sadly probably apocryphal, of a fella leaving his car and on being asked, 'Want me to mind your car for yer, mister?', telling the youth, 'It's OK, lad, I've got an Alsatian in the back.' To which the scally instantly replied, 'Oh yeah? I hope it can put out fires, like.'

This gave birth to the 1980s jokes about how if you went to Liverpool, you would have your car robbed or your hubcaps taken. It was also around this time that London-based football fans began taunting visiting Liverpool supporters by waving brick-size wads of banknotes at them.

Around this time, the up-and-coming comedian Harry Enfield was doing a gig at the Tunnel Club in Deptford. The audience consisted mainly of pissed-up Millwall supporters – a tough crowd at any time – and Enfield was trying out a couple of new characters. One of these was 'Loadsamoney'.

Later, Enfield remembered that while much of his material fell flat, Loadsamoney and his jokes about Scousers being impoverished had everyone pissing themselves. In fact, many in the audience didn't even realise it was an act.

On television, the character soon became a national favourite. Enfield, to his dismay, realised that the character he had created as a hated satirical monster – an intended pariah – had been turned into a sort of national hero for his Scouser-baiting antics and general loutishness.

Horrified by what he'd done, Enfield soon killed off the character. Instantly, he was attacked by *The Sun* for what would now be called giving in to the woke mob: 'Shut your marrrff and look at OUR wad', the headline read. 'Seriously we believe you should buy yourself a decent sense of humour.'

After the 1980s, the fortunes of both clubs declined. This was especially the case for Everton, who went from winning the league to flirting with relegation, with the 1995 FA Cup being (at time of writing) the last trophy won by the club.

Liverpool's fall was less dramatic, continuing to win trophies and occasionally compete for the league title, and never finishing lower than eighth. But for a club that had dominated British and then European football for two decades, this decline was hard to take. Having won the league thirteen times between 1963 and 1990, they would not finish first in the table again for thirty long years.

Given the success of Manchester United, which more than any other club was able to profit from the vast fortunes that began to flow around the sport in the 1990s, both Liverpool and Everton looked to acquire fresh investment to enable them to again compete at the elite level.

In this process, Liverpool narrowly avoided calamity. In January 2007, after Dubai International Capital pulled out of a takeover bid, the club considered a new offer made by American businessmen George Gillett and Tom Hicks.

They offered to buy the club for £435 million, which would include £215m set aside for the building of new stadium on Stanley Park, to allow Liverpool to catch up with the 80,000-seat capacity of Manchester United's Old Trafford ground. The club's board, led by chairman David Moores and chief executive Rick Parry, unanimously recommended that this offer be accepted.

Things soon went wrong. Despite Gillett calling for a 'spade in the ground within 60 days' to build the new stadium, this spade did not materialise and neither did the stadium. The Americans also failed to follow through on their extravagant promises in terms of transfer spending. At one point, Gillett assured fans that they would be able to buy 'Snoogy Doogy' if they wanted to (it's believed he was referring to the West Coast rapper Snoop Dogg, although no one's quite sure). In the end, they bought Christian Poulsen and Milan Jovanović.

After a complicated legal case which saw the club come within one day of entering administration, Hicks and Gillett were bought out by New England Sports Ventures. While these American owners have not been without criticism from the fans, they at least oversaw a return to success, with the team reaching three Champions League finals, winning one of them, and most importantly securing the league title during the 2019–20 season. However, by far their greatest move came in October 2015, when they acquired the services of German coach Jürgen Klopp.

But before the good times returned to Anfield (and they are still some distance away from Goodison Park), there were more travails and humiliations to be endured. In 2012, the Uruguay and Liverpool football player Luis Suárez was banned for eight matches after a Football Association disciplinary panel found him guilty of racially abusing Manchester United footballer Patrice Evra during a match. Evra alleged that Suarez had repeatedly referred to him a 'negro' and at one point pinched his skin.

Suarez and Liverpool football club – including manager Kenny Dalglish, several players and the majority of fans – insisted that this was not meant as racial abuse, that the use of 'negro' in South America has different meanings and implications, and that the skin pinching was merely part of Suarez's usual gamesmanship.

This was a line taken by many South American black players, including former teammates and opponents of Suárez, as well as left-leaning, Spanish-speaking journalists, such as Sid Lowe, who retweeted a selfie by black Brazilian player Dani Alves, captioned with the offending word.

Nonetheless, it has to be said that if all the facts in the Suárez case were the same, but he played for another club, Liverpool fans (or at least, online Liverpool fans) would have been the most vociferous in condemning him, calling for a lengthy ban and criticising those who doubted Evra's accusations. The Liverpool fan forum Red and White Kop (imagine if the *Guardian* did football forums) would have called for Suárez's expulsion from the country.

When he returned from his ban, Suárez was routinely booed by opposition fans and became the subject of chants calling him a racist. I remember this happening when I watched Liverpool play Chelsea at Stamford Bridge in November 2012. Of course, there will have been some crossover between these Chelsea fans and those recorded on the Paris Métro praising their captain John Terry for being a racist and preventing a black Frenchman from boarding the train.

Just as fans of clubs other than Liverpool used his racism as a means to attack Suárez, so too do fans in general adopt whatever cause allows them to attack their opponents. During the 1984–5 miners' strike – which many Nottinghamshire miners did not take part in – Nottingham Forest were welcomed to Anfield and Goodison with chants of 'scabs'. Today, the alleged Toryism of Chelsea fans is attacked – as they attack the supposed poverty of Scousers.

Therefore, when Klopp took over in October 2015, he joined a club out of sorts. One of the many great things about Jürgen Klopp is that he is genuinely off-the-cuff funny. This is a rare gift in football management and not something that can be coached. But it is very appropriate for the manager of a Liverpool team. After one loss, a miserable 2–0 defeat away to Red Star Belgrade in 2018, he was asked if he could put his finger on what went wrong and responded, 'I only have ten fingers.'

This is in keeping with the famous wit of Bill Shankly, who when asked, 'How would you like to manage the best club in the country?', by then-Liverpool chairman Tom Williams, drolly replied, 'Why? Is Matt Busby [then manager of Manchester United] packing it in?'

Although Klopp can be a sore loser, he is also notably phlegmatic. When there was a disastrous season, he came to terms with it and moved on, happy to start again. He didn't lose faith that he could fix whatever had gone wrong. There is a video of Klopp, after the soul-destroying loss against Real Madrid in the 2018 Champions' League final – his sixth defeat in seven major cup finals – drunkenly singing with two friends, downcast but not despondent.

This compares starkly with the waves of negativity that can sometimes wash down from the Anfield stands. It could be because he's a Christian; he has the religious faith that most of his host city has lost, but more than that he has a different understanding of religion, something private and personal to him. For many people in Liverpool being 'Catholic' is about hating Margaret Thatcher and singing Irish rebel songs. It has fuck all to do with an ethical sense of how to live life, still less to do with the metaphysical or 'God'. While so many people adopt identities – socialist, Irish, Catholic, Scouser – to try to fill an emptiness inside, Klopp seems to be at peace with himself. Though he clearly likes a drink, he is a devoted family man, which slightly jars with the beak-and-brasses lad culture.

One of my first thoughts upon hearing of the death of Queen Elizabeth II in September 2022 was: 'Fuck, they're going to cancel the match'. Liverpool were due to play Chelsea at Stamford Bridge that weekend, and I knew that at least this game would be cancelled – as it was, the entire set of fixtures was postponed – because any minute's silence would most certainly not have been 'impeccably observed' by the away fans.

Especially since the match was at Chelsea. If it was at Anfield, maybe things would have been different. Quite possibly, if it was at Anfield, it *might* have been impeccably observed, just to stick two fingers up to the media and other fans.

But given that the match was due to be played at Stamford Bridge, and given that Chelsea are seen by Scouse football fans as the embodiment of the 'Knees Up Mother Brown', 'Oi, Oi, Saveloy', Cockney Toryism to which the modern Liverpudlian identity is constructed partially in opposition (however ignorant this assumption may be of London geography, politics and culture), there was no way that the silence would have been greeted with respectful reverence.

There has been controversy around minute silences – and the more recent innovation, a minute's applause – for at least twenty years. At the intersection of football, politics and culture, they generate disagreements over how frequently they are held – with some voices complaining about their proliferation and arguing that they should be reserved for the most significant deaths and sombre occasions, while others complain about the absence of a tribute after a particular death or tragedy.

When a minute's silence was held at Anfield in 2004 after the execution of the Liverpudlian hostage Ken Bigley in Iraq, Boris Johnson – then the editor of the *Spectator* magazine – published an infamous editorial complaining about the city's 'mawkish sentimentality' and proclivity to 'wallow in a sense of vicarious victimhood'. On the other hand, once the postponement of the fixtures for the weekend after the Queen's death had been announced, social media was awash with complaints about 'Scousers' getting football cancelled because they could not be trusted to respect Her Maj.

This 'policing of silence', over whether and for whom silences are held, and whether or not they are respectfully observed, reflects broader conflicts over what exactly comprises a tragedy worth remembering. As football is now so visible, pervasive and 'important', silences before matches have become increasingly contentious.

Today, the discourse around professional football encompasses not just sport, but politics, culture, class and many other issues as well, and high-profile games are one of the few occasions when live television is watched in huge numbers across generations, classes and ethnicities. The expansion of football broadcasting and the feedback mechanism of social media means that these minutes of silence or applause are no longer witnessed merely by the spectators in the ground, but by millions in the UK and around the world.

The sociologists Richard Giulianotti and Roland Robertson call this the 'glocalization' of football, in which identities built around what team you support compete with and take over from traditional identities based on nationality, religion or occupation. These new identities based on sports teams are at once particular to certain places, like Liverpool, but at the same time adoptable by people from all round the world.

Giulianotti and Robertson argue that this results in an increased need to stress the distinctiveness of local identity, as fans try to shape how their club and area are perceived by national and global audiences. Hence the proliferation at Anfield of songs and flags emphasising Liverpool's cosmopolitan history, e.g. 'Scouse not English' banners and chants about the Tories and Thatcher.

Other academics such as Liam Foster and Kate Woodthorpe argue that as well as more 'traditional' mechanisms – banners and chants, minute's silences (or applauses) – are now increasingly used 'to consolidate and (re)confirm the community identity associated with a football club'.

So, while there was no chance that the Liverpool away fans would have respected a minute's silence at Stamford Bridge after the death of the Queen, and why the brief 'moment's silence' at Anfield was hastily concluded at the next Liverpool home game, Liverpool fans did unanimously observe the minute's applause for murdered schoolchildren Ava White and Olivia Pratt-Korbel, and gave a standing ovation to the then Manchester United player Cristiano Ronaldo – who wore the number 7 shirt – during the seventh minute of a match after the loss of his baby son in April 2022.

Liverpool fans booing the national anthem, or their reluctance to endorse a minute's silence for dead royalty, is a projection of a desired image rather than a reflection of politico-cultural reality. In the same way that Millwall fans made sure to boo their players 'taking the knee' in support of the Black Lives Matter movement, the same gesture was inevitably greeted with respectful reverence at Anfield. And yet, in reality, there is probably not as great a chasm in political opinions between the working-class people of Liverpool and Bermondsey (or Kent, or wherever most match-going Millwall fans live nowadays), as either set of fans would like to think. But there is in the self-image of the fans, and this self-image must be performed to be maintained.

This is ultimately what the policing of silences is about; when right-wingers complain about the mawkishness and sentimentality of the increasing frequency of minute's silences and applauses, of the national anthem not being duly respected or of players taking the knee, it is a vain protest against a changing world they cannot control. Reactionaries cannot stop 'wokery' and the gradual liberal drift of society on issues from race to LGBT rights to vegan sausage rolls, so they rail about Scousers disrupting the silence for Her Maj.

So too for Liverpool fans; there is little chance of any shifts in popular support for the monarchy and a restrictive immigration policy, or of any serious changes to wealth and income inequality, so they chant about how Thatcher is still dead.

Talking of this transformation, Paul Du Noyer wrote that 'Scouse solidarity used to be based on family, workplace, the union, religious and political affiliations. Now only football remained.'

Today, despite many people in Liverpool having no interest in football, the sport has stepped in to fill the void of a lot of prior forms of identity and connection. Different aspects of the city's personality are also reflected in its teams. Since the first Premier League season in 1992, the team at the top of the table on Christmas day has usually gone on to win the title. However, Liverpool FC have the record for sitting top on Christmas day and failing to win the competition, having done so (at time of writing) on five different occasions, as early promise and verve fell victim to a lack of focus and the superior resources of rivals. With Everton, it seems their struggles over the past thirty years reflect the other aspects of the city: doggedness, determination, spite, a little bit of envy. If Liverpool FC is the night on the ale, goes the saying, Everton is the hangover.

Hopefully, in the future, if the economic recovery of the city continues, its people will have more reasons to be proud than the actions of eleven men on a football pitch. Especially since Everton fans don't even have that.

INTERLUDE 4

Casuals

In the late 1970s, changes were taking place on the football terraces and surrounding streets. It was not just that the fans were getting more violent – with notable riots such as the 1975 European Cup Final and 1980 Scottish Cup Final leading to legislation banning the consumption of alcohol during matches – but that they were becoming better dressed.

It's believed that Newcastle fans in the 1970s were the first to start wearing replicas of the team shirt to the match – but at the same time football hooligans in Liverpool were adopting a very different style.

These fans would not be seen dead in a replica shirt, but nor were they about to don the suits and ties that their fathers and uncles wore to the match. Instead, they wore European designer labels, such as Lacoste, Ellesse, Fila and Sergio Tacchini.

The so-called casual era came about through a combination of factors. Firstly, the growth in away fans following English teams in Europe – which was itself a phenomenon pioneered by Liverpool supporters; in 1979, around 10,000 Nottingham Forest fans travelled to see their team win the European Cup in Munich; however, two years later, three times that number made it from Liverpool to Rome.

There was also the decline in traditional industry, with hooligan firms, and football more broadly, filling a hole once occupied by a job or class identity. Yet casual culture itself came about at a time of rising relative affluence – even if, perhaps especially because, Liverpool itself was in a worse state than the broader British economy.

As well as the growth in teams taking large numbers of fans to away matches, the change from the ubiquitous suits and ties of the 1950s and '60s to the designer brands of the '70s and '80s reflected this new affluence; instead of proudly maintaining a good-quality suit, now status and identity were demonstrated through spending on the latest fashions.

Will Sergeant recalls one game between Liverpool and Chelsea when 'ten or so Chelsea fans had come decked out in full *Clockwork Orange* regalia: bowler hats, one false eyelash, white boiler suits, the lot'. Finding themselves in the Anfield Road end, they were viciously beaten by Liverpool fans and had to be rescued by the police: 'In and among the sea of red and white bobble hats, the odd battered bowler trophy sat atop Rod Stewart-style feather-cut hairdos.'

Everton 'top lad' Andy Nicholls recalls battling an opposing fan who wore a full-on gas mask with goggles. Challenged by Nicholls over his ridiculous get-up, he could only say that it was 'fashion'.

Why was it that Liverpool fans, then and now, travelled in such numbers? It might have been due to the city's seafaring history and the long-established itinerant culture.

If you were out of work or casually employed, the chance to spend a few quick days getting to a European city and back, pissed the whole time, was a welcome escape.

Casuals usually had cash to spend not just on tickets, ale and travel but also on keeping up with rapid-changing terrace fashion; though, with a certain base level of thievery, following your team over to Europe could cost you only a return coach ticket and ale money.

Then and now, football hooliganism recruits from a particular stratum that could not be described as an 'underclass'.

Nicholls talks about his shame that he couldn't live up to the example of his father, a non-violent family man who held down a steady job and made sure that his kids 'never wanted for much' growing up.

In the '90s and early 2000s, there was a bit of a craze for tales from former hooligans now going to seed due to a combination of banning orders, improved police intelligence and the gentrification of the game. There were a couple of notable Merseyside entries into this genre, the novel *Awaydays* by Kevin Sampson, which fictionalised the activities of Tranmere hooligans, and *Scally* by Nicholls, which details his exploits with various Everton firms, including the literally named 'Country Road Cutters'.

Reading these accounts today, it already seems a world away, not least because there was a huge market for mediocre books by former football hooligans. My 2004 edition of Nicholls' book is fully *400 pages* – and, as you can probably guess, that does not include extensive pages of notes and a detailed index.

I say my edition, because Nicholls' book sold shedloads and had several reprints – clearly, I missed a trick by practising with a pen when I would have been better off with a Stanley knife.

As with the rise of football hooliganism, there were many reasons for its decline: more effective prosecution and banning orders; the rise of dance music and club culture in the 1990s; and the gentrification of football. Ultimately, many of the lads who would have become hooligans were priced out of the game.

In the words of Du Noyer, 'the scally tribes of the 1980s' remade the link between Liverpool music and football. Kevin Sampson remembers that the 'instant connection between the football crowd and the acid house crowd' fuelled a fusing of the two, which created a new culture, one equally at home in a ground or a nightclub.

The changing nature of clubbing, and in particular the ecstasy wave of the early '90s, combined with the changing nature of football grounds, led to a working-class culture that was less violent, less male and increasingly less working class.

The Taylor Report commissioned in the aftermath of the Hillsborough disaster brought the curtain down on a distinctive era in English football. In its aftermath, the crumbling stadia, pens for fans and ageing terraces were replaced with all-seater arenas, with standing at matches banned in the top two divisions in 1994.

By the 1990s, there was a change in how football was perceived within British culture; it had become universalised and shorn of its working-class associations – apart from the fact that footballers' wages, unique in the British labour market, are discussed in terms of weekly pay, for some reason, as though they are 1930s millhands earning 30 bob and sixpence.

But the legacy of the casual era lives on: of the numerous social media accounts that celebrate casual culture, Hooligans.cz showcases videos of ultras from the length and breadth of Europe and beyond. In an era of declining British cultural relevance, casual culture is one recent British intervention in that sphere that is expanding its influence. Perhaps it is no surprise that it was born in Liverpool.

6

MERSEY BEATS

In 1841, the prison inspector complained that 'in no other town' had the 'demoralising influence of low theatres and amusements upon children been so decidedly experienced as at Liverpool'. The population of Victorian Liverpool may have been poor, but it was musical. In the 1850s, thirty-two pubs had 'concert rooms' for travelling and local bands, with the largest hall holding up to 400 people. In 1849, a visiting journalist remarked on the 'concert-room industry' in the city:

> The attention of the stranger who walks through the streets of Liverpool can scarcely fail to be directed to the great number of placards which invite the public to cheap or free concert-rooms. Of all shapes, sizes and colours to attract the eye, they cover the walls of the town, and compete with one another in the inducements which they offer to the public to favour with its patronage the houses which they advertise.

As well as this commercially provided live music, middle-class reformers took music to those too poor to pay, hosting 'court and alley' concerts, as they were known, in the slums. The most famous of these, run by

H. Lee Jones, also delivered free food to poor children and the disabled, and became well known nationally.

Around 400 people attended the first of these concerts, in July 1897 – having first washed and cleaned their court and decorated the windows with paper flags – and within two years Jones had a group of around 150 volunteers to play in his shows.

These concerts were publicised with pamphlets stressing that the events were free, and that it was not a front for any kind of church, cult, religion or political party. They also noted that those fortunate enough to have previously received a show by the Jones players had scrupulously cleaned their court, provided chairs and kept all their children quiet.

On the big night itself, a horse would pull a piano into the chosen street, the performers would set up, using a rope to keep people off the platform, and around a kilo of lime chloride 'to antidote any immediately disagreeable effluvia'. Jones and other such bandleaders entertained the crowds with hymns, patriotic songs, comedy numbers, Scottish and Irish folk tunes, as well as violin, mandolin and banjo solos.

A generation earlier when instruments were scarcer, handbell ringing – which is exactly what it sounds like and sounds about as bad as you think – became a well-established working-class leisure pursuit. In the 1840s, one Liverpool group – imaginatively called the 'Lancashire Ringers' – so impressed American circus magnate P. T. Barnum when he saw them perform in the city that he took them on a tour of the USA. Barnum renamed them as the 'Swiss Bell Ringers' – possibly the first and one of the more successful examples of a Scouse band being repackaged for an American audience. (Although this history was probably unknown to the author of a negative review of the Beatles' appearance on the *Ed Sullivan Show*, twelve decades later, who dismissed them as '75 per cent publicity, 20 per cent haircut and 5 per cent lilting lament', owing 'less to Britain than to Barnum'.)

The popularity of having a bash at an instrument no matter how humble was testified to by Paul McCartney, who recalled that the early Beatles 'lost every bloody talent contest we ever went in. Never came anywhere. We always got beaten by some terrible loser, you know, nearly always the woman on the spoons. In Liverpool they'd all get tanked up and by 11.30 when the judging went on they're all going "Go on, Edna". Bloody good she was, too.'

Despite this musicality, unlike many other parts of the British Isles there was no indigenous folk-music tradition in Liverpool, apart from the sea-shanties of transient seamen. But by the middle of the twentieth century, Liverpool audiences enjoyed beat poetry and folk; the poet Adrian Henri, originally from Birkenhead and the grandson of a Mauritian seaman, once hosted Allen Ginsberg in the city, who declared that 'Liverpool is at the present moment the centre of the consciousness of the human universe', although it's not known whether that was just because he was there.

During Bob Dylan's famous 'going electric' tour of England, an audience member in Liverpool, doing his version of the 'Judas' shout, asked Dylan: 'Where's the poet in you? Where's the saviour?', which if nothing else confirms that folk-music fans in Liverpool circa 1966 were pretentious dickheads just like everywhere else.

Liverpool was a ready market for US imports, becoming an early centre for UK jazz music. The Cavern Club, which opened in 1957, was named after Le Caveau de la Huchette club in Paris, with the opening night headlined by the Merseysippi Jazz Band.

Decades before Liverpool became known for the Beatles, country and western music was so popular in the city that it was called the 'Nashville of the North' – although it's not clear by whom – and was said in the 1950s to have more country groups than Nashville itself (which seems unlikely). Apparently, in those pre-rock 'n' roll days a singer called 'The Yodelling Brakeman' was the biggest star on Merseyside.

The actor Ricky Tomlinson – of airport fame – once performed as Hobo Rick, complete with a ten-gallon hat. Paul Du Noyer recalls the Kirkby factory he worked in during the 1970s having a giant portrait of Che Guevara on the wall and the records of George Jones and Merle Haggard blasting out from the morning till the night shift.

George Harrison's sailor father brought back records by Jimmie Rodgers and Chet Atkins, which encouraged him to take up the guitar and ukulele. Harrison became so enamoured with the ukulele that a Vegas tart recalls fellating him and he apparently continued to play his uke throughout.

By the late 1950s, the transatlantic trade that had introduced the city to jazz and country music began bringing over Little Richard, Chuck Berry and Bo Diddley. This music found a ready audience across Liverpool, but the venues themselves were de facto segregated. Few black Scousers would venture into the clubs in town and not many white people went into Liverpool 8.

And it was this part of town in particular which continued to provide a home for a wide variety of music when most of the rest of the city had lost interest in jazz and blues. Toxteth featured venues such as the Somali Club, the Gladray and the basement Al-Ahram bar, the latter especially popular with Arab sailors, where calypso and reggae were played alongside Yemeni folk songs and commercial disco.

This meant that Liverpool remained a destination for touring American artists of all types; if you were around in the 1960s and went to Smithdown Road's Palm Cove, you might see Nat King Cole or Dizzy Gillespie propping up the bar.

By the 1950s, the city was launching its own imitations of the big American stars. Michael Holliday, the first Liverpudlian to have two number one singles, was a former seaman from Kirkdale who honed his Bing Crosby style while singing to American troops at Burtonwood Base.

Frank Abelson, a Jewish Scouser, became known as Frankie Vaughan, the major UK singer of the pre-rock 'n' roll era. He briefly relocated to the USA to make movies, which led to the apocryphal myth that the band name Frankie Goes to Hollywood was inspired by an *Echo* headline on the move. While in America, he famously and mysteriously spurned the advances of Marilyn Monroe, and for some reason ended up as the Lord Lieutenant of Buckinghamshire.

Ron Wycherley from the Dingle became Billy Fury, one of the first genuine UK rock stars (sorry, Cliff), who would go on to equal the Beatles' record of twenty-four hits in the 1960s and altogether spent some 332 weeks in the UK charts. Soon after, Liverpudlian manager Brian Epstein had his first taste of chart success with local band Gerry Marsden and the Mars Bars (soon named the Pacemakers).

The pre-Beatles era witnessed a variety of genres and bands coming out of the city that wouldn't be seen again until the 1980s. The long Liverpool tradition of black sailors marrying Irish women produced, among other artists, Derry Wilkie, the frontman of the Seniors, who led the first Merseybeat group in Hamburg, and whose musical tastes were honed on a diet of calypso, country and Irish ballads. Fellow Scouser Sugar Deen of the Valentinos had a Glaswegian mother and a Nigerian sailor father. Fifteen years later, Eddy Amoo, who had a Ghanaian father and an Irish grandmother, would form the Real Thing, probably the most successful black group the city has produced.

In the early '60s, Liverpool girlband the Vernon Girls had minor hits, and another group called the Liver Birds played a residency in Hamburg. Now known more for her Saturday night TV work, Cilla Black was Britain's biggest female pop star of the decade.

By 1963, it was estimated that there were over 200 semi-professional bands in the city, although there is some debate around this number. Bob Wooler, Cavern DJ, stated in *Mersey Beat* that there were 300 groups at the start of the 1960s, but a 1984 Cavern history puts the number at closer to 400.

However many there were, there is no doubting the success of Liverpool groups in this period: for fifty-one of the sixty weeks between April 1963 and May 1964, there was a Merseybeat record at number one in the UK. The number one record for two of the remaining weeks, 'World Without Love' by Peter and Gordon, was written by Paul McCartney.

At this time, as Du Noyer writes, 'the elite of the scene, Beatles included, could assemble after hours at Allan Williams' upmarket Blue Angel club in Seel Street', where 'distinguished guests includ[ing] Bob Dylan and Judy Garland' were treated to delights such as topless waitresses and miniature bull fighting.

I'm not sure whether it's more surprising that Bob Dylan and Judy Garland visited the Blue Angel, or that it was at one time considered 'upmarket'. Either way, generations of students will thrill to know that their feet once stuck to the same carpet on which Bob Dylan once trod.

At the height of the city's musical power, the Rialto Ballroom was used to record a series of *This Is Mersey Beat* albums, featuring bands from the city. The big pop show of the time, *Thank Your Lucky Stars*, hosted a Liverpool special featuring Cilla Black, the Beatles, the Searchers and Billy J. Kramer; it was so successful that it was the UK's entry into a 1964 international TV competition.

The US publicity for the Dave Clark Five, the second biggest British act after the Beatles, described the Tottenham band as having 'the Mersey sound with the Liverpool beat'. US youth discarded their boardshorts and donned deerstalkers, forming groups like Sherlock Fogge. A Monkees-style beat group was invented called the Wackers, although they were actually from Manchester.

In a nice example of musical influences coming full circle, Chuck Berry released an album *St Louis to Liverpool*, while Diana Ross and the

Supremes recorded an album of Beatles covers called *A Bit of Liverpool*. Similarly, country singers such as Rosanne Cash, Dwight Yoakam and Steve Earle worshipped John Lennon as they did Hank Williams, while the black blues singer Robert Cray was apparently inspired to pick up a guitar after listening to the Beatles.

A *Rolling Stone* magazine feature on San Francisco during the 1967 'Summer of Love' gave the California city the ultimate compliment when it referred to it as 'the American Liverpool'.

This transformation of the city, in just a few short years, from nondescript deindustrialising northern town to the centre of the pop-culture universe has had an impact on the transformation of the people, from Tory-voting, rioting, hard-nosed capitalists to their current incarnation – from 'wackers' to 'wacky'.

Despite the success of various other Merseyside groups before 1963, this transformation was ultimately down to one group in particular. Liverpool in the early 1960s was not unique among northern industrial cities in producing popular singers, comedians and actors. In fact, until around 1963, Liverpool was not particularly associated with music any more than any other UK city. Just like the country itself – before this period there was no sense that Britain was a natural home for pop music. Without the Beatles, Liverpool, Manchester and the rest of the UK would at best have been regarded as a minor outpost of a hegemonic American showbusiness industry. All of this was about to change.

In 1961, Geoff Davies – later owner of the legendary Probe Records – was a jazz purist, horrified to hear that a 'pop band' called the Beatles were playing his favourite venue. He has some vague memories of the first time he visited the Cavern while they were on, when he mostly ignored them and chatted with his mates. But his second experience of hearing the band is etched into his memory:

The following week I went to a lunchtime session and there were the Beatles again. And that was it, everything changed for me. They used to do 'Money' and extend the intro, really bloody heavy, and then Lennon comes in, 'The best things in life are free', in the dirtiest, foulest voice I'd heard in my life, full of hate and sneering and cynicism.

He subsequently saw them seventy-eight times at the Cavern, where the band played 272 shows between 1961 and 1963.

There were several reasons for the mammoth success of the Beatles, and Liverpool contributed many of them. The first of these is the long multicultural history and connections of the city, which come up in all sorts of unexpected and sometimes surreal ways in the early days of the band; the Beatles were first taken to Hamburg by their agent/manager Allan Williams and his business partner, a calypso singer and steel band player called Lord Woodbine. In 1960, the only place the then named Silver Beatles could get a gig was Woodbine's New Cabaret Artists' Club on Upper Parliament Street. One of the first gigs the band got at the Cavern in 1962 was supporting Joe and Edmund Ankrah's band the Chants.

Another reason was that since mass music practice was more common in Liverpool than elsewhere, instruments were usually easy to come by for the young Beatles. After the Second World War, it was surprisingly common for working-class households to have an upright piano; my brother once cracked his head open on a coffee table after jumping off my grandparents' one. Paul McCartney and Cilla Black's homes both had pianos – coincidentally bought in the music shop of Brian Epstein. Ringo Starr's grandparents played the mandolin and banjo and passed their instruments on to him.

In the wake of their success, British politicians were eager to comment on what the Beatles' achievements told us about Liverpool, working-class youth and the direction of the country. The historian Marcus Collins has said that these were often standard negative 'it's the children that are wrong' bromides, such as when the Labour MP Richard Buchanan warned that those who 'follow the Mersey beat' rather than 'the scholastic beat' ended up in jobs 'well below their intellectual capacity'.

But others had much more positive opinions. Fellow Labour MP William Teeling credited 'the Beatles and similar groups of musicians' for the rapid decline of 'unruly behaviour' by young northerners. The popularity of the band led to W. R. Rees-Davies calling for dance clubs to open on Sunday evenings, on the grounds that teenagers who were prevented from 'listen[ing] to the "Beatles", or whoever it may be . . . would be on the streets, getting into trouble'. Conservative MP Norman Miscampbell claimed that gang-related crime had 'largely disappeared' from Liverpool thanks to 'The Beatles, and groups like them' offering an alternative form of group membership. Miscampbell argued that beat groups could be the solution to the problem of youth alienation and atomisation as they 'provided an outlet for many people who find it difficult to integrate themselves into society when they move into adolescence'. He also argued it was appropriate that they be rewarded handsomely for their 'great skill'. Fellow Conservative Bill Deedes was then the Minister of Information, and he gave a number of speeches praising the Beatles as representatives of the export-driven, upwardly mobile and go-ahead country created by his party. He commended the group for showing that '[t]here is no place for the lazy, the incompetent, the slipshod' in a Britain 'free of divisions of class or creed'.

The Labour leader of the opposition, Harold Wilson, used the band to make a distinction between his relatively youthful and classless image with the old, aristocratic Tories, at that point led by the peer Alec Douglas Home. Speaking in the Commons, Wilson claimed that it was preposterous for the Conservative 'apostles of a bygone age . . . to pretend that they are "with it" by claiming the Beatles', adding that the desperate Tory government of Home 'would not hesitate' to appoint the Beatles to ambassadorial positions 'if he thought there were votes in it'.

Wilson fully intended to use the young, classless and successful lads from Liverpool to further his and the Labour party's cause. Six months before the 1964 general election, he used his only in-person meeting with the band to stage a famous photoshoot, while at the same time attacking 'attempts recently by a certain leader of a certain party . . . to involve our friends, the Beatles, in politics'. Two years later, as prime minister, he would personally reopen the renovated Cavern Club.

As well as being claimed by politicians across the political spectrum in support of their own views and ideologies, the Beatles provoked a great deal of soul-searching in Parliament about exactly what they said about Britian in the 1960s. In particular, questions revolved around the success of apparently humble lads from an increasingly humble town. Were they a force for good or ill? Should they be treasured as an economic asset? Did they demonstrate the existence of a meritocracy? Did they exemplify the failure of secondary-modern education or the success of a grammar-school one? Did they promote or prevent juvenile delinquency? Were they the pride of the North or a symptom of its backwardness?

But despite the fears and aspirations of politicians and commentators, the success of the Beatles did not immediately result in a transformation of the northern working class. By the time they were switching amphetamines for LSD and stopping live gigs in favour of studio experimentation, they were becoming more of a London – or San Francisco – band than a Liverpool band. In the words of Ringo Starr: 'A lot of flower power didn't translate in, say, Oldham or Bradford, and not really in Liverpool.'

Instead of wondering why bands from Liverpool became so success-ful in the early '60s, a more interesting question could be what Du Noyer calls 'the Surrey Conundrum': 'Why did the art school R&B bands of South-east England become the new rock aristocracy, while the Liverpool bands (the Beatles, as usual, excepted) got consigned to cabaret or civvy street?'

Because while the likes of the Rolling Stones, Fleetwood Mac, the Who, Eric Clapton, Jeff Beck and Jimmy Page went on to have long and established careers, people like Billy Fury died in obscurity. It could be that they weren't prepared for the changing musical tastes of the late '60s and early '70s; the Liverpool music journalist Spencer Leigh reckons this was due to the Midlands and southern artists having a greater grounding in blues music, which enabled their smooth transition into the type of tunes that would dominate popular music in the '70s. 'For some reason,' says Lee, 'the blues passed Liverpool by. They were into jazz, and appreciated Muddy Waters when he played the Mardi Gras club, but that was it.' He points out that when the Beatles were in Hamburg, they would fill the interminable hours they had to spend on stage by stretching out classic twelve-bar blues standards, but didn't themselves record a blues song until the *White Album*'s literally named 'Yer Blues'.

There could have been an element of 'all the gear, no idea'. Mick Jagger said that groups such as the Rolling Stones 'had a good overall history of the thing, blues, country, rock, black music, jazz, whatever ... it's the middle-class knowledge, the sense of history, and the desire to know everything'. In contrast, the Merseybeat bands were made up of mostly working-class lads who were imitating traditional music-hall entertainers and had little to no interest citing obscure records. In the words of Du Noyer, 'they liked the bright, accessible pop of Tamla Motown ... they had no interest in the emerging "counter-culture"; their roots were in semi-pro show business. When pop became rock and rock went weird, around 1966, the Liverpool groups were left behind.'

Maybe that's why the second wave of Liverpool music would be so weird. After the Beatles broke up, the industrial decline of the city continued apace. The transition from wackers to wacky was well under way.

By the start of the 1970s, Liverpool had drifted far from the centre of the musical universe. In 1971, Rory Storm of the Hurricanes – the first massively popular band on the Liverpool and Hamburg scene of the early 1960s – died of an overdose of Scotch and sleeping pills; it is unknown whether or not it was intentional.

When his mother Violet discovered the body, she immediately took her own life. At Storm's funeral he was carried by pallbearers from other Merseybeat bands, accompanied by Gerry Marsden's 'You'll Never Walk Alone'.

At this sad time, even Wigan was cooler than Liverpool – a situation unimaginable before or since.

Even so, the city was still fulfilling its traditional role as an importer of the latest sounds. Many of the Northern Soul records played at the Wigan Casino and other such storied venues came into the country via US troops at Burtonwood base, while the leading northern DJ Rob Bellars imported his records directly through Liverpool docks.

At this time, the young musicians in the city wanted to move as far away from the Beatles as possible. Andy McCluskey of Orchestral Manoeuvres in the Dark remembers seeing Kraftwerk at the Liverpool Empire in 1975 and recalls that already the Beatles 'seemed like ancient history; we were teenagers and they belonged to the time when we were children. We wanted something new, and that's why I got interested in synthesisers'.

As Will Sergeant argues, bands such as Frankie Goes to Hollywood, the Teardrop Explodes, Orchestral Manoeuvres in the Dark and Dead or Alive were 'all desperate to shake off the shadow of the Beatles that pervade[d] every aspect of Liverpudlian life'.

Elvis Costello, a sort of part-Liverpool, part-London, part-Ireland hybrid, gives a sense of the musical tastes of the city at the time; having gone to school in Hounslow, West London, where 'you had to like Tamla and reggae otherwise you were dead', when he came back up to

Liverpool, 'you didn't dare say you liked Tamla, it was poof's music, you had to like Deep Purple or something'.

For many aspiring Liverpool musicians in the late '70s, punk would serve the role that skiffle had in the 1950s by providing the quickest way to form your own band, even if you couldn't really play. But even so, the influences on Merseyside were slightly different: Jonathan Richman, the Velvet Underground and the Doors were more influential than the Clash and the Sex Pistols.

This new scene had several ingredients crucial to its success. One of these was the presence of hundreds, maybe thousands, of young people passionate about music and looking to start their own bands, or at least become early fans of new and exciting artists. Another was the broader ecosystem of pubs, clubs, practice rooms and record shops; when Eric's opened in September 1976, it was one of 235 nightclubs in the city, alongside shops like Probe Records.

The timing of Eric's was also crucial. People like Pete Wylie, Julian Cope, Jayne Casey, Ian McCulloch and Will Sergeant – people from across the city and beyond – were coming down several times a week to pay about 60p on the door and see whatever was on.

Bands such as the Sex Pistols and the Stranglers played Eric's, as did a young Joy Division. In 1979 alone, Eric's saw gigs by the Cure, Jonathan Richman and the Modern Lovers, the Fall, the Specials and Madness. On 21 April 1979, one of the most anticipated nights of the year, Eric's patrons were treated to a performance by Iggy Pop himself – not only a huge influence on the nascent post-punk scene, but also a key influence on many of the other bands and artists – David Bowie, Talking Heads, etc – that had themselves influenced the scene. Apparently, Iggy insisted on including Liverpool in his 1979 UK tour, and Eric's was the only venue willing to host him.

This ecosystem gave birth to the second great wave of Liverpool bands in the late '70s and early '80s: the Teardrop Explodes, Dead or

Alive, Frankie Goes to Hollywood, A Flock of Seagulls, Orchestral Manoeuvres in the Dark, and Echo and the Bunnymen. Other names on the scene included the Scot Bill Drummond (later of KLF), Ian Broudie (later of the Lightning Seeds), and Budgie (of Siouxsie and the Banshees). Dave Balfe of the Teardrop Explodes set up Food Records, which signed Blur; it was his big house in the country described in their now-unlistenable 1995 single. Various less well-known bands also had their moments; a group called the Real People had one of their songs, 'One by One', covered by Cher.

There was also the vital presence of John Peel on Radio 1, regularly turning obscure bands who'd chanced their arm sending in a demo into next big things overnight. By no means did only artists from Liverpool benefit from this, although Peel's positive feelings towards the city might have encouraged him, consciously or otherwise, to promote new Liverpool music. But his willingness, or even compulsion, to play challenging music was vital to the success of artists who even now are hard to categorise and stick into one genre or another. These bands are often called 'post-punk' or 'new wave', but even these terms are inherently broad and imprecise.

It was also important that so many of them had metalwork and other practical training in the secondary moderns, where it was not assumed that they were destined for greatness, but these lessons would later prove very useful in fixing synthesisers.

These lads had some idea, but usually had no gear; they knew what they liked but could barely afford basic instruments, never mind the latest electronic kit. Therefore, they had to improvise.

By the start of the '80s, Liverpool was getting its reputation back. Singer Courtney Love, who arrived in the city in the '80s when she was about fifteen, later recalled that she 'stole a lot from them', from Scousers, 'including this way of playing with stupid stereotypes. I [also] learned that arrogance is not necessarily a bad thing'.

On 28 January 1984, there were more Liverpool acts in the UK top twenty than at any time since 1964. They ranged from the memorable (Frankie Goes to Hollywood's 'Relax'; Echo and the Bunnymen's 'The Killing Moon') to the forgettable (Paul McCartney's 'Pipes of Peace' and John Lennon's 'Nobody Told Me'), to the piss-taking (Joe Fagin's 'That's Livin' Alright'). There was little in common between Echo and the Bunnymen, Frankie, A Flock of Seagulls and the Teardrop Explodes, and Pete Burns was surely the strangest and least likely figure to have a world number one hit song until Ed Sheeran. The eclecticism of this era was summed up by an anonymous critic who said to Andy McClusky of OMD: 'Your trouble is you don't know whether to be Abba or Joy Division.'

Reviewing McCartney's album of the same name for the *NME*, Penny Reel described *Pipes of Peace* as 'A dull, tired and empty collection', while Jeff Strowe of PopMatters reckons that the album 'presents McCartney at his most regrettable'. That the Bunnymen and Frankie's songs have stood the test of time better than those of the ex-Beatles reflects how the former saw the latter: as stale and out of time. Although to be fair to John Lennon, he had been dead for four years by this point.

While there were some superstars and prize eccentrics among that generation of Scouse talent, there were also a large number of fairly ordinary people who hit it big; Frankie Goes to Hollywood, for example, which unprecedently had two openly gay singers, also included Nasher, an electrician, Mark O'Toole, a joiner, and Ged, who had just been sacked when he joined the band. These three fairly unlikely Scouse lads provided the rhythm section that shifted millions of copies in the decade.

The Liverpudlian desire to break with the past and move on could have been one reason for the renewed and sudden success of Scouse singers in this period. As Will Sergeant recalls, it seemed to be 'an unwritten law that to be seen twice with the same look would be an outrage'.

Perhaps another element of the success of these bands was that they had needed to be tough to survive – not metaphorically in the music business, but literally on the streets of Liverpool. Violence had been a feature of the city's nightlife for decades; legend has it that the nightclub the Iron Door got its name after the original door was smashed in by axe-wielding villains looking for Derry Wilkie, singer of the Seniors.

By the 1980s, when there was a flowering of gender-bending andro-gynist culture amid the economic ruination of one of the most violent cities in northern Europe, things got more intense. Unlike contempo-raries on London's New Romantic Scene, who traversed clubs in West London, Pete Burns had a good chance of running into scallies with Stanley knives. Before he died, Burns recalled: 'I've had a taxi drive up the kerb at me, I've had someone try to push me out of a bus. I've been smashed across the head with a wine bottle and a brick.'

Former musician Stu James remembers that when performing in the city: 'Suddenly you'd see half the audience had disappeared, because there was a massive fight going on. I remember the police having to get us out of one gig in Aigburth. They were very violent. In Penny Lane Hall, you'd see the crowd swirling like a kaleidoscope with the fight rushing round and chairs in the air.'

Paradoxically, it was during this violent, depressing time around the first Thatcher election victory in 1979 that elements of the '60s counter-culture, which hadn't been seen in the city in fifteen years, came roaring back, particularly with the popularity of Frank Zappa and Pink Floyd.

The popularity of Pink Floyd in Liverpool is one of the great mysteries. When I was about fifteen, I used to go down to Otterspool prom with a group of mates where we'd drink (cans of Hollandia, which were ridiculously cheap; something like four for a pound from an off-licence that was happy to accept blatantly fake ID) and smoke rocky (cheap soap bar purchased from behind a pub in West Derby). Our mate Matty had a portable CD player and we'd use it to play Shack, the Stone Roses, the Beatles and, above all, Pink Floyd.

On one occasion, a man walked past with his young son (probably about four years old) and I sort of winced – a bunch of lads smoking weed, discarded cans everywhere, 'Shine on you Crazy Diamond' blasting out of the tinny speakers. He paused, and we were worried he was going to kick off, then said: 'Pink Floyd? Is right lads!' and walked on.

Pete Wylie, a stalwart of the Eric's scene and frontman of a load of mediocre bands such as the Mighty Wah!, first came to the attention of John Peel when he used an interview to criticise Peel for not playing enough early Pink Floyd – a prime example of the old, new and yet-to-be-born elements of the Liverpool musical universe coalescing.

As well as Pink Floyd, the popularity of Frank Zappa was also central to the 'cosmic' turn in the city's music scene at this point. Zappa's popularity was boosted by his experimental, avant-garde music and his openly scathing attitude towards the Beatles.

With the return of '60s music and culture to acceptability among working-class Scousers, cannabis and LSD once again rose in popularity. The author Kevin Sampson recalls that prior to this moment 'dope would have been seen as a middle-class hippy sort of thing [and] your majority of urchins in Liverpool were quite anti-hippy'. In contrast, John Power of the La's and Cast reckons that the substances changed first and then the music, not the other way around: 'you'd get into a bit of pot, [then] Floyd and Zep, and Hendrix and all that'.

And so, in the city during the late '70s and early '80s, you had a strange merger of the scally, football casual scene with the music of Pink Floyd and Frank Zappa, as well as globally commercially successful bands such as Frankie Goes to Hollywood and Dead or Alive. A decade later, when these two scenes met, it would give birth to the dance music scene that would dominate Liverpool in the 1990s.

Through all this time the Liverpool and Manchester scenes kept a relatively respectful distance. There had long been music enmity between the two cities; Roger Eagle, formerly DJ at Manchester's Twisted Wheel club, burned a copy of the Beatle's second album on stage in 1963.

In the late 1980s, Nathan McGough, the stepson of Liverpool poet Roger McGough, managed the Happy Mondays, who represented the essence of the Madchester sound – a mix of rock and dance with a strong flavour of ecstasy – to again bring together Liverpudlian and Mancunian sensibilities. And the journalist Paul Morley was a Mancunian who helped launch Liverpool's Frankie Goes to Hollywood in the early 1980s through his label ZTT. There was even an aborted attempt by Liverpool's Pete Fulwell and Manchester's Tony Wilson to put together a combined label, Eric's Factory – it never transpired.

Speaking of the difference between the musical trends of the two cities, Echo and the Bunnymen's Ian McCulloch reckoned that 'Liverpool bands have always written songs, whereas Manchester has always been the place that's gone for grooves'. However accurate this was, in the 1990s Manchester became associated with guitar music through the success of the Stone Roses and Oasis, at the same time that, for a lot of people in Liverpool, that music represented the past.

In 1987, the year the Smiths broke up, the La's were tipped by many record-industry insiders as the natural successors to the Manchester band. For various reasons, this never happened. And although the La's inspired a host of working-class guitar bands – Noel Gallagher said that 'Oasis were finishing what the La's started' – Liverpool bands in general were notable for their lack of prominence in the 1990's 'Britpop' scene.

Whereas groups such as Oasis, Blur, Pulp and Suede became massive, Liverpool bands like the La's, Cast, Space and, most unjustly of all, Shack, never enjoyed the same level of success.

Certainly, some of this is attributable to behaviour debauched and diva-like even by the standards of the time; back in the '80s Ian

McCullouch had the record company send him to Paris to record the vocals on 'The Killing Moon', but he wasted so much time arsing around they ran out of money, and he had to record them back in Liverpool. A few years later, Lee Mavers of the La's refused to use a 1960's mixing desk as it didn't have the original '60s dust on it. Michael Head of Shack once turned up to a photoshoot paid for by his record label with half of his teeth smashed out from a fight the night before.

Interestingly, John Power told the journalist Simon Hughes that his band 'got a lot of stick from the music writing scene for wearing a checked shirt with cords and Adidas trainers. They wanted everyone to look like Pulp instead. They tried to frame Cast as hooligans.'

This is interesting because I suspect a lot of the adoration of Pulp in the music press – especially now, thirty years on – is not just because of the quality of their tunes and the undeniably winsome personality of Jarvis Cocker, but specifically their nerdiness; Jarvis Cocker was the proletarian geek done well, which is how the sort of person who writes about music sees themselves, or wishes they could be.

The La's, Cast and Shack were different. Not scallies exactly, but representing a very different kind of working-class attitude to Cocker and Pulp, and a world away from the likes of Blur or Suede. For all their intelligence and sensitivity, you can't quite imagine Lee Mavers or Michael Head studying at Central St Martins. And I'd like to think that if Mavers or Head had met a Greek multimillionaire heiress, the whole thing would have ended in tears, her house or flat ruined, the bizzies called and her property liberated, instead of them traipsing round a supermarket making wry observations.

Or it could have been that many of these lads didn't really have their hearts in it. In the words of former Probe records boss Geoff Davies, music has been like football and boxing for Liverpool, 'a way for working-class lads without education to get out, make money, get sex, drugs, rock 'n' roll. And this explains the blandness of much of the music.'

One of the key cultural developments in the 1990s was the merging of the city's football and music scenes. Today the synchronicity between the two seems obvious, but it wasn't that way back in the 1980s. Michael Head remembers that 'being brought up in the north end and on the streets of Kenny, for me to get into music – it just wasn't what people there did . . . to get into music, to start going to places like the Everyman, I was leaving something behind, going into a totally different territory'.

But in the '90s, this changed. Part of this was due to the increasingly sanitised nature of football. Part of it was due to the interjection of ecstasy and dance music into casual culture. In the '90s, drugs finally became widespread in Liverpool: not just weed, but now acid, heroin, ecstasy and cocaine.

The big brothers of James Barton used to chase musician Jayne Casey down the streets; now he began hosting club nights in Quadrant Park that drew 4,000 people to Bootle. That many people voluntarily going to Bootle shows the nature of the change under way. Strange things were happening. Sights previously unseen were now becoming commonplace. As Casey exclaimed to Frankie Goes to Hollywood's Paul Rutherford: 'You've just got to come and see it, the scallies are taking Ecstasy!' Rutherford later came up to a night at Quadrant Park, wearing a t-shirt saying *Queer as Fuck*: 'he went on the dancefloor and he couldn't believe how all the guys were hugging him'.

Barton would go on to found Cream, which alongside London's Ministry of Sound was probably the most famous British nightclub of the 1990s, with DJs such as Paul Oakenfold, Judge Jules and Seb Fontaine all having residencies at different times.

As elsewhere in the country, the electronic music most popular in Liverpool during the 1990s catered to the particular tastes of the locals. Crowds at Cream preferred melodically infused house music to the techno or trance favoured elsewhere in the country.

Kevin McManus, a Cream DJ at the time, recalls that 'typically the sort of stuff that went down well here was the anthemic, Italian stuff, piano-driven with big vocals'. The biggest tune at this time was the David Morales' remix of Mariah Carey's 'Dreamlover'. Cream replaced the Haçienda as the north's premier nightclub; it spawned franchises in Argentina and New Zealand, and its resident DJs would be invited to play gigs from Ibiza to Red Square. According to Andrew Lees, the Canadian DJ Moby was once denied entry to Cream – even though he could hear his tune 'Porcelain' being played inside.

This was reflected in the sound of Peter Hooton's band The Farm, which had elements of the emerging dance scene, an indication of barriers between L8 and Canny Farm breaking down. At the other end of the spectrum, Atomic Kitten's two number ones mean that Liverpool now has more number ones than Detroit, the home of Motown Records.

This merging of casual and music culture in the '90s, having previously kept their distance from each other, might have contributed to the cultural conformism of much of the city today. When you either went to football or were into music, there might have been more room for self-expression. But the mixing of these two tribes, rather than resulting in a more diverse culture, had the opposite effect.

For whatever reason, in the 1990s, the city was musically in the shadow of Manchester, London and even Sheffield. This was not due to the lack of quality local artists. By far the greatest band to come out of Liverpool in the 1990s, and possibly the greatest group the city has produced since the Beatles, are Shack, fronted by Kensington-raised brothers Michael and John Head. But Shack, though critically acclaimed, never had the commercial crossover of Oasis or Pulp. Having said that, this very Liverpudlian band still have fans in unexpected places. A review of a small gig by Mick Head at St Mary's Old Church in Stoke Newington in *The Guardian* described how 'the man who signed the Strokes grabs his neighbour in a violent bromantic headlock, overcome with emotion. Another august indie label boss is here, despite never having released any of Head's music, still enthralled by the careworn romance of the singer-songwriter.'

This is not the kind of audience you would expect for a former smackhead from Kenny. That Shack elicit such a reaction from music-industry bigwigs and aged hipsters says something about the currency and clout that Liverpool holds in the UK cultural scene today. In many ways, Mick Head is the personification of how middle-class left-wingers see Liverpool: intellectual yet unpretentious; authentically proletarian but open and internationalist; sensitive but battle-scarred and realistic.

We need more than this though. Just as a city's prosperity cannot be built on Beatles tourism alone, nor can a city's identity be built on hard-luck stories, or on immense talent never truly realised.

INTERLUDE 5

'What are you wearing there, lad?'

People in Liverpool have long had to make their own fun wherever they could find it. Very often this takes the form of remorseless piss-taking. As early as the 1770s, it was said that 'wits' in pubs would 'make some irritable individual the object of ridicule, for the amusement of the rest of the company'. Popular and cheap pastimes included dog fights, badger or rat baiting and cockfights. Every Shrove Tuesday at a cockpit near Lime Street, boys with their hands tied behind their backs would chase the birds and try to capture them with their mouths in exchange for a prize. In 1891, one drunken man fought a goat, crawling on his knees with his hands clasped behind him. 'After six rounds of being butted in the face by the goat, the battered man retired soaked in blood'.

But early Liverpudlians also appreciated the higher art forms, and often had high standards. The Theatre Royal in Williamson Square usually only employed expensive actors brought up from London, but on one occasion, in July 1778, they made the mistake of starting a season with local and provincial actors. The audience on opening night made their feeling plain; before the play began, the owner took to the stage to try and calm the audience, and was met with 'volleys of potatoes and broken bottles'. Fifteen years later, audiences at the same theatre rioted when the management ended a popular offer on cheap tickets.

But just because they enjoyed the theatre, it didn't mean they behaved themselves. Patrons of the Theatre Royal used to piss where they sat, which led to an incident in 1795 when 'several boxes' had to be evacuated 'in consequence of the streams which descended from above, and some in the pit had their clothes soiled in the same abominable manner'. And in 1783, a group of drunken sailors kidnapped a bull from West Derby village and dragged it all the way to the theatre, where it surprised the audience by popping its head out of the central box.

Popular culture in the city involves a curious mixture of the highbrow, lowbrow and no brow. In the Victorian era, Charles Dickens was a regular visitor to the city, setting sail from the Pier Head to America on two occasions, and other instances visiting the city to research, write or speak. On his reading tours he sold out St George's Hall several times, and on one visit in 1858 he spoke to an audience of over 2,300 people – apparently the largest in-person audience he ever had.

The writing of homegrown authors traditionally bore the imprint of the city's maritime heritage. In the 1930s, while working-class writers elsewhere wrote of the Depression and slums, Liverpool authors like George Garrett, James Hanley and Jim Phelan (who were all working seamen), used dockside districts from around the world as the scenes for their fiction.

More recently, the playwright Willy Russell – author of *Educating Rita*, *Blood Brothers* and much else – argued that 'the Liverpool dialect' in particular, 'is a terrific medium to work in, very fast and exclusive. I suppose it's like painters who painted in certain areas because of the sunlight or sculptors who worked where the clay was good.'

There is evidence of an appreciation for poetry in Liverpool that pops up in strange places. In the 1980s, the juvenile liaison team of

Merseyside police – charged with monitoring the city's young offenders – had an excerpt from T. S. Eliot's *Murder in the Cathedral* taped to the wall: 'What kind of peace may grow between the hammer and the anvil?'

An old Liverpool street poem reads:

> I went to a Chinese laundry
> I asked for a piece of bread
> They wrapped me up in a table cloth
> And sent me off to bed
> I saw an Indian maiden
> She stood about ten feet high
> Her hair was painted sky blue pink
> And she only had one eye

This shows that wacky and psychedelic imagery was present in the city long before *Sgt. Pepper's*.

Then there's the humour. While comedy is subjective, and there are plenty of people in Liverpool who think they are funnier than they actually are – in fact, Scouse professional comedians are often particularly unfunny – some less so than ordinary people you could meet on the street. But there's a strong argument that the Liverpudlian's reputation for wit is well deserved.

A survivor of the *Titanic* recalled a Scouse member of the crew joking to his fellow shipmates who were all soon to drown: 'Sand for breakfast in the morning, boys!' One famous death notice in the *Liverpool Echo* read 'Vinny, you've bounced back from worse than this.'

I was once in the queue for the toilets in Kazimer Gardens (conveniently cubicles only – inconveniently always full) when an American woman walked past the queue. Eager to prevent any angry accusations of queue jumping, she was repeating loudly and weirdly, 'I'm only washing my hands! I'm only washing my hands!' Instantly someone piped up: 'All right, Pontius Pilate, calm down', and everyone pissed themselves (not literally).

Why is it that Liverpool should have so many budding comedians?

The history of immigration and transient work is probably one reason. As the historians Diana E. Ascott, Fiona Lewis and Michael Power have argued, immigrants into new towns were 'unduly dependent on the qualities of wit or personality' to make friends and get by.

In his excellent book *Northerners*, Brian Groom points out that while humour elsewhere in Lancashire tended to be 'slow-building and character based', in Liverpool, as in the East End of London, 'quick fire patter' was prized more highly. Again, this has something to do with the nature of work in ports and on ships, and also something to do with Catholicism: if you have large families, you have to learn to speak quickly in order to get a word in.

After listening to the conversation of drinkers in the city-centre Yates' Wine Lodge, the Liverpudlian author and former docker L. T. Roche came up with a theory that places with high levels of migration and movement develop a culture and conversational style based on travellers' tales, told 'through personal contact or from a close relative; brother, nephew, uncle, or in-law'.

A nice example of this type of humour comes in an anecdote told by the gangster turned supergrass Paul Grimes. Speaking to journalist Graham Johnson about some of his old associates, he complained that 'they would do mad things, fucking stupid things, which would cause untold [trouble], and bring the heat on – literally'. On one occasion, noted in Graham Johnson's *Powder Wars*, a villain called Poppy Hayes and two henchmen spied a rival gangster with whom he had a vendetta, in a bar managed by Grimes. Straight away, 'Poppy gets hold of Charley and sets him on fire, there and then, in the bar. Poured lighter fuel on him and put a flame to it. Whoosh! Could not believe it, la.' After Grimes' bouncer started trying to put out the flames, Hayes and his lads turned on him, trying to set him on fire. 'Luckily I was able to put it out with hands and jacket and that. But by that time, I was fuming, la. Again literally.'

Humour is also a form of agency, a method of self-defence when you can't control much, and so it made sense that, as Liverpool's economic fortunes declined in the twentieth century, its propensity to have a laugh increased. Historian John Belchem reckons that by the end of the Second World War, 'humour was firmly established as Liverpool's response to its psychological, economic and structural problems'.

As well as humour, the constant change and churn in the city, with all the eclectic influences that accumulate in a seafaring town, contributed to the city's increasingly distinctive post-war culture.

The combination of cosmopolitan influences and dry, sardonic humour drove the success of many bands of that period. For the Beatles – and other British bands like the Kinks – their sound and lyrical focus owed not only to imports from the USA, but to the particular trials and tribulations of working-class British life in the post-war decades.

Will Sergeant remembers his old English teacher playing the class 'She's Leaving Home' from *Sgt. Pepper's*: 'A sensitive description of a teenager, an only child who sneaks off from the family home in the early morning to escape her stifled existence. It was not lost on me that it was exactly what my brother and sister had done.'

As well as humour and a kind of proletarian cosmopolitanism, the likelihood of random violence was a final key component of post-war Liverpool culture. When the Cavern MC Bob Wooler made a joke about John Lennon and Brian Epstein, asking Lennon, 'How was the honeymoon?', after the two had been away on a holiday to Spain, Lennon walked on stage and headbutted him.

'Pete [Burns] was jumped a few times for being who he wanted to be', said Pete Wylie to Simon Hughes. 'He wasn't a little fella; he could have been a docker. He'd face people down and challenge them.' Wylie himself was no stranger to violence: when his friend Holly Johnson called the Queen a 'moron' – something splashed on the front page of *The Sun* – Wylie was headbutted by a scally who took exception to these comments. 'I've still got the blood on my clothes', he proudly says.

There would be regular fights between Eric's regulars and scallies in the vicinity of Merseyside. According to the writer Paul Du Noyer, the Teardrop Explodes' Paul Simpson, who would carry a corkscrew for protection, alongside Les Pattinson of Echo and the Bunnymen, once battered a couple of scallies on the train home after a night in Eric's.

The football hooligan Andy Nicholls recalls bumping into Holly Johnson, 'the minging pop superstar' on a train back from Euston after a match against Chelsea:

> He was nearly crying when he showed the bizzie his first-class ticket and was told that there was no such thing as a first-class Scouser . . . he, like us, got a boot up the arse and no cheerio as we waved our goodbyes to the capital. The trip home was legendary. We terrorised that horrible bastard Johnson . . . Some Urchins soaked his compartment with a fire hose. One of his records had a lyric about the disgrace we brought to our city with all the slashings. There was talk of him getting a bit of a cut himself, but no one would take the risk.

Although there was an element of running the gauntlet to get to Eric's, once inside it was a relatively violence-free zone, especially when compared with other Liverpool bars and clubs of the time. However, even within this eclectic setting there was hierarchy and exclusion. Pete Burns and his then girlfriend Lynne would rip to shreds those they considered unfashionable. Burns himself often wore a long black robe, 'reminiscent of the cassock I wore in Melling church choir', according to Will Sergeant.

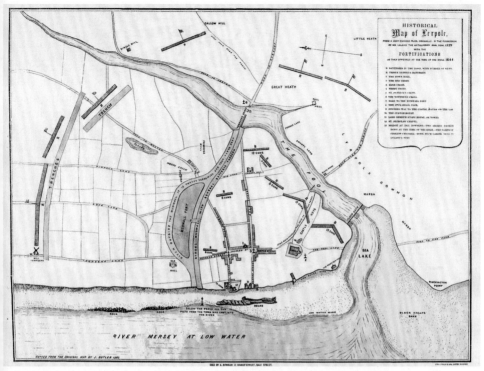

Leland's Historical Map of Lerpole: a map of Liverpool in the year 1644, before the filling in of 'the Pool' and the construction of the docks. *(De Luan/Alamy Stock Photo)*

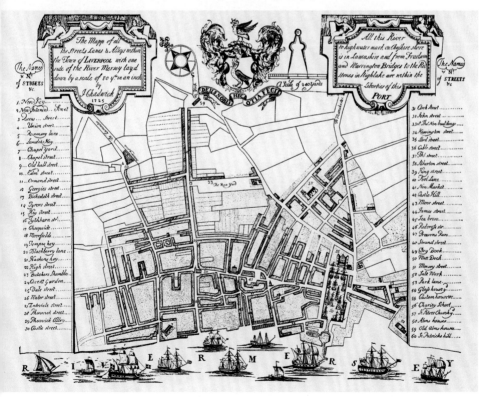

A map of Liverpool from 1725, by J. Chadwick, showing the developing dock system. *(De Luan/Alamy Stock Photo)*

The view of the Georgian Quarte from the top of the Anglican Cathedral. In the foreground is Gambier Terrace once home to Jol Lennon – and m
(Joe Dunckley/Alamy Stock Photo)

The Pier Head, featuring, from left to right: the Royal Liver Building, the Cunard Building and the Port of Liverpool Building.
(Travellinglight/Alamy Stock Photo)

William Brown Street, featuring from left to right Liverpool Centra Library, the Wor Museum, and the Walker Art Gallery. Part of St George's Hall can be seen in th bottom left-hand corner.
(David Goddard/Get Images)

Alleyway inside a Liverpool Court building in 1911.
(J Bibby & Sons, Liverpool, 1912) Artist Unknown (Photo by Print Collector/Getty Images)

Notorious pirate and slave trader John Hardman.
(Wellcome Collection)

JOHN HARDMAN,
(Corn Cutter.)

1800 floor plan he Liverpool e ship *Brooks*, ch would sport over six dred enslaved ple on each age.
ilegius/Universal es Group via Getty es)

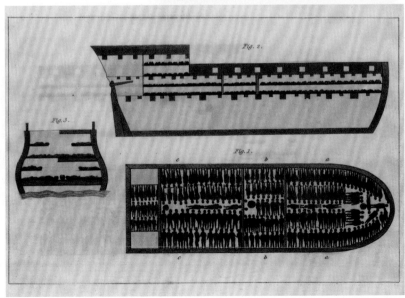

The Liverpool Overhead Railway, also known as 'the Docker's Umbrella', which ran for seven m alongside the waterfront, pictured in 1955. *(Photo SSPL/Getty Images)*

A disused and silted-up Albert Dock, photographed in 1980. *(Trinity Mirror/Mirrorpix/Alamy Stock Ph*

A demonstration of around one hundred thousand Protestants to celebration George Wise's release from Walton Gaol, 1909.
(Smith Archive/Alamy Stock Photo)

Soldiers from the 18th Hussars escort prison vans during the 1911 strike.
(Paul Popper/Popperfoto via Getty Images)

Striking dockers walk back from a picket, 1996.
(David Sinclair/reportdigital.co.uk)

Toxteth, 1981. *(Keystone/Stringer/Getty Images)*

Liverpool FC fans in Brussels, 1978. *(© Stephen Monaghan)*

oodison Park, home of Everton FC, in the top left, and Anfield, home of Liverpool FC, in the ntre right, separated by Stanley Park. *(David Goddard/Getty Images)*

he Merseybeats at the Cavern, 1963. *(John Pratt/Getty Images)*

Queues outside the Cavern, 1966.
(Keystone/Getty Images)

Echo and the Bunnymen,
1984. Left to right: Will
Sergeant, Ian McCulloch, Les
Pattinson and Pete de Freitas.
(Gunter W Kienitz/Shutterstock)

Frankie Goes to
Hollywood, 1984. Left
to right: Brian (Nasher)
Nash, Mark O'Toole, Hol
Johnson and Peter Gill.
*(John Stodddart/Popperfoto via
Getty Images)*

Paul McCartney reckons that he can still go back to Liverpool and people come up and say 'A'right, Paul, don't like yer jacket, fuckin 'ell.'

If you turn your back to the Liver Building and walk up James Street, you leave the sea air and gull shit behind and enter Derby Square, named after the local landowner the Earl of Derby. In the centre is a monument to Queen Victoria, completed in 1906.

In one corner of the square stands the Queen Elizabeth Law Courts, a 1980s brutalist hulk of pre-cast concrete. It was here, around the turn of the millennium, that Liverpool's goth community used to congregate.

Certainly, Liverpool was a bad place to be a goth. There were places for them – the courts and the earlier-mentioned Quiggins – but just because they had a place in Liverpool, like nearly everywhere else, it does not mean that the city is not conformist in a way that might surprise people from other metropolises.

As John Power – who has lived in London since 2007 – remembers: 'When you're in Liverpool, you don't want to be a victim and so, you walk in a certain way and act a certain way ... when you're in London, you can be a bit of a ponce and it's all right'.

This reflects the flip side of community solidarity: the closer your bonds, the more noticeable it is when someone is different.

Even back in the '60s, you either went to the Cavern or you went to the Iron Door; you didn't go to both. If black beat groups had arisen, they would have been able to play in Liverpool 8, but would have more difficulty in Walton. The same kind of informal segregation applied to audiences as well.

The Scottish author Darren McGarvey remembers a time travelling on the bus with other young lads from his scheme, when he accidentally described something as 'beautiful'. He froze, terrified of the coming response. In the end, it wasn't that bad: '"Beautiful?" one replied. "Ha, ha, ha. He just said 'beautiful'. Ha, ha, ha, mate, you're gay." Strangely, the chorus of laughter was, for me, a welcome relief.'

Anyone who has grown up in a similar environment will remember the fear. Had you used a word that you were not supposed to? (Even if it was a word that most people understood.) Or had you pronounced a word in an unconventional manner?

I knew a lad from Bootle who always referred to the TV show *Jackass* as *Jack-arse*, lest he be accused of some American affectation.

There is a cultural phenomenon whereby academic kids from working- and lower-middle-class backgrounds go to elite universities and, while they may be just as smart and well read as the most privileged of their contemporaries, they will not have heard certain words pronounced before. I call this the Hyperbole Test, and no matter how erudite the student or how broad your vocabulary, if you do not come from a family that listens to Radio 4 then you will simply have never heard these words pronounced before – not by teachers, parents and certainly not by people your own age.

Of course, this works both ways: I remember the ripping I endured when I mispronounced the name of the Irish footballer Kevin Kilbane, who was bought by Everton in 2003.

In 2015 or so, a set of photos went viral on Scouse Twitter. They were of a family of three on holiday – a mum, a son in his early teens and a younger son of around eight or nine. The setting itself was unremarkable – palm trees, pool, harbour, beach – but the familiar scenes were disrupted by one hilarious incongruity: the elder son was so fully committed to the 'ninja scally' aesthetic that he had refused to change his clothes and spent the entire trip swathed in North Face and Lowe Alpine.

The pictures are so mad they look as if they're photoshopped. The mum and younger son are pictured at the pool and beach in swimwear, having lunch and dinner in lightweight summer clothes – and throughout the ninja scally remains in full black tracksuit, hoody and cap.

When I first saw it, I had a few questions: was this real? Exactly how hot was it under all that polyester? Why did the younger brother look just like a normal kid on holiday? Once I stopped laughing, I felt pretty sorry for the mum: she'd saved up to take herself and her kids on a nice holiday, and throughout it all her eldest son dressed and acted as though he was still standing outside an off-licence on Norris Green Broadway.

But after a while I felt sorry for the young lad. When the pressure to conform is so bad that you act this way; when the opprobrium of random social media users, even in their millions, is nothing compared to the fear of diverging from the code of your specific subculture.

Around Christmas 2022, I noticed that some of my brother's mates, men in their early thirties, had all adopted the same type of 'three quarter' top then in style (which will definitely not be in style by the time you read this). It felt strange that people of their age, some of them with kids themselves, still felt the need to all dress the same. Not incidentally the same, but all deliberately adopting a particular look.

This is another aspect of the city's schizophrenic, conflicted identity: on the one hand it likes to pretend it is free-wheeling, free-thinking and independent; on the other hand, men and women well into middle age will continue to check what they wear and what they say in a way that in most other places is usually limited to teenagers. The way that words change every few years, and you have to keep up with the latest terms to not make an arse of yourself – in many ways, living in Liverpool is like never leaving school.

In his article 'Last of the "Real Geordies"?', the academic Anoop Nayak argues that the culture of the young people he studied in the north-east had become preserved 'like flies in amber'. I thought about this claim a lot when I was writing this book, and how far it could be applied to Liverpool but, ultimately, I think the future of Liverpool culture will be hard to predict, despite the tendency to conformity.

One reason for this is the Liverpudlian instinct for continuous change, to move on from and sometimes forget about the recent past.

Consider John Lennon, it's hard to think of a character more distinct from the modern-day Scouse sensibility: deeply cynical, recovering heroin addict and wife-beater – it's not easy to imagine him at a Jamie Webster gig.

7

'The African Trade'

The transformation of the city's fortunes in the mid-eighteenth century didn't have one single cause, but it owed its greatest debt to the opening up of a new and lucrative trade.

Over the previous hundred years, trade with English colonies in the so-called 'New World' had disappointed investors and shipowners who had hoped to build fortunes on the back of tobacco, potatoes and coffee. In 1666, a ship called the *Antelope* left Liverpool for the Americas, carrying coal, shoes, nails and linen, and returned a year laden with Barbadian sugar cane, but the profits on trading these types of goods were relatively meagre.

In contrast, after making a shaky start since its founding in 1600, the East India Company (EIC) – which had a monopoly on trade with India, China and other Asian countries – was proving increasingly profitable. Ships returning from Asia, after their long journey around the southern tip of Africa, would usually turn east into the Channel and towards London, where the EIC was headquartered, instead of continuing north to Liverpool. Therefore, it was the London docks that dominated the growing lucrative trade with India, China and beyond.

At the same time, Liverpool shipowners had usually avoided trade with Europe or the Americas, focusing instead on trade with Ireland; as late as 1707, just a quarter of the 170 ships based in Liverpool were involved in transatlantic trade.

But ambitious Scouse shipowners hoped that with the right product the transatlantic trade, based out of their western, Atlantic-facing port, could be just as profitable as trade with Asia – if not more.

They were right, and their business venture was to not only transform the city of Liverpool but alter the course of human history. The scope and extent of the success of the Liverpool merchants in their new venture continues to shape Western economies and cultures, and dominate our politics to this day.

Their plan was to load their ships with the increasingly cheaply made and mass-produced goods in which Britain was beginning to specialise: textiles, guns and knives, cooking pots, and pipes, which were being manufactured in Manchester. They would take these down to the burgeoning slave trading ports of West Africa and exchange their trinkets for Africans who had been kidnapped further inland.

They would then pack their fellow humans into the same ships that had earlier left Liverpool lightly loaded, along with tusks, tortoiseshells, indigo and other goods, and set off for the New World.

On 3 October 1699, the *Liverpool Merchant* sailed out of the Mersey and headed south. When it arrived in Barbados with 220 people in the hold, they sold for £4,239 – a huge sum at the time. When this was combined with the sale of goods such as cotton, tobacco, flour, sugar and rice that it would bring back to Liverpool, this 'triangular trade' was especially lucrative. A second ship, the *Blessing*, set off the same year. It was to be the start of thousands of such voyages.

By the time they arrived at their destination – the slave markets of the Caribbean and the south-eastern colonies of North America – at least a tenth and up to a third of their 'cargo' would have died during the journey. (One ship, the *Brooks*, transported around 4,000 Africans over the course of its slave-trading voyages, with an average mortality rate of 11 per cent.)

In the winter of 1781, the Liverpool ship *Zong* left the Gold Coast and set off for Jamaica, with seventeen white sailors on board and 442 Africans chained below decks. The ship stopped at São Tomé to take on supplies, and then sailed on to the Caribbean. Within weeks, sixty Africans had died from the conditions on board, although this was not unusual.

But after the captain fell ill, a dispute broke out between the first mate (nominally the second in command) and the rest of the crew. The *Zong* failed to dock in the Caribbean island of Tobago to take on fresh supplies as scheduled, and was still two weeks away from Jamaica, with only four days' drinking water left; it was in a difficult situation.

For the owners – the Gregson shipping line – their insurance meant that they would be covered if their cargo died from storms or piracy. If the slaves died from dehydration or any other kind of 'natural' death, however, they would receive nothing.

The sailors started with fifty-four women and children – who fetched lower prices than men. They were dragged from the hold and thrown overboard to drown; the next day another forty-two were thrown over. By the end of the week, 132 of the ship's captives had met their end this way – although ten deliberately jumped before they could be pushed, a metaphorical two fingers to their captives that their manacled hands could not manage.

The shipping company duly claimed for their loss of 'stock', and while the case aroused some controversy – noted Whig lawyer and MP Greville Sharpe denounced it as a primary example of 'the Liverpool inequity' – the courts nonetheless found that 'the Case of Slaves was the same as if Horses had been thrown overboard'.

Later fresh evidence was to emerge: when the *Zong* finally docked in Jamaica, it had 420 gallons of fresh water still on board; it turned out that the crew had just drowned the enslaved people because they could make a greater profit by defrauding the insurer.

This revelation meant that the insurers did not pay up and it caused huge reputational damage for the crew and the shipping company, but no murder charges were ever brought.

The massacre on the *Zong* is the most infamous involving a Liverpool slave ship, but the brutality of the business was so routine and so horrendous it is hard for our modern minds to comprehend. On another slave trading voyage out of Liverpool, on board the *Black Joke*, the captain, Thomas Marshall, was so incensed by the continued screaming of a malnourished nine-month-old that he whipped the child until it died, then forced the mother to throw the baby overboard.

By the 1720s, Liverpool merchants were using their slavery profits to buy tobacco in Maryland and Virginia; in the Caribbean, the amount brought in from the sale of slaves was greater than the value of sugar their ships could bring back to Europe, so they took payment in cash on top of the white gold.

During the mid-eighteenth century, it cost between £7 and £8 to buy an enslaved person on the west coast of Africa, and they could fetch as much as £40 or £50 in Kingston. In 1737, one ship, the *Lively*, made a profit of 300 per cent, and, in 1779 and 1780, two voyages of the *Hawk* made £13,000 – a 100 per cent profit. But overall profit for the trade during the second half of the century ranged between 8 and 10 per cent.

Meanwhile, food from Ireland shipped to the West Indies allowed those monocultural islands – which only grew sugar – to survive, and salt was shipped from the Mersey itself to the New World. This allowed Liverpool merchants to buy colonial goods such as sugar and tobacco up front, instead of taking them on consignment, which gave them more flexibility.

This pan-Atlantic trade transformed the ecology, economies and politics of the Western hemisphere, fuelling the growth of the British colonies in the West Indies and what would become the United States of America, and in Brazil. Back in Europe, it allowed for the massive capital accumulation and industrial expansion of European nations, most notably in the UK itself.

This industrial revolution allowed for a massive improvement in the military capabilities of states such as Britain, France and the Netherlands, which meant they could now easily defeat the great states of the East – such as in India, China, Japan – with which they had previous had subordinate status, requiring their permission to trade. None of this could have been predicted on the day the *Liverpool Merchant* left the Mersey.

Liverpool did not invent the transatlantic slave trade, which was originally pioneered by the Portuguese and Spanish. Until 1712, the London-based Royal African Company (RAC) had a monopoly on trade with Africa and any competitors had to pay a 10 per cent levy. For the first decade or so after this monopoly ended, Liverpool slavers remained bit-part players. But in a stroke of luck for the city, the South Sea Bubble crisis of 1720 seriously weakened the London slave companies.

Sometimes called the world's first financial crash, it takes its name from a company listed on the London stock exchange, 'The South Sea Company', whose stock price by August 1720 was inflated to an improbable £1000 per share. When the bubble burst – stocks plummeted, losing 80 per cent of their value; shares were worth merely £124 by December 1720 – investors were ruined and people lost thousands, including Sir Isaac Newton himself, who reportedly lost as much as £40 million in today's money. This led London traders to scale down their operations, and presented Liverpool with its chance.

The city's position in the north-west of England gave it advantages over London and Bristol – its main competitors in slave trading – as ships leaving Liverpool were more likely to avoid the French or Spanish privateers that prowled the English Channel.

As well as this, it was estimated that Liverpool ships carried slaves 15 per cent more cheaply, with Liverpool captains selling their strongest male slaves at around £5 less than the Bristol or London traders. Whether due to the lower wages of Liverpool-based sailors or because the conditions for the slaves were even more horrific – with more packed into the hold, and less money spent on food and water – it is unknown.

Liverpool captains were also less discerning in where they bought and sold slaves, venturing to Sierra Leone and Cameroon, Jamaica, Grenada, St Vincent, South Carolina and even Spanish islands such as Cuba, whereas Bristol merchants stuck to traditional markets such as Ghana, Angola and Virginia. Finally, the Lancashire textiles with which Liverpool captains were well supplied tended to keep for longer, allowing Liverpool merchants longer credit on their wares.

Soon the city came to dominate the trade; in 1732, London and Bristol ships together transported over 10,000 slaves each year, and Liverpool fewer than 3,000. But by the mid-1740s, Liverpool vessels carried over 7,000 slaves annually, while Bristol accounted for 5,000 and London less than 2,000. From 1751–6, ships departing Liverpool made a total of 238 voyages to Africa, compared to sixty-nine by Bristol ships and forty-two from London. By 1792, there were 131 slaving boats based in the city, able to carry 40,000 slaves, compared with forty-two in Bristol and twenty-two in London. In the century before abolition, Liverpool merchants paid for a total of around 5,000 slave-trading voyages.

By the 1790s, the last full decade before abolition, Liverpool controlled 80 per cent of the British slave trade and over 40 per cent of the European trade. It is estimated that of the 12 million people taken from West Africa into slavery in the Americas, 1.5 million were transported on ships owned by Liverpool companies. A Bristol merchant complained that 'the people of Liverpool, in their indiscriminate rage for commerce and for getting money at all events, have nearly engrossed this trade'.

All of this was transformational for the city's economy. In 1664–5, the Americas accounted for just 2 per cent of Liverpool's trade, compared with 90 per cent for Ireland. By 1708–9 this was already starting to shift, the proportions changing to 30 per cent and 60 per cent, and by mid-century over half of all the ships in the city were involved in the transatlantic trade. This was transformative for the city's fortunes; at the time of abolition in 1807, the town had gone from a small fishing village to the second wealthiest city in the UK, with *Gore's Liverpool Directory* containing 246 pages of affluent merchants.

As well as bringing riches to the captains and shipowners, the slave trade provided a large number of jobs. Figures show that between 1800 and 1900, while the percentage of labourers in Liverpool remained steady, at around 13 per cent of the population, the percentage of sailors declined from 23 per cent to 13 per cent. This suggests that the abolition of the trade (as well as the rise of steamships at the end of the period) had a big impact on the number of sailors employed in the city.

Alongside local men, Indians, Portuguese, Swedes and other nationalities all served on Liverpool slave ships, with up to one in five of these sailors losing their lives, mostly from disease. It was a barbaric and brutal time when death was commonplace and violence all around, but even in this context most men abhorred serving on slave ships and did anything they could to avoid them. If they were forced to crew these ships – from financial desperation, debt or violence – they often lied about where they were sailing to and what kind of ship they were working on.

Some like John Newton and Edward Rushton became abolitionists after witnessing the horrors on board. Others in the city worked to end the trade and faced danger and violence from their fellow citizens. James Cropper, a Quaker born to a Lancashire farmer, had made a fortune in trade with the East Indies, importing textiles, spices and other goods. He set up charitable endeavours to help Irish immigrants, orphans and other causes, and in the 1820s began campaigning for the final abolition of slavery (as opposed to the slave trade) in the British Empire.

The crew of slave ships would usually be composed of drunkards and convicts, and very often they had to use ship's apprentices instead of experienced sailors, due to the difficulty in getting men to work on slaving voyages. The slave-ship captain Hugh Crow described them as:

> The very dregs of the community. Some of them had escaped from jails: others were undiscovered offenders, who sought to withdraw themselves from their country, lest they should fall into the hands of the officers of justice. These wretched beings used to flock to Liverpool when the ships were fitting out, and, after acquiring a few sea phrases from some crimp or other, they were shipped as ordinary seamen, though they had never been at sea in their lives.

In a civilian form of the press-ganging used to get sailors for the Royal Navy, gangs known as 'crimps' would seize unsuspecting mariners and drag them aboard the boats. In particular, they would prey on drunk sailors in the dockside taverns. Sometimes they worked in cahoots with the publicans, who would get the targets drunk, run up their bill and then when they couldn't pay, would 'sell' them to the slavers. Sometimes the crimps themselves would ply their victims with drink until they were unconscious, or just knock them out with fists or clubs. When they woke up, they'd be somewhere in the Atlantic, heading south.

Shanghai Davies, based at the Red Lion pub, was a notorious crimp; equally infamous was the Pitt Street landlady Ma Smyrden, who once tricked a gang of crimps into kidnapping a corpse by sticking him up at the bar and pretending he had passed out drunk.

In addition to the wealth brought by the trade to the city's merchants, and the steady if dangerous and soul-destroying work provided for sailors, it also provided jobs for a large number of professionals and specialists, both on board and on land. A local historian argued at the time that 'almost every order of people is interested in the Guinea cargo . . . Many of the small vessels that import a hundred slaves are fitted out by attorneys, drapers, ropers, grocers, tallow-chandlers, barbers and tailors.'

After abolition, the number of 'skilled mariners' in Liverpool – such as surgeons, coopers and carpenters – dropped sharply. In the period 1712–1808, there were 455 church registry entries for surgeons in the city, but in the period 1809–88, when the city's population increased ten-fold, the number of surgeons stood at 553 – this suggests that in the earlier period, a huge number of surgeons were employed exclusively by the slave trade.

In fact, an analysis of wills from this era shows that most of the deaths of surgeons, coopers, shipwrights and carpenters at this time occurred on board slave ships – after abolition, the number of recorded deaths among these occupations fell by two-thirds. In the twenty-seven years between 1781 and 1808, for example, there were 242 recorded deaths of Liverpool-based surgeons, but only thirty-five between 1808 and 1825.

These economic links were reflected in politics: in 1787 only four of the city's councillors did not have ties to the Caribbean, and for the next twenty years after that every mayor of Liverpool was a slave owner.

Given that it was such a core part of their city's economy, many Liverpool merchants were prominent in campaigning against abolition; the abolitionist Thomas Clarkson was nearly killed when he was thrown into the Mersey by a gang in 1788.

Penny Lane takes its name from the slave trader James Penny, who was vocal in his opposition to the abolition movement. Eager to protect his business, he boldly claimed in evidence to the Lords Committee of Council set up in 1788 that: 'The slaves here will sleep better than the gentlemen do on shore.' In the build-up to the 1788 Act, which for the first time imposed certain legal obligations on slave traders,

Liverpool merchants submitted sixty-four petitions to Parliament arguing against abolition.

Typical of this attitude was John Tarleton, who wrote in 1788 stressing that 'the Colonies would not exist without the African Trade. The Manchester & Sheffield Manufactories would instantly go to ruin & their people be set a starving.'

One pro-slavery lecturer, who toured the UK to drum up support for his cause, warned: 'What is your Bristol, your Liverpool, your Manchester, your Glasgow, if you take from them the West India colonies? Nothing – worse than nothing – one universal scene of beggary and starvation.'

An eighteenth-century actor, having endured increasing levels of piss-taking from his Liverpudlian audience, finally snapped: 'I have not come here to be insulted by a set of wretches, every brick in whose infernal town is cemented with an African's blood.' (The response to this is not recorded, but I imagine it was a short, shocked silence, followed by a sarcastic 'ooooooooooooooh!')

But it was not just slavery that transformed the fortunes of the city; one of the reasons for the town's success in this period was that Liverpudlian shipowners engaged in all of the main commodity trades and did not specialise in any one of them – it was less important than Bristol for importing sugar, and Glasgow for importing tobacco, although by 1800 it was gaining on both.

Even though it is estimated that one in eight of Liverpool's population – 10,000 people – depended on trade with Africa and that 40 per cent of its income derived from the trade, most merchants kept a diverse commercial portfolio and few were dependent entirely on slavery. For example, in 1766, eighteen ships left Liverpool for Jamaica and Barbados, but another thirteen sailed to Philadelphia.

The historian Sheryllynne Haggerty has found that the total value of all goods imported into Kingston, Jamaica by the Liverpool shipping firm Case and Southwark during 1755 was over £34,000, and that around £23,000 of that came from the sale of slaves, with the remaining £10,000 coming from food, textiles and other goods. However, the 5 per cent commission on slaves was lower than that on dry goods, at 8 per cent, which means that legitimate trade was more profitable in terms of the weight of cargo. Apparently, even those merchants whose businesses principally depended on slave trading were reluctant to identify themselves as such in business records, describing themselves as 'merchants', 'bankers', or even in one case as a 'wine merchant'.

Despite the undoubted importance of the trade to the city, the consensus among historians is that Liverpool was more important for the slave trade than the slave trade was for Liverpool. When *Kitty's Amelia* became the last slave ship to depart from the Mersey in 1807, the city was well positioned to survive the end of the trade.

Already by the 1820s, Liverpool merchants were pivoting to legitimate trade, while keeping their hand in slavery. The city's mayor, Charles Horsfall, was a slaveowner and president of the West Indian Association, but he also pioneered the trade in West African palm oil. John Moss, the inaugural chairman of the Liverpool and Manchester Railway, was a West India merchant who played a crucial role in securing the vast compensation paid to the slave owners.

The population of the city doubled between 1801 and 1831, with another 80,000 people arriving in the 1830s – this suggests that in the decades after abolition, Liverpool's ability to generate wealth and opportunities was undimmed.

After the abolition of the trade, the city's golden era was only beginning. But although Liverpool may have been able to get over the slave trade, the broad and deep impact of Liverpool slavers – from the economy of Ghana to gangs in Jamaica and American politics – continues to leave a stark and lasting legacy.

INTERLUDE 6

The World in One City?

At the same time the end of transatlantic slavery put a stop to the city's role as a trafficker of forced labour to the New World, Liverpool began to take on a new role as an entrepôt for immigration into Britain.

As might be expected of a port city, especially one that transformed from a hamlet of fewer than a thousand people to one of the richest and most important cities in the world, immigration has played a leading part in the history of the town.

Liverpool in the years around 1700 was made up overwhelmingly of immigrants: 96 per cent of the people recorded as marrying in the town after 1717 cannot be found in the baptism registers, suggesting they must have moved from elsewhere.

The historians Diana E. Ascott, Fiona Lewis and Michael Power found that 'the town was dominated by newcomers intent on making their fortunes, at the level of the entrepreneurial trader as well as lower down the social scale'.

Despite the variety of ethnicities, languages and religions present in the city over the past 200 or 300 years, the majority of immigrants to Liverpool (and migrants still constituted over half the population well into the nineteenth century) travelled short distances to get there; the

1851 census found that 47 per cent of the adult population of the city had been born somewhere else in Britain or Ireland.

Although less celebrated than the Irish, Liverpool was also hugely influenced by Welsh immigrants. In 1813, a tenth of the town's population came from Wales and, a hundred years later, there were so many Welsh and Welsh descendants that Welsh-language newspapers could be purchased in the city – the national Eisteddfod was held there several times. The legacy can be seen in the Welsh streets in Toxteth and Goodison Park's Gwladys Street end. And though not as numerous as the Welsh or Irish, in 1871 as many as one in twenty-five people had Scottish ancestry.

As well as the English, Scottish, Irish and Welsh, immigrants and transit migrants from all over Europe came to Liverpool. This was a time when people who had journeyed from elsewhere would pause in the city until their ship left. In 1887, a reporter at the *Liverpool Mercury*, drawing heavily on the dog-eared office copy of the *Big Book of Late Victorian National Stereotypes*, described the streets of Liverpool 'during the emigrant season' as presenting 'stirring spectacles of cosmopolitan animation, and the city itself is the temporary resting place of visitors from all parts of the hemisphere. Russians, suspicious and sullen . . . Finns and Poles, men of fierce and haughty natures . . . Germans, quiet and inoffensive, brave and determined . . . the flaxen-haired Scandinavians, paragons of nature's handiwork, erect and stately'.

Between 1825 and 1913, over twelve million passengers passed through the city – 56 per cent of all those leaving UK ports – and people emigrating directly from Ireland were only around a quarter of this number.

London, the next biggest port for emigration, had only a fifth of Liverpool's total. Of the big shipping lines of the 1870s and '80s – Cunard, Inman, White Star, National and Guion – most were based in Liverpool.

For those heading for places outside of Europe, fully three-quarters were bound for America, with over nine million people leaving

Liverpool for the United States during this time. In fact, in all but three years (1825, 1911 and 1912), more people left Liverpool for the USA than all other nations combined. When we look at these numbers, we can see the central place played by the city in the family history of tens of millions of Americans – a sort of Ellis Island at the other end. Up to one in fifty aspiring immigrants would be rejected by the US authorities – for being political radicals, syphilitics, bigamists or plain old paupers – and put back on the next ship to Liverpool.

Despite America's dominance as a destination for emigrants, around 344,000 passengers left for Central and South America, the Caribbean, South and East Asia, Africa and other unspecified destinations. The historian John Herson has found that of these, while some were permanent emigrants with no intention of coming back, most were colonial administrators, troops, traders and businessmen.

In addition to the Irish, most of the transmigrants – people from other European countries who sailed to Liverpool in order to go on to somewhere else – came from Scandinavia, Germany, Russia and Poland. The first synagogue in the north of England had opened in Liverpool in 1753, and by 1851 there were around 1,500 Jews in the city – Liverpool played a crucial role in the exodus of Jewish people from the Russian Empire following the pogroms of 1881–2.

Of those millions of refugees and economic migrants who passed through the city, many remained and established businesses; in 1881, there were fifty-two commercial boarding houses registered in Liverpool, of which sixteen had proprietors with continental European names.

Even at the time, however, Liverpool's treatment of immigrants – especially the Irish – was notorious. Compared to dock work, the emigrant trade provided relatively little legitimate employment for the city, as the migrants could usually load and unload themselves. But in true Scouse entrepreneurial fashion, a whole industry developed to provide for, and usually rip off, unsuspecting migrants. These people

– very often Irish immigrants themselves – ran boarding houses, booked ships and provided food and other provisions, usually of low quality and at extortionate prices. William Tapscott, a travel agent with a dubious reputation himself, lamented in 1851 that there were 'thousands of such persons', and their activities threatened the place of the city as Europe's premier port of embarkation.

The magistrate John Bramley Moore – later to become Lord Mayor of Liverpool and give his name to a north-end dock – convicted over 900 people for cheating, swindling and giving/using short weights; between 500 and 600 of these were grocers and wholesalers, and the rest were landlords and booking agents.

All of this, says Herson, 'brought significant funds into the Liverpool economy and particularly to parts of its Irish population . . . thousands of people in mid-century Liverpool could therefore make money from the informal economy of the emigrant trade' – though, of course, the profits were unevenly spread.

Although most emigrants passed quickly through Liverpool, some were unable or unwilling to leave, and a proportion of these ended up in the Poor Law system; in the 1880s, for example, 812 emigrants were admitted to the Liverpool workhouse, mostly due to sickness – and in many cases the shipping companies paid for their stay.

In that decade a group of Syrian Arabs, who had paid in Marseille for passage to New York, found out in Liverpool that they had been refused entry to the USA. The Liverpool authorities sent them back to France, and they got as far as Le Havre before they persuaded the captain of another ship to take them back to Liverpool. They were then sent to the workhouse, but apparently enjoyed themselves, or did not find it too uncomfortable, as the authorities 'had the greatest difficulty getting rid of them'.

In a more shameful case, 140 Jewish refugees were stranded in Liverpool by an outbreak of cholera in 1892, and after four weeks the

Cunard shipping company turned them out of their lodgings and refused to provide any help or assistance in finding further accommodation. Similarly, the Liverpool Poor Law guardians refused to admit them to the workhouse, and the Liverpool Jewish Board of Guardians had to step in to keep them alive over the winter.

There was a great deal of fear of disease from new immigrants. Liverpool-based immigration officers would usually board inbound ships at Queenstown in Ireland to conduct their examinations of the passengers before they got into town. When this was not possible, those immigrants who planned to stay on in Britain were examined on the landing stage at the docks, while those who were bound for other destinations would be processed on board the ships.

Or at least, that was the theory. In reality, this led to what one health inspector described as 'confusion bordering on pandemonium' as 'men, women and children, all anxious to get on shore, crowd together round the tables where the Immigration Officers are attempting to carry on their work under conditions of great difficulty'.

And the interrogation of the new arrivals by immigration officers was overheard by all of the other people queuing up to enter, which added to the humiliation and resentment of the migrants, as well as providing people with knowledge of the 'right' answers to give.

For the on-board checks, the shipping companies habitually failed to provide a designated cabin for medical examinations, meaning that the health inspectors had to find an empty cabin themselves, and when inspecting women had to find and persuade a female steward to sit in during the procedure.

Sometimes the only available cabin had no porthole, and so the examination had to be carried out by the light of a dim bulb, which led to some conditions being missed – and the cacophonous noise from the disembarking passengers and the ships engines made it nearly impossible to pick up heart or lung problems with a stethoscope.

It was common practice for vessels coming directly from Ireland to go straight into dock without ever being seen by any medical officer, and so, as one health inspector pointed out, anyone with a health condition who might be refused entry to the UK had only to take a boat from Ireland and thus escape any checks.

All of this may have been both overzealous and ineffective, as many of the conditions they were searching for (such as trachoma, a common eye infection that caused blindness) were less likely to be found among European immigrants, but instead among British or Irish citizens, who were exempt from inspection.

As Dr Stock, the senior Ministry of Health inspector observed, 'we do not medically inspect the Irish, but in view of the statement that 65 per cent of the Irish emigrants are verminous, I think it would be a good thing if we did'.

Between April 1921 and April 1922, only 8,516 of the 26,595 aliens who arrived in Liverpool underwent a health inspection, and of those, only six temporary migrants and seven permanent immigrants were found to have conditions requiring them to be issued with a special medical certificate. And many of these people were coming back from working in the United States, either to visit their home country or resettle with their earnings.

These chaotic scenes on the quayside meant the dockside districts always had a large transient population, with various accents, languages, ethnicities and religions jostling for space.

There's a strong argument that the dock and riverside districts of Liverpool were one of the most multicultural places in Britain at the start of the twentieth century. Granby at this time was one of the few places outside West Africa that had a market for yams and plantain. John Belchem reckons that at this time, 'for the true Scotty Road Scouser', the most desired food, rather than Scouse, was a type of salt fish dish known as 'bacalao'.

At this time, the historian and Liberal politician Ramsey Muir (who held a lectureship at the University of Liverpool) wrote of the city that 'those who inhabit this vast congeries of streets are of an extraordinary diversity of races – few towns in the world are more cosmopolitan'. But it might have been that he was particularly impressed given the homogeneity of much of the UK at this time; after all, he was born in the rural Northumbrian village of Otterburn.

But for the city as a whole, it is debateable exactly how 'multicultural' it was historically. Clearly there was racial and national diversity in the city going back many centuries, but this does not mean that it was 'multicultural' in the sense of having various ethnic groups maintaining their own distinct cultures and ways of life.

Recent historians such as Diane Frost have argued that the city's 'narrowly defied cosmopolitan identity was confined to the waterfront areas only and was limited to its global trade and the subsequent settlement of diverse ethnic peoples'.

The 1901 census found that only 1.7 per cent of Liverpool's population had been born outside of Britain and Ireland – compared to 2.5 per cent in Manchester and 3.7 per cent in London. Of these, around 30 per cent, or 3,680 people, were born outside Europe.

Even in Frederick Street, which runs parallel to the docks and was at the time considered to be the most diverse road in Liverpool, the census found that most people were born in Britain or Ireland.

In many ways the cosmopolitanism observed by Muir and others came more from the number of transient workers, rather than settled citizens – Herson has estimated that sailors made up over 15 per cent of the foreign-born in the city.

And even then, they were more likely to be from continental Europe than farther afield. The census of 1881 found that almost three-quarters of the overseas sailors in Liverpool at that time came from Germany, Scandinavia or Spain.

There were 234 people whose place of birth was registered as 'India' or the 'East Indies', but only nineteen of them seemed to have been raised in those places; 148 (63 per cent) were British subjects. But this in itself tells us one important fact about the cosmopolitanism of Liverpool at that time: its connections to the British Empire. Sir Edwin Lutyens based his 1930s plans for the Catholic cathedral – sadly not realised due to funding cuts in the Second World War – on his Durbar Hall in New Delhi. And the fingers of Liverpool investors and insurance brokers found their ways into many pies, and were continuing to fund the British presence in West Africa as late as the 1930s.

Liverpool is not, despite its history, a city of immigrants in the way of New York or post-1948 London. It is a place that has always had high levels of immigration, and has also consistently featured violent resistance to immigration. It is both diverse and eclectic, and also homogenous and conformist. Any honest history of the city needs to accept this paradox.

8

PRODS AND PADDIES

In the centuries after the Reformation, Liverpool had mostly avoided the religious disputes that characterised other parts of Britain. Certain national events triggered brief upsurges in sectarian violence; after the Battle of Culloden (the last battle to be fought on British soil, which saw the defeat of an attempt to restore the Catholic 'Bonny Prince Charlie' to the throne) a mob burned down the town's only Catholic church.

Nonetheless, the lack of religious and status alignment at this time – with people of various faiths working alongside each other on ships and on the docks – meant that religious disputes would have been bad for business.

This began to change after 1800, with the increasingly large numbers of Irish immigrants reawakening anti-Catholic sentiment in the town. The first Catholic–Protestant riot erupted in 1819, when Orangemen attending a service marking the Battle of the Boyne were attacked at the bottom of Dale Street by around 2,000 Catholics. Partially as a result of this, Orange marches were banned in 1822.

There were almost 5,000 Irish in the city by 1800, out of a population of just under 80,000. By 1841, there were ten times as many, out of 288,656 residents in total. The Great Famine of 1845 to

1852 contributed to the Irish-born population rising to at least 83,813 people, or 22.3 per cent of the total (compared with 13 per cent in Manchester and almost 5 per cent in London). At that time, you could get from Ireland to Liverpool for as little as sixpence, although conditions on board were terrible; in 1848 over seventy passengers suffocated to death on a ship from Sligo when the crew forced them into the hold during a storm.

Nearly all of these impoverished migrants settled in the dockside districts near where they landed, so that by 1851, half of the 25,000 people in Vauxhall had been born in Ireland. Such was the pressure on the already impoverished dockside areas that one local suggested that the Irish be met off the boats, given bread, soup and a one-way railway ticket to London.

The importance of Irish immigration to the city can be overstated; after peaking during the Famine years, it declined for the rest of the century – by 1911, only 34,632 people, or just 4.6 per cent, of the population of Liverpool were Irish-born. Another two million Irish people are estimated to have passed through the city en route to somewhere else, without settling on Merseyside. Nonetheless, many more than 4.6 per cent had had Irish parents or grandparents in 1911, and in that year the Irish still outnumbered *overseas* immigrants (those not from elsewhere in Britain) by eight to one. Today, as many as three-quarters of the population are estimated to have Irish roots.

There was an old joke that the Irish who stayed in Liverpool were too poor or lazy to go elsewhere, or else too thick to realise that they weren't in New York; I remember my nan (herself the daughter of Irish immigrants) making this joke when I was growing up in the 1990s.

Probably of greater importance was the number of jobs the city provided for unskilled migrants, on the docks, in construction, domestic service, transport and so on, and the close proximity to Ireland which allowed people to maintain personal and business contacts.

Whatever the reasons behind their remaining in the city, Irish immigrants had a profound impact on local politics. In September 1851, the Pope restored the Catholic hierarchy in England and Wales, ended during the Reformation 265 years earlier, and appointed a Bishop of Liverpool.

This produced a counter-reaction among the Protestant majority, reinvigorating the Orange Order, which had fifty lodges in Liverpool by the early twentieth century. Mayor Sir Archibald Salvidge created the Liverpool Working Men's Conservative Association (which barred Catholics from membership) to consolidate both his own support and the growing political influence and social respectability of working-class Protestants, which seemed threatened by the Irish influx.

As the pre-eminent chronicler of Northumbria Dan Jackson points out, Anglo-Irish relations in the north-east were usually cordial. Jackson attributes this to the strength of the local economy, which had dependable, skilled jobs in mining, shipbuilding and factory work, as well as the strength of religious nonconformity (which was opposed to the Church of England as much as Catholicism).

Nonconformist Protestantism – Baptists, Methodists, Quakers, etc – was hugely important to the local identity, culture and politics of areas such as South Wales, East Lancashire, West Yorkshire and the Durham coalfield. But, with some notable exceptions such as the Lever family, it was not prominent on Merseyside.

The relative absence of popular nonconformism in Liverpool had a big impact on the political and sectarian disputes that roiled the city at the start of the twentieth century. The Ancient Romans understood religion as a public matter, about loyalty and belonging, rather than one of individual faith. The Protestant Reformation privatised religious belief, with people like Martin Luther arguing it was a matter between individuals and God. Fancy vestments, stained-glass windows, incense and the special power of priests were not important; what mattered was the belief of the individual. Though the Anglican Church maintained much of the old Catholic symbolism, as well as some of the doctrine.

In Liverpool, the population, especially the working class, was divided between Anglicans and Catholics, and these two faiths both upheld the importance of the communal, ritual and symbolic aspects of religion. Therefore, it was possible both for religion to be massively divisive and for religious doctrines not to be taken very seriously.

This reached its apogee in 1909, when Liverpool was rocked by weeks of murderous Protestant–Catholic violence. Traditionally, sectarian strife occurred during times of celebration. For Catholics this included St Patrick's and other saints' days, and for the Protestants there were around thirty annual Orange parades, culminating in the Kirkdale carnival celebrating the 'Glorious Twelfth', when effigies of the Pope would be burned in the streets.

In June 1909, the Conservative MP for West Toxteth warned his constituents that 'Jesuits' were plotting to take over England, starting with the Church and the monarchy.

The city authorities made some ineffectual attempts to regulate parades but were accused by both sides of failing to prevent the 'provocative' marches. In one incident, Protestants tried to steal a statue of the Virgin Mary from a Catholic parade on Dale Street, after the head constable had previously said the statue would not be allowed in the march.

Pat O'Mara, in his *Autobiography of a Liverpool Irish Slummy*, recounted that he 'had always been brought up to believe that Protestantism was a dying cult, and its adherents were cowards and easily frightened, but this mob up here led by the magnificent white horse bearing a little boy dressed up as a perfect replica of King William did not look frightened at all'.

During these times of increased tension, violence at parades and public meetings spilled over into random attacks, with men being beaten on their way to or from work, and women and children brawling outside school gates.

John Belchem argued that these conditions made sectarian strife in Liverpool 'more bitter and more chronic than anywhere else except Belfast'. Even an exhaustive Home Office inquiry had failed to find a remedy, with sectarian rioting raging on and off for generations.

Anti-Catholic sentiment was deliberately cultivated by the town's Conservative political establishment, who made good use of firebrand street preachers, none more so than George Wise.

Wise had been born in Bermondsey, south London, in 1855. Although a keen reader as a child, his family were unable to afford much of an education and he began work in a biscuit factory in his early teens. He then converted to Evangelical Christianity, became a Sunday School teacher and then an urban missionary among the poor of London's dockland.

He became known as an impressive debater and platform speaker and toured the USA and Canada to preach and proselytise. However, it was when he arrived in Liverpool in 1888 that the short, bespectacled, 'confirmed bachelor' found his true calling – inciting Protestant Scousers into a murderous anti-Catholic rage.

Although this was a competitive business in late-Victorian Liverpool, he soon acquired the sponsorship of wealthy patrons, notably J. A. Bramley-Moore (of the dock fame). Wise set up his own evangelical group, the Protestant Reformer's Church, which held two services each Sunday, both overflowing with more than a thousand congregants. His bible studies class was said to attract another 1,500 people.

There were also a range of social organisations that, with typical modesty, had names such as the George Wise Tontine Society (this provided health, unemployment and life insurance) and the George Wise Cycle Club, which he boasted was the largest in the city.

Wise's vast influence made him politically useful to the Liverpool Tories, particularly Sir Archibald Salvidge and the Working Man's Conservative Association. By lending his support to Conservative candidates, or by running himself for certain positions, Wise helped solidify the Protestant–Tory–Unionist political domination of Liverpool. In the local elections of 1900, he won 107,000 votes in his campaign to be elected to the local school board – twice as many as the next candidate.

In May 1901, he began preaching in Islington Square, where a Catholic and Presbyterian church faced off against each other. During these performances he would mock Catholics, dancing with fake 'rosary' beads around his neck, wearing a crucifix and denouncing Jesuits as liars and murderers.

Wise's church attracted members from across the city but was particularly popular in the Everton and Kirkdale neighbourhoods, especially as upwardly mobile Catholics were starting to move into these traditionally Protestant areas.

In June 1910 the Catholic Bishop of Liverpool was stoned by a Protestant mob. The following month, a by-election for the Kirkdale seat coincided with the Orange marching season. Archibald Salvidge insisted that the mission of the local Conservatives was to 'prevent the people of Ireland from ruling Kirkdale'.

The following spring a by-election, this time involving Conservative national leader and future prime minister Andrew Bonar Law, brought more violence; Protestants were attacked on their way to work through Catholic neighbourhoods and Catholic homes on the largely Protestant Netherfield Road were attacked and burned. In June 1911, the second anniversary of the 1909 riots saw fresh outbreaks.

Wise and other Protestant leaders warned of a secret Catholic plot to take away 'English' liberties, ranting against 'the Roman Catholic hooligans of the Council' and the 'tyrannical demands of the Church'.

The Orange leader S. G. Thomas proposed that, in order to keep the peace, that year's marches be curtailed – Wise was having none of it, claiming that such a concession was 'playing into the hands of the police and the Catholics'.

A few days later, 300 young men from the Catholic Defence League attacked and broke up a meeting held by Wise at Edge Hill, and then marched around the neighbourhood singing Irish republican songs.

The Lord Mayor wrote to the Home Office warning them that 'a revolution was in progress', and later admitted to Lord Derby that 'for three weeks turmoil and almost anarchy prevailed' on the streets of Liverpool.

The violence of 1910 persuaded many of the city authorities that the sectarian divisions might be more trouble than they were worth. The head constable of Liverpool police, Leonard Dunning, retired in December 1911, apparently after a nervous breakdown.

The Home Secretary appointed the two leading sectarian MPs – T. P. O'Connor, Irish Nationalist MP for Liverpool Scotland, and Colonel Kyffin-Taylor, Conservative MP for Kirkdale – to meet with the Home Office labour advisor David Shackleton to investigate the causes and try and settle the strike.

Afterwards, Lord Derby chaired a round-table conference made up of leaders from across the political and sectarian divides, resulting in the Liverpool Corporation Act (1912), which set up a Watch Committee to regulate religious meetings, processions and confiscate weapons.

Wise tried to benefit from this, pointing out that his meetings would now get police protection from Catholic attacks, but according to the historian John Bohstedt, 'there was now a weighty consensus against the continuation of his provocations'.

Sectarian violence was finally reduced from mass rioting to occasional small-scale fights. By 1912, the head constable's report could conclude: 'It is gratifying to be able to report that for the first time for many years the City was during the whole of the year entirely free from even the semblance of sectarian disorder. Several very large processions and demonstrations were held without a single regrettable incident occurring.'

This sectarian divide has usually been offered up as an explanation for Tory Liverpool. According to this analysis, conflict between Protestants and Catholics divided the working-class vote, resulting in Catholic support for Irish nationalist politics (Liverpool was the only place in Britain to elect an Irish Nationalist MP), and Protestants for the Conservative and Unionist party. Irish independence resulted in the transference of Catholic votes to the Labour party, while Protestants, with the end of the spectre of Irish nationalism, felt less inclined to vote Tory.

But as an explanation for the hundred-year transformation of Liverpool from the citadel of working-class Toryism par excellence – at the December 1910 general election, the Conservatives won seven out of eight Liverpool constituencies – to the home of Labour's safest seats, sectarianism and religious division is too simplistic.

The historian John Bohstedt argued that if we want to understand the politics of people in the past, we need to rescue them 'from the enormous condescension of labour history' – as in, we shouldn't assume that people should vote one way or another because of their job or their religion.

Another historian, Sam Davies, has also challenged the 'exceptionalist' account of Liverpool politics, which overemphasises religion as an explanation for the city's resistance to Labour. Davies claimed that the left's weaknesses before the Second World War were overstated and that while there was Catholic transference to Labour after Irish independence, sectarianism in general was not the key factor in Liverpool Labour's lack of success.

Writing of the sectarian rioting that afflicted the city before the First World War, the editor of the *Daily Post* reassured his readers that the Protestant mobs were made up of 'good, hard-headed fellows [who] don't care twopence about religion at all; but they to a man hate "Popery" intensely'.

In the decades before the First World War, there was a decline in Protestant church attendance in the city centre, whereas between 1891 and 1902, attendance at Catholic services increased 24 per cent. But this probably reflected an increase in the Catholic population, rather than an increase in the proportion of Catholics attending church.

It has been estimated that at the time of the First World War, fewer than one in five people in Liverpool attended church services and John Bohstedt argued that it was 'the social functions' of churches and religious organisations, rather than religious belief, that had greater importance to sectarianism.

Catholics had their own versions of the Protestant sporting and cultural associations in the Gaelic League, the Gaelic Athletics Association and the Parnell Tontine Society, named after famed Irish nationalist Charles Parnell. There were even separate floating 'reformatory schools' for dissolute youth: HMS *Akbar* for the Catholics and HMS *Clarence* for the Protestants.

This suggests that the mob violence that characterised this period owed less to religion per se than to politico-cultural divisions.

According to a Catholic in Liverpool in the inter-war period: 'Going to church and going to the pictures were the highlights of the week. They took you out of yourself. In church you could do a bit of thinking. In the pictures you could escape to Hollywood.'

The Irish issue ceased to be a key dividing line in the city's politics during the 1920s, and the political allegiance of Irish Catholics appeared to be up for grabs. They quickly switched to Labour and, according to Sam Davies, 'throughout the inter-war period the Irish were one of the most consistently pro-Labour elements within the working class'.

Meanwhile, after 1918, as the Irish vote became more influential, a powerful and socially conservative Catholic 'caucus' emerged within the Liverpool Labour party, complicating the standard left–right divisions within the party. There was an element of mutual mistrust between Irish Catholics and Labour colleagues in the local party; at first, Irish members and others did not even sit next to each other at meetings.

Divides over denominational schooling proved to be a contentious issue, with the left of the Labour movement meeting Catholic resistance in its advocacy of secular education. This was seen as an attack on the cultural identity of many Catholic recruits to Labour, and this was a vulnerable issue because, in the words of Davies, 'it had been on the level of culture, rather than explicit ideology, that the party had made its most powerful appeal to Irish Catholic loyalties' and so 'despite their support for Labour, it is likely that proportionately fewer working-class Catholics became socialists in its strict ideology form than did non-Catholics'.

There was also intra-Catholic strife, demonstrated in a 1930 division over the new cathedral. In addition to a war of words over Paddy's Wigwam, as the building became known, the Liverpool Labour party during the interwar years was also beset with divisions over abortion, with the leader of the Labour group on the council and one-time Lord Mayor Luke Hogan calling abortion the 'negation of socialism'. James Sexton, a former docker and St Helens MP, refused to talk about contraception at the Trades Union Congress.

The legacy of sectarian divisions affected the place of women in Liverpool Labour politics as the party began to make inroads in the city at a local level after the First World War. In those wards with high levels of support for the party – usually Catholic areas that switched to Labour after Irish independence in 1922 – it was felt either unnecessary or inappropriate to get women involved in local party activism, and so they were only invited to participate in Protestant areas.

There were divisions within Liverpool Labour over birth control and family allowances, but because the party in Liverpool was so unrepresentative of local workers, with disproportionately few dockers and sailors, it allowed women more influence.

An April 1936 vote over continuing a £100 grant to the Mothers' Welfare Clinic carried by 72 votes to 41; 15 Labour, 4 Protestants,

5 Liberals and 48 Tories for; 34 Labour, 4 Independents and 3 Tories against. In this case, a strange combination of socialist Left and Protestant Unionist Right triumphed over the majority Catholic caucus in the Labour group on the council. The four Labour women in the council were also divided: Bessie Braddock and Mary Cumella for; Mary Hamilton and Agnes Milton against.

This complexity was reflected in characters like James Sexton, Jack Hayes, the city's first Labour MP, and docker's leader George Milligan. Hayes, who won a by-election in the Edge Hill constituency in 1923, was a Catholic, former Irish Nationalist, who had been a constable in London's Metropolitan Police and general secretary of the National Union of Police and Prison Officers during the 1918 police strike.

Milligan, a trade unionist who later became president of the Society of Lovers of Old Liverpool, was a devout Catholic, an avowed anti-socialist who nonetheless fought fearlessly in defence of dockers' rights.

The sectarian identities of the early decades of the twentieth century were undermined by changing employment patterns, declining religious faith and the modern welfare state, which provided many of the services previously filled by faith-based organisations. The breaking down of traditional neighbourhoods through slum clearances, which uprooted residents of inner-city areas to new estates in Croxteth, Speke and Cantril Farm, where Catholics and Protestants lived side by side, led to increased intermarriage, and in interfaith families, for whatever reason, children were more likely to be raised as Catholic.

One such family was my Grandad Stan's, whose father was a Protestant – hence the name 'Swift', an Anglo-Irish name associated with Protestant settlers in Ireland – what Americans with their usual half-arsed imprecision call 'Scots Irish'. Paul McCartney himself was the product of one such marriage, his father a Protestant cotton salesman and mother a Catholic midwife.

This process led to both the declining relevance of sectarian divisions in Liverpool, and its recasting as a 'Celtic' city, in opposition to the Anglo, Protestant Conservatism of the rest of England.

INTERLUDE 7

Uprising

In 1981, on a hot and humid July night in Liverpool city centre, police officer Ray Davenport pulled over a car he suspected was stolen. He approached the driver's door and reached inside to take the keys out of the ignition. At this point the driver sped off, with PC Davenport's arm trapped inside the vehicle. He was dragged down the street and died from his injuries soon after. Given this context, Merseyside police were even less inclined than usual to proceed gently when they pulled over Leroy Alphonse Cooper on Granby Street the next day. The violent arrest of Cooper led to officers being pelted with stones, and within hours a full-blown riot had developed. Over the next nine days, somewhere between 486 to 1,000 police officers were injured – compared with 279 during the Brixton riots a few months earlier – and there were over 500 arrests. During the disturbances, milk floats and a JCB were commandeered and driven at the police. Riots also began in Netherley, Speke, Halewood, Walton, Kirkdale and Cantril Farm.

The name Toxteth (or Tocky) was not often used to describe the area – it was more commonly referred to as L8 or Liverpool 8 – until after the riots. The area as a whole was mainly white, although there was a notable difference between the mostly white Dingle and the mostly black Granby 'Triangle', the area delineated by Upper Parliament Street, Princes Road and Lodge Lane.

In the decade before the riots, Granby had lost almost 50 per cent of its population, declining from 24,000 people to around 15,000; the Dingle also shrank from around 15,000 to 12,000. Between 1974 and 1981, unemployment rose 120 per cent in Liverpool as a whole, but by 350 per cent in Granby.

According to Liverpool City Council's deprivation index, Toxteth was considerably less deprived than other areas such as Walton – but then Walton was (and still sort of is) almost entirely white.

Toxteth did have, alongside many dockside districts, a long history of violence, both spontaneous and organised. In the decade before the riots, the area accounted for more than half of all violent offences recorded on Merseyside.

But while cannabis was big in Toxteth, unlike many other parts of the city, harder drugs had little presence in the area at the start of the '80s.

As dealers began to expand sales of heroin (rebranded as 'smack') in Liverpool 8, graffiti began to appear warning heroin pushers to leave the area. One message in Granby read: 'Newflash! This is Toxteth not Croxteth. Strictly Ganja'. In the summer of 1985, a 150-strong mob of vigilantes attacked a block of flats housing some enterprising smack pedlars from outside the area and used a hammer to break the kneecaps of one dealer.

Given that attempts to keep heroin out of Toxteth were unsuccessful, it is debatable whether this attack was focused more on protecting the nascent market from rival dealers, but nonetheless at the start of the 1980s hard drugs had not yet become a problem in Toxteth as they were in other areas of the city. Former police officer David Scott reckons that as late as 1983 there was no major presence of hard drugs such as heroin or cocaine in Toxteth.

The police in Liverpool have until recently had a reputation of racist hostility towards black people, notorious even among the ranks of British law enforcement. David Scott, a white man born in Toxteth in the 1940s, served in Merseyside Police between 1975 and 1988. His wife Michelle, a fellow Toxtethian, had a Jamaican father and a white mother. As a result of this, Scott received years of racist abuse from his colleagues. He was once reassured by a superior to 'take no notice of what the other officers say', because his wife may have 'a black father but she's a half-caste, she's not a nigger'.

One officer told the author James McClure: 'If you come across a bad white, he's bad; if you come across a bad black, he's bad; if you come across a bad half-caste, he's evil . . . I know some half-castes, great guys, but they always carry a weapon for some reason, or they'll use anything to hand.' A detective concurred: 'the problem with the half-caste is that he's got this big chip on his shoulder, you don't know whether you come from A or B, so you find your own level with the villains'.

One inspector told McClure that:

> the original Liverpool coloured person was never involved in crime. Those who are involved tend to be largely Lagos Nigerians and Kingston Jamaicans, although I'd imagine that they're the type who would be criminals back in their own country, so that's not all of them. We get West Islanders who're noisy and cause trouble, only mainly among themselves and usually over women. I don't find them a bad type at all; they're hardworking, very happy and cheerful people.

In the aftermath of the riots, Chief Constable Ken Oxford said: 'This was not a racial issue' – as in, it was not due to discrimination or racism against black people, or their targeting by the police – but rather it was 'exclusively a crowd of black hooligans intent on making life unbearable and indulging in criminality'.

This interpretation was confounded by the statistics: the majority of the 244 arrested during the riot were white. Photographs of rioters published at the time in the *Echo* clearly show both white and black faces.

Out of the 5,000 officers in the Merseyside police force in 1981, only four were black. As the former officer Jim Fitzsimmons told the journalist Simon Hughes: 'We were a semi-disciplined organisation', and Oxford was 'ex-military, not sophisticated with the social aspects of what was required'.

Many officers inside Merseyside police believe that the riots enabled criminals – especially drug dealers – to operate with greater impunity because of the decreased police presence. Recounting a fight against Birmingham City's hooligan firm in August 1981, Andy Nicholls notes that it was the first game of the season after the summer Toxteth riots, and

> nobody gave a toss for the bizzies in the aftermath of Tocky . . . one bizzie who everybody thought was in plain clothes tracking us was put in hospital for weeks when he was set upon and battered. Other officers in uniform and on horses were attacked as we made our way back to the station . . . Toxteth was fresh in everybody's minds and respect for the law was nil.'
>
> Soon the bobby on the beat was phased out and replaced with the gentle souls of the Operational Support Division. It is safe to say that the OSD have got even with us on many occasions.

It also accelerated the decline of Liverpool's black community: in 1992 there were 6,782 black people in Liverpool, 1.5 per cent of the total population, half that of a decade earlier.

The previous December, John Lennon had been shot dead in New York. A month after Toxteth, Bill Shankly had a fatal heart attack. The old Liverpool, of dockers and union barons, guitar bands and small-time villains, was dying.

The new city would be post-industrial and yet, in some ways more globalised than in its port's heyday.

9

'THEY CALLED HIM PURPLE'

I can't remember exactly when it was – I think 2006 or 2007 – but I clearly remember being on Oxford Road in Manchester, not far from the train station.

I first noticed the car due to the shite music blasting out of the speakers at 100 decibels, but as I took in the rest of the scene, I became progressively more shocked. From his trackie, the waft of rocky emanating from the souped-up Vauxhall Corsa and the aforementioned shite tunes, I knew I was looking at a scally.

But something was off, something didn't make sense. And, at first, I couldn't work out what it was. Then it hit me: I was looking at my first Asian scally.

After this experience was occasionally revisited on trips to Manchester, Sheffield, Leeds and the like, it made me think: why don't we have Asian scallies in Liverpool? In fact, why are our scallies almost uniformly white? (I did know of at least one *black* scally, an Old Swan weed dealer called Jason the Jamaican.)

In fact, growing up in the city in the 1990s and early 2000s, it was fairly rare to see someone who wasn't white in any context.

The contemporary image of Liverpool is a bit confused when it comes to race. In general, people are probably aware that, as a port city, it has a long history of immigration and racial diversity. But Liverpool lacks the diverse image of places like London, Birmingham and Manchester. And while there have been are a few famous black Scousers – such as Craig Charles, John Conteh and Mick Johnson from *Brookside* – that is not a particularly long list, and one of those is a fictional character.

Although a younger generation of black Scousers such as the footballer Trent Alexander-Arnold and the athlete Katarina Johnson-Thompson are disrupting this picture, the average Scouser is assumed to be white by most people.

Liverpool today is much more diverse than it was even during my youth twenty years ago. Today there is something called the 'World in One City' cup, a football tournament featuring teams from different immigrant communities. We even have Asian scallies.

Yet many black or brown people who move to the city note their surprise that it is not as diverse as they expected. The photographer Ean Flanders, who moved up from London, told the BBC that he expected to see more diversity, given he knew the city had one of the oldest black communities in Europe. Instead, he 'didn't see that reflected . . . I rarely saw people who looked like me in the heart of the city, the Knowledge Quarter, the trendy Baltic area'.

The complicated attitude of race in Liverpool today is shown in the nickname of Akinwale Oluwafolajimi Oluwatope Arobieke, universally known as 'Purple Aki'. Aki is notorious in the north-west for approaching well-built young men and asking to squeeze their muscles, watch them perform squats or even for him to do squats with them on his back.

Although admittedly he's served time before, Aki has never been convicted of a sexual offence – in fact, he has won compensation from the police and authorities for harassment and malicious prosecution on at least two occasions.

But there is one death that has been associated with his activities. In 1986, Gary Kelly, a sixteen-year-old from Birkenhead, was electrocuted at New Brighton railway station when he ran onto the train lines, reportedly to get away from Aki. Initially, Aki was convicted of involuntary manslaughter, although this was later overturned on the reasonable basis that his presence at a train station was not itself an act of harm.

Despite his bogeyman status, Aki is not a figure of hate, but a figure of fun – he is seen as a joke or an urban legend rather than a nonce. He has never been a target of vigilante justice, which you might expect of a figure notorious for feeling the muscles of young men.

But it would be naive to think that there is nothing racial in the way Aki is perceived; his race and his size are an important part of his place in Liverpool folklore. And, of course, his nickname 'Purple Aki' does not derive from his love of the music of Prince, nor because of his previous stint as a Roman senator, but because of the colour of his skin.

In another, more racially diverse city, Aki would be perceived in a different way: as a weird pervert, certainly, but his blackness would not be remarkable in London or Birmingham. In fact, this might have served to protect him; if everything about Aki's behaviour was the same, but he was a big white grock, you can imagine that he would have been the target of mob violence by now. But the legend of Aki shows the complicated attitude towards race and ethnicity in Liverpool today. Ostensibly, it is a multi-cultural, anti-racist city, welcome to all, but that the most (in)famous urban legend in the city is universally known as 'Purple Aki' suggests there is a way to go before this projected image is made reality.

Many black Liverpudlians have ancestry in the city that goes back to the eighteenth century – much further back than that of the vast majority of the population. The city's black community owes its presence here to other factors.

There are several documented sales of enslaved Africans in Liverpool, which took place outside Customs House on the Pier Head and on one occasion in 1766 at the Exchange Coffee House on Water Street, when eleven people were auctioned.

In some cases, they had been brought back to the city because they had been used to replace white sailors who had died en route to the Americas. Once in Liverpool, they would usually be employed as domestic servants, maids and sometimes coach drivers. Many of their owners lived in the large mansions that had sprung up in Toxteth Park.

If any of these early black Scousers walked into town along the shops of Water Street, they could see in the windows the manacles, branding irons, muzzles and shackles used in the trade. Today on Water Street, the only remnant of this history is the tobacco shop.

Church records tell us of the several people born on the African continent who were baptised in the city: on 31 August 1778, Samuel Coffee, 'about the Age of twenty-five Years, a Native of Annamaboo' in Africa and servant to Captain James Paisley; five years later, Jacob Wilson, 'a Native of Benin, on the Coast of Guinea ... aged about Twenty-one'; a year later, Peggy Deccas, from Jamaica, also twenty-one, and Shuannah Oats, from Charleston, South Carolina.

On 15 December 1752, a priest at St Peter's Church baptised Peter Smith, a baby whose mother was named as Mary Smith, spinster, and father as 'Mercury; Mr. Reeds Negro'. In this case, we can assume that Mary Smith was white, as when non-white people arise in the parish records they are consistently designated as such. (For example, in the same parish in November 1826, servant Samuel Brown married spinster Eliza Robinson, and it was noted that they were 'both black'.)

In total, between the years 1717 to 1840, there are 639 people recorded as being baptised, buried or married in the city, who were likely black or mixed-race. Of these, 562 were men and 77 women, and

543 of the mentions concerned baptisms; for over 300 years, therefore, black people have been born and raised in the city of Liverpool.

The place or region of birth was noted for 364 individuals: 162 from Africa, 124 from the West Indies, 69 from North America, nine from South America and one 'man of colour' born in Lisbon. With people of African origin, any more specific details of their place of birth were usually omitted, but when it was recorded the most common entries were 'the Bight of Biafra' (between modern-day Nigeria and Cameroon) (14 people); Sierra Leone (14); the 'Windward Coast' (Liberia and the Cote d'Ivoire) (12); and the Gold Coast (12).

Most Africans arrived during the period of the legal British slave trade, and their broad geographical origins shows how Liverpool was involved in purchasing people from various parts of the west African coast.

Of the seventy-seven people with a stated occupation, forty-six were listed as sailors and twenty-three as servants. Before 1785, the majority worked as slaves and no 'occupation' was listed. These included Adam, ('Mr. Fillingham's Blackamoore') who was baptised in 1717; Ellen, 'a Negro belonging to Capt. Carr' died in 1738; Dinah, 'Mrs. Fry's negro' was baptised in 1761 at 'about 38 years old', 'Hanamoe a black belonging to Mr. James' died in 1774.

The last parish register entry using the verb 'to belong' occurred in 1785, for someone named 'Errat', who was buried on 30 September 1785, and described as 'a black belong'd to Mr. Savage'.

But most of the black people in the city during that period arrived voluntarily. Many black sailors, traders, artisans and former slaves began to settle in Liverpool, especially after the Somerset vs Stewart case of 1772, when Lord Chief Justice Mansfield held that slavery was not permissible under English law, and that enslaved people who reached England could not be forced to return to bondage. After the American War of Independence (1775–83), some of the black soldiers who had fought for the British side left the colonies on ships bound for the city.

These early black Scousers soon developed a small neighbourhood just south of the city, in the green fields and woods of a former royal hunting ground, known as Toxteth Park; as early as the 1790s there were fifty to seventy African children attending Liverpool schools.

In 1830, the American novelist Herman Melville wrote that, in stark contrast to the experience of black people in the USA, 'in Liverpool the Negro steps with a prouder pace, and lifts his head like a man; for here, no such exaggerated feeling exists in respect to him, as in America'.

Around 1850, there were more than a hundred African children in Liverpool schools. Family names like Amos, Charles, Cole, Nelson and Wilson were prominent black family names in the city for at least 200 years; in fact, many black people around the world have these names not due to white slaveowners but these black and mixed-race sailors.

James McCune Smith, a son of former enslaved people, became a politician and the first African American to secure a medical degree. He visited Liverpool in 1851 and wrote of his attending a service at St George's Church: 'There were no cold looks, no supercilious or sanctimonious frowns, none appeared to have reached that pitch of devotion in which creatures frown upon the words of their creator – upon their fellow creatures, not for the hue of the soul, but of the skin.'

Despite the importance of slavery in building up the city's fortunes, up to 4,000 people attended a meeting in support of Abraham Lincoln's Emancipation Proclamation in 1863.

A man called James Johnson from North Carolina made his way to Liverpool, whereupon he was promptly robbed of all his possessions. He then earned money dancing and singing in the street, before joining a boxing troupe that performed around the country, and then settled in Oldham, where he married a millworker.

In 1846, an Indian door-to-door salesman approached two American sailors who destroyed his whole stock before beating him; they later spat in the face of a passing black man before assaulting him, too. In

1850, another black man was drinking in a pub on Roe Street when he was forcibly ejected by a group of American sailors; a mini riot broke out, with glasses and chairs thrown. Police arrested and fined one of the attackers, after which around fifteen sailors returned to the pub to menace the owner, who they accused of lying about the incident. After buying drinks, each sailor threw beer over the hapless publican. The group were subsequently arraigned with the magistrate commenting that they were acting as though they were in the southern USA where such behaviour was acceptable.

Liverpool's long history of mixed relationships also goes back over 200 years, and can be seen in various luminaries of the city who have diverse ancestry, from Dixie Dean, the legendary Everton FC centre forward, to contemporary celebrities such as the actor Stephen Graham or footballer Ross Barkley.

The background of gangster Curtis Warren reflects the diversity of ethnicities and nationalities that have historically mixed in the city, particularly in Liverpool 8: Warren's mother, Sylvia Chantre, was half Spanish, and his father, Curtis Aloysius Warren, was a black seaman in the Norwegian merchant navy.

But, in reality, despite Liverpool having had for a long time such an unusually diverse population for a British metropolis, it has until recently been a particularly racist city.

By 1919, it is estimated that out of the 20,000 or so black people in the UK, roughly 5,000 lived in Liverpool (compared to 3,000 in Cardiff, another key area of black settlement at this time), concentrated around the south docks and Park Lane in Liverpool 8.

Yet that year was scarred by vicious race riots, instigated by white men, often recently demobilised from the army. In response, West Indians attacked whites with straight razors and African sailors attacked the Scandinavian Home in Great George Street. One black man, Ernest Marke, wrote later of his experience in Liverpool in 1919: 'a young

West Indian friend and I . . . saw a mob about a dozen strong. They started chasing us the moment we were spotted . . . A tramcar was going southward . . . we ran for it . . . I caught it but my friend was unlucky . . . I learned later that he was beaten unconscious and left for dead'.

Marke noted that women had been far more sympathetic than men: 'I was saved many many times by women . . . A lot of women used to wear clogs in those days, and they took off their clogs [to beat the men] and started shouting "Leave him alone! He hasn't done any harm!"'

Liverpool's assistant chief head constable, demonstrating the racism that would characterise the city's police force for many years, wrote that 'the trouble' was 'mainly on account of the blacks interfering with white women'.

A local newspaper, the *Evening Express*, took up a similar line, arguing that 'undoubtedly these associationships [sic] – romantic enough in the case of Othello and Desdemona – are undesirable and harmful to the dignity of the white – that is to say, the dominant race'. The editor of the rival *Liverpool Courier* paper wrote that 'the average Negro is nearer the animal than is the average white man'.

In the aftermath of the riots, some black workers were fired from Tate & Lyle after white colleagues refused to work with them and the Elder Dempster shipping line repatriated a hundred black sailors to West Africa in 1919.

In Liverpool especially, there was considerable evidence of police racism, and these riots further eroded trust in the police, who were viewed as having failed to protect black people from white racist violence. In the words of the historian Jacqueline Jenkinson, an 'undeclared state of war' existed between the police and black people in Liverpool.

This was encapsulated by the murder of Charles Wooton, a West Indian ship's fireman, whose body was retrieved from the water at Queen's Dock after being chased by an angry mob of around 300 white men.

Whether due to the riots, broader racism or the Great Depression that followed the 1929 Wall Street Crash, by the time of the Second World War the black population is estimated to have declined to around 2,000 – although this was still double the 1,000 or so estimated to be living in London. And despite the abuse, violence and ostracisation faced by mixed-raced couples at this time, it was estimated that there were around 1,500 mixed-raced people in the city by the 1930s.

During the Second World War, black Liverpool girls and black GIs from the USA met in clubs like the Ibo, Yoruba and the Sierra Leone. The Colonial Office received numerous complaints about the 'threatening attitude of American troops' to black Britons and black troops from the British Empire. By January 1943, there were reports of a 'steady deterioration in the relationship between white soldiers and our own Colonial People'.

Throughout the war, 300 West Indian technicians – mostly from Jamaica – came to work in Liverpool's munitions factories. Learie Constantine, the renowned Trinidadian cricketer, was appointed the local welfare officer for the technicians, and it was through him that they lodged complaints about racial discrimination in wartime Liverpool. He lamented: 'I have lived in this country for a long time and claim many friends among the white population, and I shiver to think that I am liable to attack by these men if I am seen in the company of my friends'.

Cebert Lewis, a Jamaican technician, complained to the Colonial Office in 1941 that he had been racially abused by two police officers during a cinema trip with his white 'lady friend'. Lewis received a verbal apology from Liverpool City Police and was reassured that steps would be taken to prevent the reoccurrence of such an incident.

Lewis' case caused particular concern within the Colonial Office who were eager to ensure that black people, especially war volunteers, were not unduly harassed by the police as this could have 'serious political repercussions in the colonies'. The Colonial Office's concern about Cebert Lewis' treatment was part of wider efforts to contain the impact evidence of racial discrimination in Britain had on the nation's reputation with its imperial subjects.

In 1947, there were serious anti-Jewish riots in Liverpool as well as Manchester, Glasgow and other cities, in response to the killing of two British soldiers by Zionist fighters in Palestine. By 1948, the racial situation in the city had worsened, with an investigation by sociologists Harris Joshua and Tina Wallace finding that policing was more of an issue for black people in 1948 than it had been in 1919. In 1948, before the arrival of the HMS *Windrush* at Tilbury docks, there were an estimated 8,000 black people in the city.

This population was mostly West African although there were some people from the Caribbean and East Africa. A newspaper article from 1954 suggested that up to a third of the black population had been born in the city.

Police persecution helped to break down the separate national, regional or religious identities of Liverpool's black population and create a separate identity. The journalist Anthony Richmond quoted a Scouse Somali in this period as saying: 'This is as much our business as the West Africans or anyone else. If it can happen to them it can happen to us.'

The National Union of Seamen (NUS) was increasingly antagonistic to migrant labour and created a special committee 'to vet all coloured entrants to the country who claim to be seamen'. This inevitably soured relations between black and white seamen already working in the port.

West African and West Indian stowaways were also arriving in Liverpool. Stowaways were seen as cheap labour, and there was a widespread perception that they had it easy because after a short period in prison upon their arrival, they were released and able to claim unemployment insurance. Newspapers often publicised court proceedings against alleged stowaways, highlighting magistrate's pronouncements on the scale of the problem and the limits of the law in allowing them to tackle it.

It was in this climate that, at around 10 p.m. on a hot Saturday night in July 1948, a crowd of around 300 white people amassed outside an Indian-owned café on St James Street. It was known to be a popular meeting place for black men and white women. Eventually, someone threw a stone through the window of the restaurant causing Michael Lasese, a 25-year-old West African ship's fireman (who shovelled coal into the furnaces) to come outside and confront the crowd.

At this point the police arrived, and two officers reported finding Lasese with a knife, surrounded by the crowd. Instead of dispersing the crowd, the officers attempted to restrain Lasese who at that moment allegedly stabbed one of the rioters in the face and arm, and then another rioter as the police tried to remove him from the scene. While this was going on, the rioters had attacked the café itself, and the owner would later receive compensation for £275 and 10 shillings in damages (equivalent to over £10,000 today).

The next day, a white mob of up to 2,000 people attacked the black seamen's hostel, Colsea House, on Upper Parliament Street. The police managed to break up the crowd, only for officers themselves to then force entry into the hostel and arrest several of the black residents. Sporadic street fighting also took place between random groups of white and black men outside the Rialto and the violence continued until after midnight on 2 August when order was restored.

The next evening saw the peak of the rioting after rumours spread that a white mob intended to attack Wilkie's, a popular social club. In response, some black people barricaded themselves into the club, arming themselves with a variety of weapons to defend themselves from the white crowd outside. That night, of the fifty-one people arrested, forty-three were black, and two of them women.

This was an even greater disparity than in 1919; in fact, Liverpool City Police appear to have been even less willing to arrest white rioters in 1948 – only ten white people were arrested compared with thirty-six in 1919.

Three men – Edward Johnson, Alfred Gurley and Clifton George Brown – described how after their arrest they had been made to 'run a gauntlet' between two lines of officers who beat them repeatedly. Despite the numerous and consistent allegations of police misconduct, most black defendants were found guilty.

However, of the dozens of black people arrested during the violence, one group – Wentworth Barrington Dawson, Harry Arthur Bell, Hermon McKay, Samuel Walker, Ekundi Elliot and an unnamed fifteen-year-old – who became known as the 'Liverpool Six', attracted more attention.

The police claimed that these men were seen armed and chasing a white man along Upper Parliament Street before retreating into Wilkie's, from where they threw bricks and bottles at the police.

Their barrister, Harry Livermore began by describing the injuries sustained by one of his clients at the hands of the police, asserting that Hermon McKay had 'received an injury of the right upper lip, as big as a hen's egg, a black eye, bruised shoulder . . . and a bruised knee' because of 'a little baton practice'. Livermore also used the testimony of doctors who had examined the defendants at Walton prison to confirm that their injuries were consistent with having been struck with batons.

During its second day, the 'Liverpool Six' trial was stopped by the presiding magistrate, who told the court that having heard the evidence 'I find the case one of great difficulty [and] I feel I am left in doubt that the charge has been established'.

This hostility was not confined to black Liverpudlians and migrants. Liverpool tourism promotional materials will proudly tell you that the city has the oldest settled Chinese community in Europe, and the largest Chinese arch outside of China, but is less likely to describe the historical hostility against the Chinese, who were regularly employed as strike breakers, and so 'anti-Chinese hostility from dockers and seamen was unremitting', according to historian Anne Witchard.

In 1906, the dockers' trade-union leader James Sexton initiated a public enquiry into supposed 'vice' in Chinatown, including prostitution, opium and the debasement of white women. Sexton had in the previous year won election to the council for the St Anne's ward on an explicitly anti-Chinese manifesto, and his pronounced Sinophobia led to complaints from, among others, the chief constable of the local police force.

In response to a study by Rachel Fleming, a prominent eugenicist of the time, the Liverpool Association for the Welfare of Half-Caste Children was set up in 1927 by the Liverpool University Settlement.

Its report of 1930 by social worker Muriel Fletcher echoed the newspaper commentary on the 1919 race riots in characterising 'the white women who consorted with coloured men' as prostitutes, or 'women of a poor type'. The report, perhaps surprisingly given the sentiments of the time, found 'no serious problem . . . presented by the Anglo-Chinese community', but expressed grave anxiety about what it termed Liverpool's 'Anglo-Negroid' population, especially the mixed-race girls.

During the Great Depression, David Logan – who was the Labour MP for the Scotland Road constituency – complained of the meagre shipping that entered Liverpool, half of it manned by 'coolie labour, black labour, and chinks'.

The first Chinese sailors had arrived aboard the *Duchess of Clarence*, a tea ship, and after the Opium Wars established exclusive British trading rights in Guangzhou and Hong Kong, many more came to join the babel of tongues on the dockside.

After the Second World War, local pressures contributed to the deportation of more than 2,000 Chinese seamen from Liverpool; many of them had wives and girlfriends in the city, but were deported so suddenly that many of their partners assumed they had abandoned them.

The city evolved from being one of the most ethnically diverse populations in the mid-nineteenth century to one of the least by the start of the twenty-first century. One of the reasons for this was the city's economic decline during that same time period; a 1953 investigation found that the city's Caribbean population had declined by a third, and the West African population by half, since the First World War. Some of this might have been due to the race riots of 1919 and 1948, but declining economic opportunities would also have played a part. This was the main reason why so few of the 'Windrush Generation' of migrants came to the city in the '50s and '60s.

And while it continued to be home to people with a variety of languages, religions and ethnicities, the city has a long history of segregation, at one point between English and Irish, Catholic and Protestant, and more recently between white and black. The historians John Belchem and Donald MacRaild argued that Liverpool's very cosmopolitanism contributed to its propensity to racism. Not so long ago, the Boundary Hotel on Lodge Lane literally marked a boundary between Granby – the accepted 'black' area of Liverpool – and the city centre.

As the journalist Simon Hughes wrote of the Liverpool 8 postcode, although it was 60 per cent white at the time of the Toxteth riots of 1981, 'because it was the area of the city with the highest percentage of black people in a city which had just one black community, it was regarded as Liverpool's black area'.

In *Scally*, former football hooligan Andy Nicholls recalls one occasion before a League Cup match at Goodison when he was informed that the Manchester United firm had been spotted: 'We bounced over to see a black lad getting ragged across the road by a little gang of Urchins. It was always the same story at Everton: when it went off, there was no hiding place for black people.' Another season, after a match at Tottenham Hotspur's White Hart Lane, he realised that an unfamiliar group of lads were not fellow Everton hooligans when 'they were joined by a mob of black faces and the game was up; Everton they were not'.

On another occasion, after being attacked by a group of black hooligans from a rival firm, he quips that 'I had a lip as big as the lads chasing me'. Nicholls' book was published in 2004, and he felt no need to apologise for his language or note that it went against the image of 'Scouse not English', etc, because no such image existed as recently as twenty years ago. Certainly not among scallies, anyway.

Even as immigration into Liverpool declined, the city retained one of the most racially diverse populations in the UK in terms of the heritage and origins of the non-white population. As Diane Frost pointed out: 'While it is well known that Liverpool had one of the largest biracial or mixed-race populations by the late twentieth century, what is often overlooked is the diverse racial or ethnic mixing that had taken place there.' This included combinations such as African-Irish, African-Arab, African-Caribbean, African-Jewish, African-Scottish and African-Chinese. One woman interviewed by Frost in the 1990s told her how her Scottish-Jewish father took her to synagogue without her (non-Jewish) mother's knowledge. Another woman, who was of mixed Irish, Arab and Caribbean ancestry was raised as a Muslim at home, although she had an Irish surname and went to a Catholic school.

But these relationships were, in the words of Diane Frost, greeted with 'overwhelming' hostility, and 'many women with black partners continued to be ostracised into the post-1945 end-of-empire period and beyond'.

As late as 1978, an article in the *Listener* magazine – produced by the BBC – described Liverpool's mixed-race population as being 'the product of liaisons between Black seamen and White prostitutes'.

In the Covid summer of 2020, as protests erupted around the world in solidarity with the Black Lives Matter demonstrations in the United States, there was a new impetus for cities and towns that had benefitted from the transatlantic slave trade to pull down statues of former slavers and change the names of streets and buildings named in their honour.

In Liverpool, this process had already begun with some of the more egregious names: in 1925 the main road running alongside the docks in the heart of the city centre was renamed 'The Strand', after previously being named 'The Goree', after an infamous island and slave-trading fort off the coast of Ghana.

In fact, as early as the mid-nineteenth century, only fifty years after the abolition of the British slave trade, the city was trying to recast itself and reshape its narrative; among the statues outside St George's Hall is a female figure of 'Africa', complete with broken chains, representing the 'liberation' brought by the British Empire, which is pretty ironic considering the city's history.

Today, some of the most prominent roads in the city-centre streets, such as Bold, Cunliffe, Hardman and Tarleton Streets, are among the many still named after merchants who were involved in slavery.

Frankly, if you were to rename every street and building in Liverpool that has a connection to the slave trade, you'd have to rewrite all the maps of the city. And there are also many buildings that were funded by it, such as the town hall.

A common route to end walking tours of Liverpool – I've taken a few people on it myself – is to walk down Water Street towards the Liver Building. As you do so, you pass by the rather blatantly named 'West Africa House' on the left. Although named after post-abolition trading in Africa, based on palm oil and cocoa rather than humans, it shows how much the historic wealth and architecture of the city is inextricably intertwined with exploiting that continent.

To take a long view, Liverpool's role in slavery had a notably more significant impact on the history of the world than the Beatles or Liverpool FC. But today, of course, this is something we would rather forget. We can't brag about it. But maybe learning about and discussing this legacy more openly will help the city to truly live up to the image it projects of itself.

INTERLUDE 8

Bizzies

Given the rich pickings to be had on the docks, there was a need for a proper police force in Liverpool much earlier than elsewhere in the UK. The city was one of the first outside of London to have a modern police force develop after the Municipal Corporations Act of 1835, but before then the job of keeping the law in the town fell to the city watchmen, who were usually hapless at best and fully corrupt at worst.

Initially, these watchmen were armed only with a lamp and a rattle, which warned some criminals of their approach, and attracted others to try and rob them. At this time, the sport of 'Pummelling a Charlie' (as the watchmen were known) became a popular pastime; as well as beating them up, Liverpool miscreants would try and tip over their sentry boxes with the watchman inside, or nail the doors closed. In one instance, a watchman was found drunk and tied to a lamppost.

Many were also reprobates themselves: one was dismissed for keeping chickens in his sentry box and killing them with his truncheon; another ended up in Ireland after drunkenly boarding a boat and falling asleep. In 1835, the last year of the night-watch system, sixty-one men were dismissed for drunkenness and another for having an 'improper connection with a female prisoner'.

After the introduction of the modern police force, the standards of law enforcement improved somewhat, although this was inconsistent, depending on the character of the copper and the area they patrolled; it was recommended that police should only do a maximum of three months' duty in the vicinity of the Sailors' Home, for example, as it was so easy for them to become corrupt and desensitised to crime.

By the twentieth century, although a much more professional force, the Liverpool constabulary had a claim to be one of the most racist in the United Kingdom. Until the passage of the British Nationality Act 1948, black Commonwealth citizens could not become police officers in England and Wales as an applicant had to be a natural born British subject or a child of 'natural born subjects of pure European descent'. For many black people, the way that the race riots of that year had been policed highlighted the need for reform. Activist Edwin DuPlan told the *Daily Post* that 'responsible black people' should be taken on as auxiliary officers to assist in the policing of 'coloured districts'.

By the time Ken Oxford arrived as Chief Constable in 1976, he claimed to be 'appalled' at the extent of violence in the city. His response was as ineffectual as it was authoritarian, leading to miscarriages of justice, a deteriorating relationship with local people and even death after a Huyton man, Jimmy Kelly, died in police custody after being violently arrested for drunk and disorderly behaviour in June 1979. Harold Wilson himself – the former prime minister and MP for Huyton – called for a public inquiry.

This treatment was repaid in spades by the city's criminals; when Jim Fitzsimmons, a young police constable who had recently joined the force, entered the Arkles pub in Anfield he was beaten over the head by burglars he had disrupted. Although violence against the police usually did not make the news, this attack was reported by the *Echo*, and led to the then captain of Liverpool FC, Phil Thompson, visiting Fitzsimmons in hospital. A whip-round by Arkles regulars collected almost £500.

This case nicely encapsulates the paradox of Liverpool, in terms of crime and more broadly: a bizzy is more likely to be beaten about the head by intruders than elsewhere, but he's also more likely to receive a generous, spontaneous response from the local community than elsewhere.

10

THE DARK SIDE OF THE MERSEY

Back in the nineteenth century, an old sea captain wrote that while he had a great deal of affection for the port of Liverpool, 'its seamen are reputed to be responsible for more than half the misdeeds and mysterious happenings on board ship. When something goes wrong, or some wrong is done and none comes forward to admit culpability, then it was the Liverpool feller wot done it.'

The latest figures at the time of writing show that Liverpool today has lower incidences of most types of crime than other major UK cities – and has done for a while. For antisocial behaviour Liverpool had 11 incidents per 1,000 people, compared to 19 in Greater Manchester and 27 in London. The robbery rate in Greater Manchester, at 1.8 per 1000, was twice the Merseyside rate of 0.9. Sexual offences (4.1 to 3.3) burglary (7.4 compared to 4.1) and theft (36 to 24) were also notably much higher. Mostly insulting of all for Mancunians, the incidences of shoplifting in Manchester were also higher than in Liverpool.

At the county level, Merseyside had 126,436 total crimes in 2023, a rate of 88 crimes per 1000 residents; West Midlands had 266,479, a rate of 91 per thousand; and London 782,816 and 87 per thousand. Greater

Manchester, for whatever reason, does not disclose all of its data around crime rates and cannot be compared in terms of total crimes.

Despite this, the city's national reputation for crime is unmatched. In some ways this shouldn't be surprising, since the economy of the town, long before it became one of the world's leading ports, was built around piracy. During the economic downturn at the end of the sixteenth century, Liverpool ship captains were urged by the government of Elizabeth I to become privateers, hijacking ships belonging to England's enemies, which they did with some success.

Privateers were a kind of officially sanctioned pirates, bearing 'Letters of Marque' issued by the Crown, which made their actions legal (according to English law), whereas ordinary pirates would be hanged. Privateers would sail the oceans, intercepting and robbing Spanish (and later Dutch and French) ships, and bringing their loot back to England. In the eighteenth century, Liverpool privateers took more enemy ships than those from any other British port.

At the start of that century, before the slave trade really took off, the city's maritime trade was roughly divided between whaling off Greenland, slavery and privateering. The experience of the city's sailors with the violent practice of privateering probably helped equip them for the evils of the slave trade. This was the opinion of Sir James Picton, who said that the history of piracy among Liverpool seamen 'could not but blunt the feelings of humanity of those engaged in it'.

During the Seven Years War (1756–63), a globe-spanning conflict between Britain and its allies and a French-led alliance, Liverpool privateers gained a reputation for boldness in taking and looting French ships that was unmatched in the merchant marine. They were a kind of seagoing predecessor of the scallies who would so effectively rinse continental shops in the '70s and '80s. In one haul, the *Mentor* captured a ship of the French East India Company loaded with diamonds that would be worth around £12 million today.

Therefore, both Liverpool haters and passionate defenders of the city's reputation might be surprised to learn that its association with criminality has a longer heritage than the recent decades of decline and Thatcher-era Scouse-baiting jokes.

In particular, it was the ruthless exploitation of the influx of up to half a million impoverished Irish peasants fleeing the Great Famine of the 1840s that did the most to give Liverpool its early reputation for dishonesty and crime.

Among other scams, Liverpool crooks ran 'training schools', like Paddy West's in Great Howard Street, for criminals, drunkards, debtors and runaway youths who wanted to become sailors. They included intensive training such as rolling up a window blind to replicate furling a sail, having cold water thrown in your face to get used to North Atlantic storms and placing your hand briefly on a ship's wheel so you could say you'd done it. Paddy was no fool and, in exchange for his expert tuition, graduates had to give him their first two months' pay.

As well as the opportunities for exploiting the thousands of migrants who landed in the city each week, the booming docks – with their endless quantities of a vast variety of goods – provided an ideal opportunity for theft. By the middle of the Victorian era, although the combined population of Manchester, Salford, Bolton and Preston was now 25 per cent larger than that of Liverpool, there were 17 per cent more convictions for theft in Liverpool than in all of those towns put together.

Meanwhile, as one of the world's busiest ports, thousands of seamen from across the world would regularly spend time in the town, and a whole industry of pubs, brothels and drug dens sprung up to cater for them.

In the opinion of Herman Melville, who knew a thing or two about sailors:

of all the sea-ports in the world, Liverpool, perhaps, most abounds in all the variety of land-sharks, land-rats and other vermin which makes the hapless mariner their prey . . . And yet sailors love this Liverpool; and upon long voyages to distant parts of the globe, will be continually dilating upon its charms and attractions, and extolling it above all other sea-ports in the world.

The use of Liverpool as a standard by which to mark depravity – even among sailors – gives you a sense of the reputation of the dockside districts during its imperial heyday.

Among other vices on offer, the demand from sailors and dearth of options for female employment meant that Liverpool probably had more prostitutes per capita than anywhere else in the world. As one shocked observer reported: 'Abandoned women paraded themselves in considerable numbers, indulging in disgusting language, noises, and riotous conduct, without any effectual interference from the police.'

As early as 1800, though the population of the town was only 80,000, the authorities believed there were 2,900 prostitutes, constituting one in every 28 people. A survey from the 1860s found that Liverpool had more than double the number of prostitutes of Manchester, and more than twice as many brothels. There were estimated to be around 600 brothels, which by this point mostly contained Irish women and girls, some of whom made a name for themselves, such as Harriet Lane, Blooming Rose, Jumping Jenny, Cast-Iron Kitty, Tich Maguire, the famous Maggie May and one woman enigmatically known as 'the Battleship'.

Of course, this had many horrible consequences. At the time, baby farming was a common practice, whereby kids were sold to childless parents, and an expert in the trade advised that 'in Liverpool, where there are lots of bad women, you can get any quantity you want'.

The city's venereal wards were also kept busy; the one at the Brownlow Hill workhouse was a sight to behold, with patients suffering 'enormous condylomata and warts, buboes of some weeks standing in each groin, immense rupial crusts all over the body'. One doctor recalled that a woman he had treated for venereal disease propositioned him on the street just three days later.

Prostitutes would supplement their income through theft, and they were believed to be responsible for a quarter of all of the property stolen in the city. This was risky, and they took care not to carry too much money, as it could reveal their profession if found by the police. Since they had a high chance of being robbed, many women concealed gold sovereigns internally, with some women reckoned to hold as many as thirty coins 'where decency forbids to name'.

The high number of prostitutes in the city meant that others ran a risk of being mistaken for one. This happened to Catherine Flaherty, a street hawker, who was accosted by a constable when leaving a pub in February 1864. She was shocked and asked the officer: 'Do I look like a prostitute?', but he smacked her across the head and began to drag her to the station, before realising his mistake and letting her go.

To avoid the perils of the street, women tried to find whatever shelter they could, no matter how humble, to conduct business. In 1849, it was found that the sheds of the Brownlow Hill workhouse had been taken over by fifty to a hundred 'disorderly prostitutes'.

The healthier, better-looking women could find work and accommodation in the many brothels in the city, which were usually run by an aged member of their profession; police stats estimate that in late Victorian Liverpool, around 90 per cent of the brothels were run by women.

Fanny Wilson, aka Mrs Mandeville, was a notorious Liverpool madam, reported as keeping between fifty and sixty girls at any time. Mandeville paraded around town 'covered in diamonds' and was assisted by her ruthless enforcer Ginger Jack.

One day, she came across Mary Lomax, a beautiful daughter of a prosperous farmer from the Midlands, who had been seduced by a

Liverpool 'gentleman' when she was just fifteen and ran away to the city, but was later abandoned. She was taken off the streets by Mandeville, who put her up in one of her fancier brothels on Blandford Street. Mary was apparently much sought after, and when her uncle came looking for her, she was drugged and hidden in an empty boiler, lest Mandeville lose her valuable new asset. After nine years, Mary caught tuberculosis and began coughing up blood; her clients complained and she was once again thrown out onto the street. She ended up in Brownlow Hill workhouse and died three months later, at the age of twenty-four.

Worse than this was the shocking number of child prostitutes: one mid-century survey found at least 200 'regular' prostitutes under twelve, although these figures may have been exaggerated; six years later a police estimate suggested there were only twenty-one prostitutes under sixteen in the city. Until 1875, when the age was raised to thirteen, it was legal to have sex with twelve-year-old children, and there were few prosecutions anyway.

The levels of crime in the city were made worse by the Second World War, which brought a fresh influx of American goods and made theft made easier through blackouts and bomb damage. The 1945 *Report on the Police Establishment and the State of Crime* found that crime had increased almost 70 per cent since 1939, with the bombing of the city making many premises easier to break into. Thieves and muggers also used destroyed houses as bases to launch raids and to store stolen goods. The Liverpool Youth Organisations annual report contrasted the 'heroism, endurance, and cheerfulness' displayed at Dunkirk, Arnhem and the Battle of Britain, with the domestic 'outbreak of hooliganism, theft, sexual immorality and various forms of anti-social behaviour that make social welfare workers wonder for a moment whether all their labours have not been in vain'.

But if this opportunistic increase in crime owed much to the wartime destruction and the enterprising spirit of Scouse criminals, it was also driven by the desperation and hardship of the times. As the police report found: 'The shortages of all kinds of food and clothing made it easy for thieves to dispose of stolen property and also made it worthwhile to steal what before the war would not have repaid the trouble and risk.'

If the Second World War provided a huge boost to organised and petty crime on Merseyside, the decline of the docks and the broader economy in the following decades ensured that crime would continue to provide a viable and profitable career option for many. The docks themselves might have been in decline, but for thieves it was a golden age; there were still vast quantities of goods coming in and out, the much more secure containerisation had not yet arrived and the accessibility of consumer goods meant that consignments were increasing in value.

Timpson's were among the companies to begin splitting up their cargoes, with the shoemaker sending left-footed shoes on one ship and right-footed shoes on another. Remington had to store the motors for their razors in a separate warehouse miles away from the plastic casing.

This period, between the war and the rise of the drug importers in the 1980s, provided a kind of golden age for old-school villainy. It was Liverpool thieves Billy Grimwood and Paul Grimes who made the first use of a thermal lance to break into a bank safe, snatching £140,000 from the vaults of Water Street bank in 1969.

Today, the city's current reputation owes more to the high-profile crimes that have recently occurred in Liverpool, than to the reality of crime on Merseyside.

Most infamous of all was the murder of two-year-old toddler James Bulger in 1993. On 12 February 1993, two ten-year-old boys, Robert Thompson and Jon Venables, abducted Bulger from the New Strand Shopping Centre in Bootle, after his mother had briefly lost him. His mutilated body was found two days later on a railway line in Walton.

Thompson and Venables were charged on 20 February 1993 with abduction and murder. They were found guilty on 24 November, making them the youngest convicted murderers in modern British history. They were sentenced to indefinite detention. (In 2001, when they were eighteen, the parole board recommended their release, although Venables has since been returned to prison several times for breaches of the terms of his release and at the time of writing is still behind bars.)

As horrible as the case was, it was not unprecedented in the long history of human cruelty. An accurate history of the British working class would reveal many such cases. In Liverpool alone, there were several recorded incidents of children killing younger children.

In July 1855, a boy called Alfred Fitz, nine years old, got into an argument with James Fleeson, aged seven. Fitz threw a brick at Fleeson's head, and after this felled him, finished him off with another brick to the head. He and his friend John Breen then threw the boy into the nearby canal. He was fished out of Stanley Dock a few days later. Fitz and Breen were convicted of manslaughter and sentenced to twelve months in prison.

In 1891, friends Samel Crawford, nine, and Robert Shearer, eight, killed a stranger called David Dawson Eccles, also eight years old, when they lured him to a building site and pushed him into a water-filled pit, leaving him to drown. Deemed to be too young to be legally responsible, they were remanded into a boy's home under the care of Father Nugent.

This kind of thing, regrettably, has always happened, probably in every culture and every country in the world. Back in the 1960s, in the Edward Bond play *Saved*, a group of young Londoners, bored and drunk in a park, torture and stone a baby to death.

As Simon Hughes pointed out in his history of Liverpool, in the 'long 1980s', a year before the Bulger murder, an eleven-year-old girl in Northumberland killed an eighteen-month-old baby, yet for whatever reason this and similar crimes have not lodged in the public memory in the same way as the Bulger murder.

In recent years, this included the murder of nine-year-old Olivia Pratt-Korbel, accidentally caught in the crossfire of an attempted underworld assassination as she stood in her own hallway; another little girl, twelve-year-old Ava White, was stabbed to death in the city centre by a little boy, just a few feet away from where I was married a year later.

In 2007, eleven-year-old Rhys Jones was shot dead in a Croxteth pub car park, and two years before that Anthony Walker was murdered in brutal style. With these last two crimes I was, coincidentally, very close to the scenes at the time they were committed.

Any history of Liverpool, or the rest of the country, tells us that this kind of thing has happened all the time. You can take a snapshot of any era and find untold misery. Robert Thompson's mother, Ann, tried to take an overdose in the weeks *before* her son and Venables killed Bulger.

Crime in general, and violent crime in particular, are at historically low levels. Today, despite the city's violent past, it has much better stats on violent crime than Manchester, London, Birmingham and most other UK cities.

One difference today is that we are more likely to hear about it, and increasingly see it. Still, some cases, for whatever reason, attract more attention and linger longer in the memory.

The one area of crime where Liverpool remains a statistical outlier is when it comes to drug consumption: in 2023 there were 8.6 offences per thousand people in Liverpool – higher than any other major UK city.

Liverpool has a drug problem in more ways than one. Far be it from me to criticise anyone in this regard – it would be not so much a man in a glass house throwing stones, more like someone in the Sefton Park Palm House manning a medieval trebuchet.

Liverpool's reputation for broader criminality is undeserved, but when it comes to illegal drugs the stats are clear: as of 2021, cannabis use was as prevalent in Yorkshire and London as in Liverpool; but Liverpool had the highest cocaine use per capita, with one in seven people having used the drug at some point.

Liverpool had the highest rate of use for MDMA and ecstasy, with one in every six people reporting as having tried the drug and one in fifty having taken it within the last year. Of the respondents who reported increasing their use of ecstasy in the last year, two-thirds (66 per cent) lived in Liverpool.

With heroin, the city that had the highest use of the drug was Sheffield, where one in twenty had taken it, closely followed by Liverpool and Cardiff with one in twenty-five.

In addition to illegal narcotics, abuse of over-the-counter medication to 'self-medicate', using medicines such as Nytol and Sudafed, was most common in Sheffield, Southampton, Liverpool, Brighton and Glasgow.

So, across different types of drugs, from cannabis to heroin, Liverpool is consistently among the top consumers in the UK – unlike any other city. As with much of the city and its identity, the popularity of narcotics in Liverpool is a recent development. After the anti-opium laws of 1916 were passed, a lucrative new smuggling opportunity was created, which almost exclusively catered to the city's Chinese community, as well as a few eccentric artist types.

All of this, like the modern identity of the city, is a very recent development; the city has long had a drinking problem, but until the 1980s it didn't have a drugs problem.

A 1963 council report on issues affecting the city – at 579 pages a pretty hefty tome – devoted only two pages to drug use, and concluded that the main problem was opiate use, but even this was confined to elderly Chinese men who used it to treat minor illnesses.

As late as 1970, the local police had just one drugs dog, trained to find cannabis. The BBC presenter Winifred Robinson recalls that when she left Norris Green in the early 1980s, 'drugs were still something only hippies took. We wouldn't begin to know where to buy them.'

By the end of the '80s, however, Merseyside constabulary had twenty-four dogs trained to sniff out heroin, amphetamines and cocaine.

Some of this transformation can be attributed to the social and cultural changes of the '60s, whereby young people started to combine their drink with various additives, at that time largely legal. At the Cavern, compère Bob Wooler might introduce a band as 'the boys with the Benzedrine beat'.

Another element was the shifting economic tides, as Atlantic shipping declined and trade with Europe expanded, benefitting southern and eastern ports but destroying the Liverpool docks. The year after the Misuse of Drugs Act was passed, Parliament voted to join the European Economic Community, which accelerated the movement of trade from Britain's west to east coast.

Nonetheless, a new type of transatlantic product began to take off just as the docks' legitimate trade reached its nadir. And as with the slave trade two centuries earlier, although Liverpool made a late entrance to the industry, it soon came to dominate, becoming the major UK centre for the international drug trade.

As early as the 1980s, London distributors were travelling up to Liverpool to buy wholesale heroin and cocaine, mostly imported through the Bootle and Garston docks. (The first crack factory in the UK was discovered in a house on Kelvin Grove in Granby in the 1980s.)

There are many similarities between the drugs business and the legitimate shipping that used to dominate the Scouse economy. Brendan Wyatt, who became addicted to heroin in the early 1990s, told Simon Hughes that from the whole period he only remembered Sunday mornings, because 'the dealers had their day off – just like the dockers used to on a Sunday'.

The big increase in drug importation during this time fuelled the '90s gang war in nearby Manchester, as rival groups competed for distribution of drugs transported by Scousers into the larger Manchester market, the two cities' underworlds replicating the relationship that existed between them in the nineteenth century.

When Operation Crayfish – the police campaign against Curtis Warren – seized a van in West Derby containing 110 kilos of ecstasy, 97 kilos of amphetamine, 10 kilos of cocaine, 3 kilos of heroin and 40 kilos of cannabis – one officer estimated that it was about a week or two's supply for Merseyside.

By the 1990s, the city's pre-eminence in the newly vitalised UK drug trade was assured, and it was well placed to capitalise on the MDMA/ ecstasy boom fuelled by rave culture. Scouse villains had extensive contacts in the Netherlands, where most of the MDMA was made, and soon set up labs of their own, usually in North Wales.

Between October 2000 and February 2003, over one tonne of cocaine was found in customs seizures at Liverpool seaport. Although many drugs seized are/were destined to be consumed elsewhere, it is likely that drugs entering through the city's port help keep local prices low (e.g., in 2002, a gram of cocaine cost £40–60 in Liverpool compared with £65 across the UK).

A friend of mine whose family was vaguely connected with these things used to joke to me that if drugs all disappeared from the face of the earth, then the economy of Liverpool would collapse, never to recover. For many decades now, peddling substances has provided many in the city with a lifestyle that would otherwise have been well beyond their means.

A journalist in the *Independent on Sunday* remarked that:

> One of the greatest mysteries is where the money comes from.
> Strangers are struck by the run-down feel of a once-great port
> that has fallen on hard times. Yet, amid boarded-ups shops,
> there are pockets of wealth: a designer-clothes shop, a flashy
> night club . . . Expensive cars cruise the streets, and a remarkable

proportion of the kids flaunt mobile phones. They cannot all be the dependents of Premier League footballers.

The transformation of music and drugs during the 1990s had a broader effect on working-class culture, as hooligans became ravers and depleted the ranks of the casual firms. Whereas around 2000, certain nightlife venues and their patrons would have been strongly associated with either alcohol or drug use, now both are commonly consumed by the same individual on a night out.

As well as the more hedonistic and even aspirational drugs, such as ecstasy and cocaine, Liverpool proved a ready market for heroin. Enterprising Liverpool dealers rebranded heroin as 'smack' – it was 'like a Saatchi & Saatchi campaign' in the words of The Farm's Peter Hooton, according to Simon Hughes. It was hard to persuade people to take heroin due to its association with addiction, poverty and HIV; but smack was promoted as a party drug to be sniffed, with no needles, infections or addiction. People were told that, 'You don't get addicted . . . you have it at the weekend then leave it', says Hooton.

Conspiracy theories argue that, as with crack in the United States during the same period, the importation of heroin into Liverpool and other UK cities during this period was a deliberate ploy to quell a restive population and make the neoliberal medicine of the era more palatable.

It is true that in the aftermath of the Toxteth uprising there was a reduced police presence in that area, but Merseyside's smack problem was not dominated by Liverpool 8; instead, hotspots included notably white areas such as Cantrill Farm and, across the water, Birkenhead; it is estimated that 9 per cent of 16–24-year-olds in Birkenhead were regular heroin users at this time.

The spread of heroin inevitably led recorded crime to climb by 25 per cent in 1981, 15 per cent in 1982 and 13 per cent in 1983. Burglaries went up by 20 per cent and crimes involving firearms almost doubled.

Against stiff competition, Liverpool has a strong claim to be Britain's thirstiest city.

The day after the 2017 General Election, the Grapes pub in the city centre attracted criticism after banning Dan Carden, newly elected MP for Liverpool Walton, due to complaints of people in his company engaging in overenthusiastic celebration of his victory.

In a public statement the landlords said that they 'do not tolerate screaming, shouting, chanting or standing on furniture . . . We do not allow large noisy groups to dominate the pub and ruin everyone else's evening. This includes stags, hens, political parties.'

Knowing Carden personally, I was certain that the accusations must have been false. But I was also worried: would this incident damage his political career before it even started?

Turns out I shouldn't have worried. In an article the next day, the *Liverpool Echo* reported on their readers' reactions to the city's newest MP being barred from a pub – and noted that 'it seems to have done wonders for his popularity'.

Hundreds of different *Echo* readers commented on the story, with the majority of readers supportive of Carden. One said: 'He's a proper Scouser now,' while another pointed out that his 'mum works for the NHS, dad was a docker, now he's banned from a pub for partying too hard. He's a proper Scouse MP'. One constituent added: 'He should have invited the Walton girls. He's deffo one of us. Lovely lad, we'll have to take him on a bender.'

The landlords of the Grapes, meanwhile, were roundly criticised: 'Absolute bores. What a terrible advert for a pub, you can't have a good celebration in one.' It even caused some people to change their mind about Carden: 'I take it back, I like him!'

Apparently, the next day, the Grapes contacted Carden to apologise, and offer a photoshoot of him behind the bar, pouring a pint, to show that all was well. He didn't take them up on their offer.

In 2023, my wife and I went to Primavera music festival in Barcelona and took the opportunity to visit our friend Paddy, who lives just outside of the city in the beach-side suburb of Badalona. The three of us went for lunch with a woman from Liverpool who was also in town for the festival. She had travelled with her friend, and when we asked where her friend was, she explained that she had a liver condition and didn't normally drink, but last night she had had a few and 'her eyeballs turned yellow'.

'Don't worry,' she added, clocking the worried look on our faces, 'she'll be back on it tonight though.'

Liverpool's love of a drink should not be glamourised. A recent nationwide study of alcohol dependency estimated that 2.53 people in every 100 people in the city were alcohol dependent. Only four places in the UK had a higher rate: Blackpool, with 3.5 people per 100, and, perhaps surprisingly, Southampton with 2.65 – showing how the cultural legacy of hard-drinking sailors and dockers outlasts the death of their industries.

Meanwhile, the city's venues, particularly off-licences, are not exactly sticklers for preventing underaged drinking. I knew someone whose uncle used to work for trading standards, and he roped us in to work as grasses for the council, targeting off-licences that sold alcohol to underage kids. We were fifteen and definitely looked like it. If we were asked how old we were, we had to tell them the truth. So all people had to do was ask us our age – they didn't even have to ask for ID.

You might be shocked by how many people clearly didn't give a shit and would happily sell booze to blatantly underage lads, even though they might have suspected that the council would target them due to their reputation, and despite the fact one of the lads had a suspicious bag that definitely looked like it could have a camera in it. It was not quite at the level of the Simpson's episode when Homer conceals a camera inside a giant cowboy hat, but it wasn't far off.

It's been this way for a very long time. In the eighteenth century the dockside districts of the city were rammed with pubs and gin shops dispensing ale and liquors at all hours of the day and night. By the Victorian era, there were forty-six different pubs within a 150-yard radius of the Sailors' Home in Canning Place.

In an attempt to divert people from the gin and hard liquors on offer in pubs, Parliament passed the Beer House Act in 1830, which allowed anyone who could pay the two guineas registration fee to open their home as a 'beer house'. This only made access to beer even easier; by 1834, Liverpool boasted at least 700 beer houses as well as around 1,500 pubs.

They also had a high level of turnover: one survey from 1873 found that 904 people passed through one pub in just four hours of a Sunday evening.

At this time, there were no licensing laws and many pubs opened early in the morning, to allow dockers and other workers to have a quick eye-opener before starting work. In one bar by the docks, the owner would have 300 to 400 glasses of spirits lined up on the bar ready at 6 a.m.

Loose licensing was based on free market ideas; the hope was that good pubs would replace worse pubs due to the pressure of competition – in reality, it just led to more pubs.

Naturally, all this boozing led to and exacerbated serious social problems. In 1851, the chaplain of Kirkdale gaol reported that: 'two thirds of those who come before me are in some way or other indebted to the public house or the gin-shop for their appearance within these walls'.

There were untold cases of drunken violence and rowdiness: in his 1869 report the head constable said he hoped that public drunkenness had peaked, with a record 18,303 charges in that year – but, by 1874, it had increased to some 23,303 cases, and yet only three publicans were convicted for permitting drunkenness.

This affected women almost as much as men, and led to some particularly sad reports: in one instance, a mother of seven children who, having already sold everything else, went to a barber and sold him locks of her hair so she could buy some beer. On another occasion, a woman who had sold all her clothes stood at a bar drinking in only her chemise – when asked jokingly by the publican if she would sell that too, she took it off and finished her drink naked.

Nor was this confined to the adult population: in 1876, 353 of those convicted for public drunkenness were under twelve years old. The lack of proper licensing laws was one reason for childhood drinking; another was that their parents would send them to pick up booze for them and they would get a taste for it.

One commentator observed 'ragged children' who would come to pubs in the city with 'old shaving mugs or broken-nosed teapots' to get a little beer for their parents' evening meal. The anti-poverty campaigner Father Nugent observed a five-year-old girl having two gulps from a bottle of rum she was carrying home for her parents, and a three-year-old getting served in a pub.

At one children's home, a newly arrived seven-year-old girl asked the matron at bedtime, 'if it wasn't time to have her gin?' A nine-year-old girl admitted to the Children's Shelter had delirium tremens from withdrawal symptoms – previously her parents would get her drunk and make her sing in pubs for money. Brewers even gave publicans toffees stamped with the name of the pub to hand out to their child clientele.

The national and local authorities made some token efforts to deal with the problem, but they met with fierce resistance: on 3 November 1872, there were two protests against 9 p.m. closing times on Sundays, attended by around 20,000 people. Toxteth Park banned pubs in the 1890s, becoming the largest 'dry' area in England, but it didn't do much to stop the imbibing of its 50,000 residents, who just crossed into Liverpool to get their hooch, while merchants were regularly seen dropping off booze and collecting empties.

In 1896, Liverpool became the first city to force publicans not to serve alcohol to children under thirteen. But the next year, the brewers, merchants and publicans fought back, presenting the local authorities with a petition calling for the age to be lowered to ten.

Although alcohol abuse was common across the UK, and especially in port cities, Liverpool was an outlier. In the year 1889, the number of charges for drunkenness was six times the number of Birmingham. At the start of the twentieth century, the fruit pastille magnate and poverty campaigner Joseph Rowntree catalogued regional levels of drunkenness in England and Wales in his book *The Temperance Problem and Social Reform*, ranking areas from 'Level 1', which had fewer than 150 drunkenness offences per 100,000 people, to 'Level 6', with more than 1,000 offences per 100,000 people. Only two areas – Durham and Northumberland, and Lancashire – were graded Level 6.

The author Hippolyte Taine reported after a visit to the city during this period: 'I know of no place where drunkenness is so flaunted, so impudent, not only in the crooked side streets and mean courtyards where one expects to find it, but everywhere' – and he was French!

This hedonistic, nihilist attitude has long been present on Merseyside. The American novelist Nathaniel Hawthorne observed that a labourer, eating oysters before lighting a pipe, exhibited 'perfect coolness and independence' characteristic of people in Liverpool. 'Here,' wrote Hawthorne, 'a man does not seem to consider what other people will think of his conduct but whether it suits his convenience to do so.'

This attitude is not incompatible with a strong work ethic; Curtis Warren became the most successful drug dealer in Europe through many factors, not least hard work and professionalism. But even Warren and his cronies were not above randomly taking a day off to go fishing and get pissed. One of the police officers involved in Operation

Crayfish noted that 'they were one of the most active drug gangs in Europe yet some mornings they would get up and one would say, "Why don't we go fishing?" And off they would go to spend the day by the canal.'

This attitude is not laziness, but more of a way of sticking two fingers up to authority and trying to take back control of your own time. Workers in factories such as those that dominated the rest of the industrial north had a tradition where workers observed by a foreman would deliberately slow down, work to rule and use other methods to lower and frustrate production without doing anything so obvious as to get sacked. It was a way of resisting the dominance of the boss and the employer – what could now be called 'Quiet Quitting'.

Given the unusual labour conditions in Liverpool, workers in the city usually didn't have this option, so dockers and sailors would rebel in other ways. One of these was thieving, which was understood as legitimate reward for the hazards, low pay and hard work of their jobs.

This taste for booze owes a lot to the city's economic heritage; both dockers and sailors were notorious drinkers, and cared more about quantity than the quality of their hooch: on board ships sailors would often drink 'swipes' – the dregs from beer barrels that were collected and sold cheaply to ship's captains.

Even Liverpool housewives, despite their lengthy days of domestic drudgery, still managed to find time for what historian John Belchem described as 'bibulous conviviality, good cheer and personal indulgence' – as demonstrated by the traditional Monday 'tea party', held after the weekly visit to pawn their clothes:

> On these occasions there appeared to be no lack of meat or drink, and immediately after the arrival of each visitor a little girl would be sent off to the grog shop for spirits . . . There was generally a

great bustle to get all indications of the tea party cleared off before the time at which the husbands might be expected home – that is supposing them to be at work – and the women separated with very loud protestations of friendship for each other.

In preparation for the city's 750th anniversary celebrations in 1957, the council cracked down on the numerous unlicensed drinking dens in the city centre, forcing them to decamp a few hundred feet into Toxteth, where illegal drinking clubs began to profligate.

By their peak in the 1980s, there were estimated to be over five hundred pubs and clubs in Liverpool. Today, the city is one of the busiest in the UK for stag and hen parties, and this attitude is absorbed by the people who live there, who likewise give visitors to the city the sense that everyone is out to get rat-arsed, even if, for them, it's a normal weekend.

INTERLUDE 9

Birds

The life of a working-class Liverpool housewife – much like her equivalent elsewhere in the country – had a set routine: Friday was payday, when her husband would turn over most of his wage, keeping a little back for his own beer and tobacco money. Then she would go to the pawnshop to repay the debt incurred on Monday and get back their Sunday clothes. She would then pay the week's bills and buy food. Three days later, the weekend over and the family money spent, she would take their Sunday best again to the pawn shop and borrow enough to make it through the week.

This was complicated by unreliable husbands. Although there was a great deal of social stigma towards men who did not provide for their family and kept too much (or nearly all) of their wages back for themselves, many men still did it. Sometimes they were alcoholics, or sometimes just wanted to make their wife beg for every shilling and penny.

This was complicated even more by the casual labour market. In most areas, apart from when unemployment spiked during periodic recessions, a miner or steelworker could usually expect to be in work and be paid the same amount each week. This was not the case with the docker, who might have only worked one or two days that week, or not at all, or with the sailor, who'd come home with a decent wage packet, enough to cover the next few weeks, but with no guarantee he'd be able to find another ship before that money ran out.

For those women who had the financial support of a husband, they still had to deal with (or sometimes enjoy) the prolonged absence of up to a quarter of the men in the city. And there was a non-negligible chance on any given trip that their husband would die or simply disappear, never to be heard from again.

Around 40 per cent of Liverpool men made stipulations in their will that property left to their wife should be earmarked for the upkeep of their children – apparently, out of concern that their wife would remarry and take their bequest to their new husband – a much higher figure than elsewhere in Britain. Liverpool women themselves were more likely than men to leave property to daughters in preference to sons, sometimes stating the reason why: their sons were feckless or had run off, whereas their daughters were loyal and sensible.

Compared to other cities, a much higher proportion of wives and mothers were left as the head of households for long periods of time. And the large number of women rated as liable to pay taxes suggests that many also owned property in their own right, rather than through their husbands. One woman, the aptly named Cicely Cook, was abandoned by her husband but went on to have considerable success after setting up her own bakery. Legal documents show a woman called Katherine Cottingham registered as a milliner and established her own flourishing business making and mending hats. Margaret Heald, described as a midwife in her will, amassed a fortune of £817 – equivalent to hundreds of thousands of pounds today.

For the wives of prosperous merchants, a husband's early death usually did not come with the threat of penury but instead a large inheritance. Mary Fleetwood, widow of glass magnate James Fleetwood, took over the family business on the death of her husband and ran it in her own name for two decades. Sarah Clayton inherited her husband's coal mine and used the money to build Clayton Square, while Margery Formby inherited her husband's sixteen-room mansion, which was later reported to be 'well stocked' with 'wine, beer and ale'.

Having said this, there is little record of women in paid employment – of almost 20,000 marriage and burial records from 1660–1750, under twenty state a female occupation. This is another way that Liverpool women were different from those elsewhere in the North; in the cotton and wool districts of Lancashire and Yorkshire, young working-class women would normally work in mills and factories, and have the same regular employment as the men (until they got married). This kind of steady (albeit poorly paid and highly dangerous) work was not open to women in Liverpool, who were usually even more dependent on the irregular wages of a casually employed husband.

This meant that Liverpool women had to find work in more eccentric ways; of the twenty stated occupations for women in the 1660–1750 period, one woman is described as a 'brewer' and another as a 'comedian' – two very apt jobs for a Scousewife.

But for most women forced to work for a living, outside of prostitution, the most common occupation was hawking goods on the street, which was technically illegal and punishable by a fine. When they couldn't pay, they'd be locked up, and this contributed to Liverpool's record number of female prisoners.

The ferocity of Liverpool women was yet another way in which the city was an outlier. According to one local journalist, 'when a Liverpool woman's tongue is loosed nobody in this world can rival her in the production of foul and bestial language. She is an oral cesspool – a philological sewer.' Such was the reputation of some of the city's female crooks, they were handed punishments more usually dealt to male criminals, as in 1776, when Ellen Berry and Ann Melling were flogged for stealing hand towels and a guinea coin from a gentleman's household.

On one occasion in Brownlow Hill workhouse, a dozen women, described by Josephine Butler as 'the most violent, strong amazons' in the place, were arrested for beating one of the matrons to death. Another four beat and nearly killed a female worker for threatening to inform the matron when they refused to work.

Up until 1933, HMP Walton was a mixed prison, and the one-time deputy governor Basil Thomson testified that 'as a rule, the men were easy to manage, but when it came to the women, the mere male prison official had to take his chance'.

In addition to prostitution and street-hawking, 'child stripping' was another common occupation for Liverpool women. This involved targeting children playing in the street, ideally those wearing as many clothes as possible (children wearing extra layers during the winter were particularly good catches), and stealing their clothes to sell. The ideal age was three years old, when a child would be let outside to play, but was still too naive to know what was happening.

In 1849, a woman called Eliza Thompson was charged with luring kids down back alleys and getting them to take their boots off by pretending she wanted to buy a pair for her own children. In December 1861, Mary Slater was found guilty of taking an eighteen-month-old to a communal toilet, stealing his clothes and leaving him crying in the dirt. In August 1869, after Ann Quinn was arrested on suspicion of child stripping, a search of her home found sixteen hats, twenty pairs of stockings, three frocks, three pairs of boots and twenty pawn tickets.

Child stripping, though shocking, usually did not involve violence. But just as domestic violence against women was endemic and unremarked upon, violence against children within the home was shockingly common. In 1868, courts returned murder verdicts in the cases of twenty children under one year of age. Given that most killings likely went undetected, the true number of child murders would have been even higher.

Sometimes this was done for financial gain: an 1888 committee of the Liverpool Society for the Prevention of Cruelty to Children found that a 'disturbingly high' percentage of the children 'accidentally' smothered by their parents had been insured, with their parents gaining cash settlements upon their deaths.

In other cases, it was done more out of desperation. Bridget Hale, a domestic servant, was found to have given birth in the home of her employers when the afterbirth was discovered in the toilet. The baby could not be found, and Bridget at first denied being pregnant, but eventually admitted that she had just had a child. The body of a newborn female was found in the coal vault, its skull fractured with a hammer, and Bridget was given two years' imprisonment for concealment of a birth.

11

GRAFTERS

In September 1991, on a hot, humid day in Caracas, Venezuela, three men met at the headquarters of the Conar Corporation. One was Mario Halley, of Colombia's Cali cartel (recently made famous by the Netflix series *Narcos*), another was a bespectacled man from Middlesborough, Brian Charrington. The final person was a bull-necked, mixed-race skinhead from Liverpool called Curtis Warren.

The Cali cartel had a business proposition for Warren: the increased attention from the Colombian government and the United States' Drug Enforcement Agency meant that their routes into the USA were becoming increasingly fraught and profits were taking a hit.

They wanted to branch out into Europe in a big way, seeing the continent as a relatively untapped resource. Unlike the US, in Europe cocaine was still relatively rare and expensive in the early '90s. The Colombians, having previously experimented with human 'mules' bringing through small amounts, wanted to scale up their operations and secure consistent and reliable routes to send hundreds of kilos into the European market. They wanted to make cocaine use as commonplace as cannabis for young Europeans.

Unlike weed, speed, ecstasy and MDMA, which tended to be used by specific groups of people, cocaine could appeal to a varied cross-section: it might be used by football hooligans and hippies, students and musicians, bankers and builders.

They needed somewhere with established port facilities and transport links. They needed people with connections in Europe and Asia, who were experienced in the intricacies of the drug trade, and with the necessary proficiency in violence. Warren knew just the place.

Curtis Warren was born in May 1963, a few weeks after the release of the Beatles' first album. By this point, Liverpool had already been branded the 'number one UK centre of excellence for drug smuggling' by a British customs officer. Much of this was due to the collaboration between the traditional, white-dominated Liverpool mafia and the younger, so-called 'Black Caucus' based in the Granby area of Liverpool 8.

Historically, the Liverpool mafia had tried to avoid violence as much as possible, preferring to focus on less risky and more lucrative economic crimes. Their main income came from the docks, where they made millions through smuggling and thieving. Their profits were heightened by the huge black market created by the Second World War and subsequent rationing. The Liverpool police report for 1945 found that 'on many occasions a whole lorry load of goods was stolen' directly off the quayside.

During the war, American soldiers based in the city had to resort to assigning special units of troops to guard their cigarettes, food and other supplies from Scouse thieves. After the war, US musical and cultural influences continued to stream across the Atlantic, contributing to the development of a youth counter culture and increasing the use of drugs such as cannabis and amphetamines. By the 1950s, Liverpool accounted for a third of all UK drug prosecutions. At this point, there was already an established cannabis market in Toxteth, allegedly run by a man whose nickname was 'Bull', originally from Jamaica.

In 1960, the Beatles were introduced to drugs backstage at the Jacaranda, on Slater Street, by the beat poet Royston Ellis, who the band were supporting that night. According to George Harrison, 'Ellis had discovered that if you open a Vick's inhaler you find Benzedrine in it, impregnated into the cardboard divide.' As Lennon recalled: 'Everybody thought, "Wow! What's this?" and talked their mouths off for a night.'

It was the same factors that led to casual culture – the opening up of cheap foreign travel and an increasingly wealthy population – that also helped to create modern drug consumption habits in the UK. And then it wasn't long before organised crime moved in and took control of the market. Old-school hippies like the Oxford-educated Howard Marks were quickly supplanted by hardened criminals, as 'the headbands gave way to the headcases' in the words of *Guardian* crime reporter Duncan Campbell.

That said, many of those on the bottom rung of drug smuggling were ordinary people in desperate circumstances: when ten men were caught underloading a shipping container loaded with cannabis at Seaforth docks in 1981, most of them were unemployed dockers.

At this time, drugs were not a particularly lucrative product in L8. Cannabis was still the main drug being traded in the city, and its market was limited. In the new Liverpool that would emerge after the '80s, the criminals would have bigger ambitions. Their banking contacts – amassed over decades of industrial money-laundering – were one of the many factors that enabled them to get into the drugs market during this time.

At first, Liverpool gangsters had looked down on drugs, associating them with 'black' crime in a city where the underworld was heavily segregated. By the 1980s, however, there was just too much money to be made. After fourteen-year-old Jason Fitzgibbons died of a heroin overdose, his uncle Tony Murray swore: 'When I find out who did it, then they are dead. I will do it with my bare hands if I have to. These people are nothing but rats. They are scum of the earth. They should be wiped off the face of the earth.' A few years later he was imprisoned for plotting to import heroin worth one million pounds.

Despite their initial reluctance, drugs, particularly cannabis and heroin, had become the most lucrative operation for the Liverpool mafia. The city's gangsters were also becoming better connected with their equivalents elsewhere; in 1980, Delroy Showers (who along with his brother Michael was believed to be a key member of the Granby crew) was arrested in London in the company of Charlie Richardson, notorious head of the eponymous south London gang.

At the centre of this network was Tommy 'Tacker' Commerford. According to Ranald Macdonald (his real name) of HM Customs, 'you can chart the entire development of drug smuggling in Britain through Tommy Commerford'.

After being jailed for cannabis smuggling, a re-energised Tacker – now armed with the knowledge and connections gained from his time inside – expanded his empire to organise the importation of heroin, cocaine, amphetamine and LSD. From his Belle Vale council flat, he coordinated with contacts in Colombia, the USA, the Netherlands, Germany, Italy, the UAE and Pakistan.

Another key character was Brian Charrington, originally from Middlesbrough's Hemlington estate. By 1998, Charrington – now a long way from Middlesbrough – was ensconced in a heavily guarded luxury villa on the Costa del Sol. He had a mini fleet of boats, a private helicopter and pet crocodiles in the garden. It was with Charrington that Warren first met the Colombians and set in motion the chain of events that led them to the Caracas office building and the Cali cartel.

The cast of characters was completed by Ussama 'Sammy' El-Kurd, a Jerusalem-born, London-based Palestinian who started off as a tobacconist and, from his High Street Kensington store, became the most prolific money launderer in Europe – and an integral part of the Liverpool mafia's transformation of British drug consumption.

The international reach of Warren's operation was crucial to his dominance of the industry. One senior officer from Operation Crayfish, the campaign tasked with bringing him down, reckoned Warren was one of 'only six or seven people in Europe' with such a diverse network of contacts.

Their plan was to hide the cocaine inside four-foot-long lead ingots – believed to be beyond the reach of the longest drills possessed by UK customs.

In September 1991, nine days before the first shipment was due to sail from Venezuela, Warren and Charrington boarded a ferry at Dover. They arrived at Felixstowe, by this point the UK's biggest port, with automated cranes and forklifts in place of hundreds of teeming dockers. On 30 October 1991, the containers were cleared by customs, and sent by rail and then lorry to Liverpool. Another shipment of 907 kilos had already left Venezuela on board the MV *Advisor*, this time heading directly to Liverpool. This second shipment was intercepted, leading to Warren's arrest.

Although prosecuted alongside Brian Charrington and others in 1992, the trial collapsed due to lack of evidence. In the court building, Warren walked up to the third floor where a few devastated customs officers milled around trying to console each other. Warren walked up to them: 'I'm off to spend my £87 million from the first shipment, and you can't fucking touch me.'

He could now bring in hundreds of kilos of cocaine directly from Colombia, without any middlemen, and flood or starve the market as he saw fit, thus lowering prices to expand his reach or increase them to boost profits.

Warren had a high-level informant within the police and was able to access supposedly confidential reports from law enforcement in the UK, Spain, the Netherlands, Canada and other countries.

It's believed that as early as 1988, a police insider was speaking directly with the Granby firm. The frequency with which this happened made the bizzies suspect something was up. The terrifying thing was that it had to be someone very senior.

It turns out it was Detective Chief Inspector Elmore 'Elly' Davies, then deputy head of the Merseyside Police drug squad. He had thirty years' service in the force and his son had followed him into policing.

In 1998, he was convicted of disclosing information to pervert the course of justice, becoming the most senior British police officer jailed for corruption in modern times. Warren bought him for around £20,000.

Hilariously, Warren's link to Davies was Mick Ahearne, better known as 'Warrior' from the hugely popular '90s TV show *Gladiators*. Before his time beating PE teachers with inflatable clubs, Ahearne shared a flat with Davies. Although their paths subsequently diverged, one to Saturday nights on ITV and the other into the seedier parts of the Liverpool underworld, the light entertainer and the corrupt cop had stayed in touch.

Ahead of Christmas 1996, Ahearne invited Warren and his long-term associate Tony Bray down to Kent to see him appearing in panto alongside fellow Scouser Stan Boardman. Although it makes a compelling image – the most important man in European drug distribution sat among the families, roaring with laughter at the antics of Window Twanky, etc – unfortunately, Warren declined the invitation.

When Warrior was arrested as part of the investigation into Warren (there is no record of whether he was wearing his *Gladiators* outfit at the time) he protested: 'You can't arrest me, I'm a children's icon!' The bizzies were unmoved.

Warren used his inside information to threaten and intimidate the officers investigating his ill deeds. After his arrest for the lead ingots shipment, Warren saw one of the West Midlands customs officers who were in Liverpool, and greeted him: 'You're with the West Midlands

County Council, staying in the Adelphi, right?' This became even more sinister when a letter was sent to the *Echo* with the names and addresses of senior customs agents and a promise of £25,000 for the death of each one.

On another occasion, two suspicious-looking old steel containers in Granby were drenched in petrol and set on fire by local scallies – inside were five police officers who had been spying on a property used by Warren – they just about escaped with their lives.

In addition to his connections and comfort with ultra-violence, Warren was a hard worker with a keen eye for detail; on one occasion early in his career, frustrated by the shoddy wrapping of packages of cannabis being smuggled from Spain into France, he went to a warehouse himself to personally show the mules the best way the wrap the goods.

He became the only drug dealer to feature on the *Sunday Times* rich list. Although estimates of his fortune varied, he was believed to own hundreds of properties in Liverpool, Wales, Turkey, Spain and Gambia, as well as diverse other investments such as a football club (Barrow AFC) and at least one brothel.

By this point, the Liverpool mafia's reach stretched across the world; in Ireland they came into conflict with the IRA after they successfully infiltrated the highly profitable Dublin heroin market and ended up the biggest suppliers to the city. They made one of their largest markups in Australia, where ecstasy selling at £10–12 per tablet and speed at £10 a gram could fetch as much as £40 or £45 in Sydney. Soon they were the leading suppliers of MDMA and amphetamine in New South Wales.

The volume of drugs being brought into Liverpool by the city's criminals led to a vicious gang war in the city during the 1990s. One of Warren's key lieutenants, Johnny Philips, was shot in March 1996, and only avoided bleeding to death because his blood was so thick from steroids. Tit-for-tat strikes broke out across the city; a fight in Childwall, a shooting in Old Swan.

On 18 April, a Granby hit squad set out and shot one teenager four times at his home in Old Swan, kneecapped someone else in Bootle and took prisoner another suspected rival and his girlfriend. They were worried that they had the wrong man but shot him anyway, three times in the left leg, three times in the right and once in his right arm. Their victim, who was left on the carpet and nearly bled to death, was 24-year-old police constable Stephen Hardy. In another notorious gangland incident from this time, four men tried to chop off a victim's feet.

By this point, Warren himself had moved to the Netherlands. Despite being a multi-millionaire, able to retire and live in comfort for the rest of his life, he continued to graft. The Dutch police, alongside international colleagues, were onto him, recording his telephone conversations with associates back in Liverpool, and arrested Warren on drug importation charges in 1996.

The raid on his home in Sassenheim found three guns, hand grenades, 400 kilos of cocaine, 1,500 kilos of hash, 60 kilos of heroin, 50 kilos of ecstasy pills, plus 400,000 Dutch guilders and $600,000 in cash.

This time, it looked as though he was going away for good. His arrest produced panic in Liverpool, concern in Colombia and had ripple effects as far away as Soviet Russia, where one man was killed after he could not fulfil his cocaine supply promises due to the loss of Warren's connection.

Sentenced to twelve years in prison by the Dutch authorities, the only way that Warren had any hope of early release was if he could pay the money the Dutch were demanding in their request to seize his assets. And he had an ingenious idea.

Back in 1992, when the police had raided Brian Charrington's home in Middlesbrough and found £2.5 million in cash, everyone denied it belonged to them – no one was about to claim that these proceeds of drug trafficking were rightfully theirs. Therefore, the money was put into a bank account for criminal proceeds, where it had been gathering interest.

By 2003, however, circumstances had changed: the newly created Assets Recovery Agency had been set up to allow the UK government to seize these unclaimed gains of illegal activity.

Warren had to convince the High Court that the money was rightfully his, and then use it to pay the Dutch – reducing his sentence by as much as six years.

To do this, he would need to confess that he masterminded the first shipment. Taking advantage of 'double jeopardy', by which a person cannot be tried twice for the same offence, that is exactly what he did. It was audacious, and complicated by the fact that both Charrington and Mario Halley were doing the same thing.

This led to a bizarre *Life of Brian*-style situation, whereby three different drug dealers were all trying to claim that they were the real owners of the £2.2 million – now £3.5 million with the accumulated interest.

It didn't work – the government claimed the money and Warren's chance for early release was gone – but he did at least get the Crown to pay for his legal expenses.

While in prison, he was involved in an altercation with notorious Turkish gangster Cemal Guclu, who was serving a sentence for murder and attempted murder; in the fracas that followed, Warren beat the Turk to death, getting another four years for manslaughter.

Six years after the Guclu incident, Warren was charged with conspiracy to smuggle drugs from his prison cell – although his conviction was overturned on appeal and he was released in 2007. That same year, he was arrested while back in the UK, accused of planning to smuggle tons of cannabis into the UK via Jersey. This time he was sentenced to thirteen years in prison.

Warren was finally released from jail in 2022 – although not before having an affair with a prison officer, Stephanie Smithwhite, who was given a two-year sentence in 2020 after admitting misconduct in public office. Smithwhite had denied cutting a hole in her uniform trousers for sexual purposes, but the sentencing judge said it was hard to imagine why else it was there.

At the time of writing, Warren is a free man, but he has spent most of the last thirty years behind bars. In that time, he amassed a fortune, becoming Britain's most successful drug dealer. He was instrumental in flooding Europe with drugs in the 1990s, and did more than any other individual to change cocaine from something rare and unusual into Britain's national drug.

INTERLUDE 10

Scallies

Understanding the concept of the scally is fundamental to understanding the modern Liverpudlian identity.

The first thing to understand about the word 'scally' is that it is not a Scouse version of 'chav'. It is much more definitive than 'chav', and is definitely not a term of classist abuse. Instead, it means someone whose violence and criminal behaviour goes beyond the accepted toleration of such things among Scousers.

Although it comes from the Irish and Lancastrian term 'scallywag', that word implies a loveable scamp or a bit of a rogue. Scally, however, could refer to anyone from an ordinary lad who liked the odd bit of theft or violence, through to full-time gangsters or community terrorists.

The word scally being used in this way is itself fairly new – only a few decades ago, a scally was called a 'buck'. Nowadays, if you used the word 'buck' in Liverpool, you could expect to emerge ridiculed at best. Especially if you said it to a scally.

As one old Liverpool police officer told the authors of *Cocky*, a 2001 biography of Warren: 'A buck's a buck and it's the first thing you notice about him. You can spot one a hundred yards off, even before he turns round and speaks to you. It's the way they behave.' A buck could be described as 'a young man, strong and lawless, who lives for the day and hangs the consequences. A buck trades on wild masculinity, gratuitous violence and contempt for social mores.' By 1975, a quarter of all prosecutions and a quarter of all police cautions in Liverpool were for juveniles.

For the 1982 version, a bricklayer called Phil Jones reported that 'the younger scals tend to have flicks, wear their jeans too tight and too long. Short-collared shirts, Slazenger jumpers and trainers "zapped" from Europe. Also if it's cold they either wear sheepskin coats or anoraks . . . and maybe sheepskin mittens, borrowed off their sister.'

(I strongly advise you not to approach contemporary scallies in a sheepskin coat and ask them where they 'zapped' their trainers from.)

'The older scals are different,' conceded Jones, but no stranger to the modern scal sensibility: 'they wore tweed or corduroy jackets'. So there you have it: scallies used to wear tweed coats.

The journalist Stuart Maconie, in his book on the north of England, wrote that:

> they are a distinctive tribe, identifiable for their penchant for Rockport, Henri Lloyd and Lacoste brands . . . hang around Huyton bus station and you will see scores of weasel-faced youths dressed like this, pallid from lack of vitamin C and generally looking for something to urinate on or set fire to. Plastic Scousers of this ilk have no interest in being witty, vital or revolutionising popular music but merely in being thought of as hard or criminal.

Attributing Anthony Walker's death to 'the wrong kind of Scousers', Maconie continued: 'Scousers have "plazzies" because they aren't real Scousers but cheap wannabes with no style.' This is tempting to believe, but it is not true. It's a fantasy to say that 'real' Scousers would not and have not engaged in scally behaviour, up to and including racially motivated murder.

Like anyone, I've had run-ins with scallies myself. On one occasion after my A Levels I was drinking at the VR Bar on Bold Street where you could pay £10 – I had to double check it really was £10, even in 2005 – and then drink all night for free. Someone must have also been spiking my drink with MDMA because for some reason I was showing signs of having consumed loads of it.

Anyway, we were at a petrol station on Queen's Drive when we were accosted by some scallies, one of whom apparently headbutted me. I don't remember much but, apparently, I bled all over my mate Nick Matchett's bath. I had a badly bruised nose for a few days but told my mum I fell over drunk, and she accepted that as likely.

A few years before that, I was punched in the face by one of two schoolboy louts who accosted me in West Derby. They went to the rival Cardinal Heenan (or could have been West Derby comp) school and took exception to my purple blazer. Another time, two other lads and I were 'legged' from some girl's house to the relative protection of the Eaton Road shops.

I always wondered: do scallies know that they are scallies?

In the TV show *Little Boy Blue*, the dramatisation of the events surrounding the murder of Rhys Jones, his killer Sean Mercer is shown having dinner with his family, who offer their support to him. Mercer's mother Janette was jailed for three years for perverting the course of justice after lying to provide her son with an alibi.

James Yates and Dean Kelly were jailed after supplying the firearm and helping to hide Mercer when he was on the run after the killing. And Yates' mum Marie and her husband Frank were jailed for eighteen months after admitting perverting justice and burning evidence.

Some blame such actions on the decline of families and traditions; however, in many cases, the people who do these things come from strong families. Except that their families are scallies and their traditions are based around violence, crime and thuggery. Sean Mercer's father,

Joe McCormick, was an associate of Curtis Warren back in the '80s and '90s.

But if today's scallies are bad, given the horrendous lives lived by many children in the city over numerous generations, it is surprising that they aren't worse.

One Victorian observer recalled after a tour of the slums: 'There are children everywhere. Children carrying children: mothers of fifteen carrying their diminutive offspring of three and four months . . . their tiny backs and chests deformed and distorted by the strain . . . Children – poor little wretches – whose faces are one mass of scrofulous sores – recording symptoms of hereditary venereal disease.'

For nearly the whole of the nineteenth century, Liverpool had the worst rate of infant mortality in England and Wales. For much of that time, one in every three children died before their first birthday, so a family of a dozen children (the average family size in Catholic parts of Liverpool) could expect to have buried four or five of them. A study covering the years 1899–1900 found that the infant death rate among alcoholic women in Walton prison was 56 per cent, but among the non-alcoholic inmates it was still 24 per cent.

Disease was the main killer, but children also died from easily preventable accidents; in just six weeks at the start of 1847, twenty-one children under twelve died from burns in the home, which were caused by them lifting kettles from fires, trying to cook or just warming themselves.

Horrendous violence against children was also commonplace. A baker on Great Howard Street was so annoyed by lads playing near his shop that when some of them were loitering on top of his cellar grid, he thrust a sharpened stick through the grating, causing a serious injury to the genitals of one of the young scallies. In another incident, when a ten-year-old lad went to the cellar of Eliza Peacock to ask for his mates' football back, she threw a cup of carbolic acid in his face.

Around Christmas of 1866, a woman called Mary Burke was found wandering Scotland Road, holding a six-week-old baby by the legs and threatening to bash its head in. She raised the child above her head but a policeman intervened and snatched the baby before it hit the ground. She was sent to prison for a month.

John Clark of Upper Frederick Street would send his seven-year-old stepdaughter out onto the street to find 'chews' – gobs of chewing tobacco spat out onto the pavement. If she didn't bring any home, he would beat her with a strap. She was taken to hospital with black eyes and her body covered in welts.

Fanny McCaig was a prostitute and alcoholic who had eighteen court appearances for drunkenness. On one occasion, when her ten-year-old daughter couldn't find the iron she had asked her to fetch, she beat the girl with an iron poker before smashing her head against a wall. The child ran outside and was found by a stranger in a field nearby, her nose bleeding and the lower part of her face 'covered in gore'. Upon examination she was found to have wounds all over her body. McCaig was given a month's imprisonment and her daughter sent to the workhouse.

A man named John Mitchell, after a drunken argument with his partner, attacked her four-year-old son and nine-year-old daughter, kicking them with his clogs until they were unconscious, and stamping on their heads. He threw them, lifeless, out into the street, where they were found by police. When he was arrested, he asked if they were dead – on being told they were still alive, he flew into a rage and screamed: 'I'll kick their fucking brains out!' Clumps of their hair were found still stuck in his clogs.

Child sexual abuse was also common at this time, and was particularly pronounced in Liverpool, given the large families, cramped accommodation and widespread drunkenness endemic in the city. John Clare, who owned a brothel on Hotham Street, was imprisoned for two years after he tried to rape his thirteen-year-old daughter while she slept. Charles Dillon, a shopkeeper, was imprisoned for ten years for the rape of a twelve-year-old who had been sent to his shop to buy something for her parents. A man called William Wright was charged with indecent assault on a seven-year-old; the child was too young to give evidence and Wright was discharged.

An old man of seventy, judged medically infirm, tried to rape a ten-year-old girl in Toxteth Park; he was ordered to pay a £5 fine or serve two months in prison. Another old man, John Morris, indecently assaulted a two-year-old girl; he was fined forty shillings plus costs. A Spanish seaman was charged with indecent assault on an eighteen-month-old.

There was an unfortunate superstition at this time that you could cure sexual infections by having sex with a virgin. In July 1848, 21-year-old Thomas Looney was charged with raping his nine-year-old niece after the girl became ill with what was described as a 'loathsome disease'. Peter Conlon was found guilty of passing a 'loathsome disease' to Martha Rooney, a ten-year-old girl, who he lured into his house on the pretext of helping him light a fire. In October 1857, Amos Greenwood joined a travelling show that had been in town, befriended one of the showmen and moved into their lodgings. A syphilitic, he raped Mary Johnson, the family's nine-year-old daughter, and was arrested in Wigan when the girl became unwell and reported what had happened. She died soon afterwards, and Greenwood was jailed for life.

When they weren't raping or beating them, or sending them to buy booze, parents might financially exploit their children to earn a few pence; it was not uncommon for poor mothers to hire out her emaciated youngsters to professional beggars.

All of this meant that, in many cases, the death of one or more parents could be a blessing. One young delinquent, on being asked by a probation officer why he looked so 'bright' that day, said that 'his mother was dead, and now he would have a chance in the world'.

While children were at risk of violence or sexual assault from their own parents or relatives, those without parents were even more vulnerable – one 1867 survey found that 25,000 children were living on the streets of Liverpool without any parents or guardians.

'Already evil in its twofold form of vice and sorrow blocks their pathway in life, to corrupt and afflict them,' said Catholic priest and social reformer Father James Nugent. 'What an existence, what an education, what a future!' In desperation, Nugent set up a child emigration system to remove children from the streets of Liverpool to healthy, wholesome (and Catholic) homes in Canada and elsewhere.

Another priest, Father Berry Homes, published regular reports on the state of the urchin problem, arguing in 1894 that: 'Our criminals are bred in our streets . . . an over-scrupulous regard for parental rights makes English lawgivers hesitate to act . . . In some cases boys who have come to us have been claimed by their parents, and have been forced by them, to our great regret, and, in spite of themselves, to return to the miserable life of a street arab.'

These kids were usually either orphans or their parents were unable to look after them and willingly supported their emigration as a chance for a better life. However, some kids were sent away even when they had living parents who objected to their emigration.

In 1914, Liverpool Girl's Industrial School tried to emigrate one thirteen-year-old girl, Amelia Mason, to Canada, and informed her father of their recommendation that she be sent away for her own good. He was told that if he had any objections 'it is open to you to send to the Home Secretary any representations you desire to make against the emigration of this girl'.

In the application to remove the girl that was sent to the Home Office the school noted that Amelia herself had formally given consent (although given Amelia's age, level of education and the fact that she was living at the school, we cannot be sure how genuine this consent was) and described her father as 'Drunken, Worthless.' Later on in the process, after her father (with the help of local MP Stephen Walsh, who himself grew up in a children's home) appealed against the decision, Amelia said she wanted to stay with family in Liverpool.

Amelia's father sent a letter to the Home Secretary writing 'I object very much,' and argued that his married son Nathaniel could look after her. But the school's opinion of the father counted for more. The school said both parents' 'fecklessness' removed the need for their consent, claiming that both parents were 'of drunken habits' and had previously been convicted of child neglect.

In May 1914, the Home Office agreed that the father should be ignored, praising the school for their 'wise' decision: 'This is a case in which . . . the parents' consent may be dispensed with. The father is a low black-guard, living apart from his family in common lodging-houses, is a drunkard and has been convicted 6 times for child neglect and drunkenness; the mother is also of drunken habits and has been convicted for neglecting her children.'

Given this heritage – of poverty, separated families, drunkenness and dispossession – it should not be surprising that one of its legacies is an unusually high rate of street violence. Considering the lives lived by virtually all of the predecessors of today's Liverpudlians, it's more surprising how stable and happy most people are, as is the relative lack of violent psychopaths given the brutalisation of generations and the centuries when being a violent, snide bastard would help you survive.

I spend more time than I should looking at videos of fights and crim-inality on social media, and you often see in the comments arguments that anyone caught carrying a knife should have a mandatory prison sentence. It's tempting to agree with this, but then I remember that I myself briefly carried a knife. It was found in a tent we had pitched in a park and, fortunately, because a tent is considered a dwelling, and the police had no warrant, they could not use it as evidence against me and I faced no repercussions.

And for many young working-class men, in Liverpool and elsewhere, being a scally is a temporary phase: marriage and kids soon sort them out. The short-lived nature of scallydom for most youths was acknowledged by the former hooligan Andy Nicholls, who noted that when he attends Goodison today, there are men sitting there peacefully with their kids who not so long ago 'were standing there tooled up and ready to cut up the opposition'.

Despite his blatant racism, incompetence and barely veiled disdain for the people he was charged with protecting, former Merseyside chief constable Ken Oxford hit on one notable element of the Liverpudlian character: 'Mythology has it – and I exclude nobody from this – that the area is tough. It has the unfortunate effect that people feel they must react to this and be tough.' Or as the singer John Power put it: 'no one in Liverpool wants to be seen as a victim'.

This has long been a key priority on Merseyside, because the dominance of the maritime industry and shipping – as well as making it the national recordholder for theft, drunkenness and prostitution – meant that Liverpool, for much of its recent history, was the most violent place in Britain.

As well as brutal robberies and assaults, the city was a hotbed for random and often unprovoked violence. Historian John E. Archer argues that the late Victorian era saw a nationwide 'civilising process', whereby street fights and casual violence became more regulated, with unwritten but accepted codes, such as not using weapons. This happened elsewhere in the country from the 1870s, but even by the end of the century, notes Archer, this process 'had not been successfully accomplished in Liverpool'.

According to a 1923 book of sailors' lore and experiences, Paradise Street in the city centre was internationally renowned as a barometer to grade the threat level faced by visitors to other 'sinks of iniquity' and was described bluntly as 'one of the toughest streets in the world'.

Part of this was due to the especially volatile nature of the portside districts and the experience that many Liverpool men had during months away from home in hostile environments. Joseph Conrad wrote in his memoir that 'the crew of Liverpool hard cases' he was with on one voyage 'had in them the right stuff. It's my experience they always have. It is the sea that gives it – the vastness, the loneliness surrounding their dark stolid souls.'

As well as being quick to use fists, Liverpool men had a reputation for kicking in an ungentlemanly manner. Lancashire as a whole was known for 'up and down fighting', which meant kicking opponents even when they were on the floor, with the heavy clogs or iron-tipped boots worn by northern men coming in handy. This offended the middle-class mores developing at the time, by which white men should only use their fists; after a man was kicked to death in a fight in Bolton in 1832, a Manchester newspaper compared the brawlers to 'New Zealand savages, or Hottentot spearmen'.

Likewise, the routine use of knives and other weapons in the city drew comparison to the indigenous nations being encountered by British colonialists; when a police officer was stabbed to death in 1853, the coroner decried the commonplace use knives, stating he preferred a 'stand-up fight with fists' to the use of a weapon 'peculiar to barbarous nations'.

In some ways, the authorities were right to see the influence of 'foreign practices' beyond the heightened use of knives, if only because so many seamen – onshore in a strange city notorious for deception and violence – routinely carried blades for self-defence. In 1863, a magistrate had to produce a notice in seven different languages specifically warning sailors against carrying knives and weapons.

Needless to say, most took no notice. On Christmas Day 1863, a local called Joseph McGrath drunkenly stepped onto the toes of a sailor from Manila – a few briefs words were exchanged, and later the Filipino stabbed McGrath to death.

For both foreigners and locals the move from 'a coarse word or a ribald jest to a kick, from a poker to a knife, is made with alarming rapidity', reported journalist Hugh Shimmin. As well as knives, guns were especially prominent in the city: in 1890 there were 251 shootings and serious woundings in Liverpool – compared with twenty-eight in Birmingham and ten in Manchester. The total for the ports of Cardiff, Hull, Southampton, Bristol and Grimsby was a combined forty-seven.

Preparing for a weekend night out in Liverpool involved more precautions than other cities: a hospital by the north end docks had two extra nurses to provide bandages every Saturday night; one corpse of a local sailor was found with his name and address tattooed onto his arm, so he could be returned to his relatives.

And, of course, this proclivity for violence was not restricted to the men. One horrified witness wrote of a fight between two Liverpool women: 'her ragged bodice was torn from her back, and then thin blood streaks showed the marks of her enemy's fingers on her naked chest. The further the combatants approached to nudity the greater was the delight of the bystanders.' Another observer wrote of how one 'ferocious Liverpool woman' armed with a rasp, 'knocked down seven men with her own hand'.

On one New Year's Day, Ann Bayland and Bridget Cowley, who shared a home on Leeds Street, stayed up drinking until 8 a.m., when the trouble began. Bayland grabbed a poker and whacked her friend about the head with it, lacerating her scalp, and then smashed a cup into her face, knocking a tooth out of her mouth and nearly cutting her top lip clean off.

A ten-year-old girl, Mary Foy, was ambushed by two teenagers called Mary Mullen and Mary Costello, who dragged her by the hair before smashing her head against the pavement. One Raglan Street woman stabbed another in the head over an argument about a handkerchief. A woman called Sarah Welsh borrowed a book – ironically called *Life of Peace* – from her neighbour, Sarah Regan, and refused to return it; Regan cracked her across the head with a poker.

When Liverpool women turned to violence, pokers were very often involved, given that nearly every household had one, and working-class women quickly learned how to use them. If a poker was not to hand, a pot or kettle full of boiling water usually was; Margaret Wilson, who lived in a brothel on Hotham Street, threw a pan of boiling water over the household servant, with no apparent motive. In another incident, an argument between Catherine Fitzgerald and Susannah Kelly ended when Kelly cracked Fitzgerald on the head with a hatchet before throwing boiling water over her.

When boiling water wasn't to hand, Liverpool women had recourse to cleaning fluids, including sulphuric acid, which was sometimes used against unfaithful or abusive husbands. One such man was Gabriel Webster, who was lying in bed after a six-week drinking session, when his wife Ann poured acid on him, leaving him badly disfigured: 'the whole skin was off the poor fellow's face', according to one witness. A seventeen-year-old girl tried to blind a cad who had left her pregnant and denied he was the father; an incident that prompted a letter to a local newspaper supporting the young woman.

It was less common for women to use acid against other women, but it was not unheard of, such as when a prostitute called Mary Lovell was charged with throwing acid in the face of a rival.

And when they couldn't find any weapons, Liverpool women were quick to use their teeth. Mary Ann Douglas bit off a four-inch strip of flesh from the forearm of Isabella McCann, leaving the muscles and tendons exposed. Rose Ann Burns had only been out of prison a few hours when, after a celebratory boozing session with her friend Catherine O'Brien, she bit a two-inch chunk out of her mate's ear. Mary Ann MacNab was holding a baby in her arms when she was attacked by a group of women, one of whom called her an 'Orange bitch', and bit off 'the whole of the left side of the cartilage' of her nose, leaving her permanently disfigured.

Things improved after the horrors of Victorian Liverpool. But even by the 1960s, the city retained a fearsome reputation. In a 1964 music documentary, presenter Daniel Farson narrated: 'To my mind, Liverpool is the strangest of all the cities of the North . . . hard-living, hard-drinking, hard-fighting, violent, friendly and fiercely alive.'

As late as the 1970s, the everyday nature of violence can be seen in the attitude of local media to confrontations and incidents that today would provoke sustained hand-wringing about the decline of moral fibre. Two days before the 1979 general election, the comedian Ken Dodd – who was out campaigning for Margaret Thatcher's Conservatives in Speke (probably a tougher crowd than the Royal Variety) – was 'kicked, punched, pushed and kneed'. In addition, Dodd and his twelve-strong group had posters ripped from their hands and were shouted down with loudhailers that were shoved into their faces. The *Liverpool Echo*, which if this incident had happened today would no doubt headline their coverage: 'This is the moment violent yobs assault dear Doddy', instead went with: 'Ken Dodd was not tickled pink when he led a Tory showbiz campaign to Speke Market'.

For a while, this easy resource to violence was very useful to British businesses and the government. But as the need for such men to fill the forecastles of slave ships and the red tunics of the British Army declined, official attitudes changed.

At an event, just before I finished this book, I overheard someone tell someone else about a mate of his, a former drug dealer, who went to collect £20 from a baghead who owed him money. They got into a fight and the dealer stabbed said baghead in the backside, then went to stab him again, whereupon the narrator slipped, and the knife went into his heart. The lad was dead and the former drug dealer got a life sentence for murder. The narrator himself then spoke about how he, in debt to drug dealers, had to 'go work county lines', in places like Cumbria, North Wales and Cornwall. The person who was telling this story appeared as though he was one of the kindest, friendliest lads you could meet, but at the same time he was talking about being involved in all kinds of horrible behaviour over the years.

The point is, apart from some psychopaths, most of the people who find themselves caught up in violent lives could and would have been entirely different people in different circumstances. When they are given different options, they usually make different choices. The problem is that so many young men do not have these options, and never have.

Today, despite high levels of drug and alcohol use, the combined efforts of the police, local authority and other public-sector services mean Liverpool is considered one of the safest cities in England; on a Friday or Saturday night, Liverpool city centre is patrolled by only around eighty police officers (but with around 1,500 door staff – and I know who I'd rather get on the wrong side of).

High-profile crimes mean that people still think of Liverpool as somewhere where terrible things happen with a bleak regularity. But at the same time, people do not think that they themselves are in danger around Liverpudlians.

This might be why, despite the city's continued reputation for violence and criminality, it consistently polls highly in terms of friendliness. In a 2005 experiment by *Reader's Digest* magazine which gauged the 'friendliness' of various UK towns and cities based on factors such as the politeness of taxi drivers or the likelihood of receiving help from strangers, Liverpool finished in second place, just behind Newcastle.

12

ALWAYS THE VICTIMS

In the 2000s sitcom *Peep Show*, the character Mark – emblematic of a kind of generic middle-class office worker, too posh to have any cultural cachet, not posh enough to give him any real economic advantages – vies for the affections of his love interest Sophie with Jeff, a Scouser.

The rivalry between these two is a good demonstration of the place of 'the Scouser' in the class/cultural hierarchy of early twenty-first-century Britain: whereas Mark is nerdy and awkward, Jeff – despite being a fellow white-collar worker – is masculine, confident and funny.

It is implied that this is not fair; being from Liverpool gives Jeff a certain edge and masculine credibility Mark can't offer, but at the same time Mark can't criticise Jeff for being from Liverpool.

Eventually, Mark hatches a scheme to provoke Jeff into hitting him in view of the office security cameras, so he can get him fired and out of the way. Mark tempts him to violence first with some generic insults before he finally cracks: 'Stolen any good cars lately, Mr Scouser? Where's your native wit now, eh, Mr Stupid?' and Jeff headbutts him.

This outburst says a lot about the English attitude towards Scousers: they're thick, and everyone knows they are, but you can't say it; they actually do love to thieve, but again you can't say this; they all think they are hilarious, when actually they are not, and if you point this out they will kick off due to (ironically) their poor sense of humour.

And of course, saying that we're stupid and thieves is still more sayable than the one thing that you definitely can't ever say, or make reference to.

This is by no means confined to people who might be expected to make jokes about gypsies or foreigners or whatever, and it crops up in expected places. As early as 1982, an editorial in the left-wing *Daily Mirror* argued that 'they should build a fence around [Liverpool] and charge admission, for sadly it has become a "showcase" of everything that has gone wrong for Britain's major cities'.

A year earlier, at the time of the Toxteth riots, the *Daily Star* – now better known for its wacky pieces on lettuce and such – published an article on an eleven-year-old girl, Sharon Walker, who was alleged to have been behind a spate of crime and anti-social behaviour, featuring a photo of her with the headline 'Big, Black and Really Nasty'.

By 1995, left-wing journalist Ian Jack could write in the *Guardian* of how the Pier Head, 'swamped by mountains of rubbish left by striking municipal workers' made Liverpool seem like 'the personification of civic squalor', while the Anglican cathedral, 'marooned in an urban free-fire zone more like the South Bronx than anything in an English city, was witness to decay on a frightening scale'.

A year after that, Peter Popham wrote in the *Independent*: 'Liverpool, it seems, has succumbed to its unequalled talent for self-dramatisation. In response to a succession of petty firearm attacks, almost exclusively involving gangland figures and causing minimal harm to the innocent, they have wheeled out a force worthy of a role in *Terminator 3*.' Another article in that newspaper, entitled 'Scouse Equals Louse in Genteel Bournemouth', described how the relocation of hundreds of Liverpudlians to the Dorset town had led to the UK's first ever town-centre CCTV cameras and the local football league introducing a new rule of a maximum of five Scousers per team.

Before becoming better known as host of *The Weakest Link*, Anne Robinson, herself from the Merseyside town of Crosby, only a few miles north of Liverpool, wrote that the Kirkby area of the city 'made Alcatraz look like the Park Lane Hilton'. (When I appeared on an episode of *The Weakest Link* aged nineteen, after asking me what I did and where I went to university, Robinson asked me if there were many other Scousers in Cambridge to go out robbing cars with.)

Why is it that so many people hate Scousers? I suppose one reason is that you've got to hate someone.

No one is free from prejudice. As Morrissey sang, 'It's so easy to laugh, it's so easy to hate' – and on this topic he really knows what he's talking about. Finding pleasure in stereotypes and taking the piss out of certain groups is enjoyable, and as it's become less acceptable to do this with women, gays, foreigners, gypsies, ethnic minorities and disabled people, perhaps it's inevitable that there will be more criticism of liminal groups such as Scousers. (And perhaps people with things like Autism Spectrum Disorder, ADHD and dyslexia – in which case I am doubly fucked.)

As journalist Rod Liddle wrote of his experiences with call centre staff: 'Somehow I feel less bad about being abusive to, say, a Scouser, after he's failed utterly to sort out my problem, than some bloke in Delhi. [And only] partly because I worry that the Indian bloke will think I'm racist if I tell him he's a witless idiot.'

So if someone or something has to be hated, why should Scousers and the city of Liverpool fill such a role for so many British people? (Or at least the English people; Scottish and Welsh people usually don't have the same attitudes. As a Liverpool woman transplanted to Glasgow told me recently, up there being Scouse is an asset, as you 'sort of get a pass for being English'.)

Assumptions around and insults levelled at Liverpool and Liverpudlians are different from those aimed at Scottish, Welsh or Irish people. Similarly, there is not the same attitude to people from other northern cities such as Newcastle or Manchester.

But then why is there such a clear sense in the English imagination of what a Scouser is like and what you can reasonably assume of them?

Maybe Scottish and Welsh people are too varied; although there're stereotypes around tight-fisted Scots or sheep-bothering Welshmen, Scottish and Welsh people are assumed in the English popular imagination to have a greater variety in terms of class, accent and attitude than Scousers. And just as anti-Irish sentiment was abating in the 1990s, Liverpool was obtaining its new political association.

In terms of other English cities, it is usually tough to tell from somebody's accent exactly where they come from and what you can assume about them – and the geographical boundaries of most places are too confusing in any case. Is someone from Bury a Mancunian, to whom you can safely apply any stereotypes you might have about that city? What about someone from Rochdale? Or Oldham? For most southern English people these places may as well be on the moon for all they know about them. Likewise, most English people know fuck all about the difference between a Geordie and a Mackem and care even less. But they do think that they know about Liverpool.

After the murder of James Bulger, 1,086 people wrote into the *Echo* expressing condolences and sympathy. Commenting on this, the journalist Jonathan Margolis wrote that the city was 'getting off' on mourning, adding that 'like blacks in the USA, Scousers are now on the proscribed list. You publicly find fault with them at your peril.'

In fairness to Margolis, he later apologised for his words, and claimed that the response to his article gave him an insight into the extent of anti-Scouse sentiment, writing that the piece 'seemed to release a Pandora's box of cold loathing', with many self-professed liberals and left-wingers congratulating him for 'sticking it to those whingeing Scousers'.

The point about whingeing is important, because it is not just that people from Liverpool are assumed to be impoverished thieves, we are also meant to have an insuperable sense of grievance. What some people find most objectionable is that we complain about being criticised.

This is clearly expressed when football supporters, in reference to Hillsborough, Heysel and other tragedies, chant: 'Always the victims, it's never your fault.'

After Hillsborough, as often happens in response to these types of tragedies – when people don't know what to do, can't comprehend what has happened, and are filled with devastation for the bereaved and a secret relief that they don't number among them – people make whatever little gestures they can such as lighting candles and laying flowers.

None of this impressed the playwright Alan Bennett, who confided to his diary the next day: 'It would be Liverpool, that sentimental, self-dramatising place.'

This quote by Bennett – as well as another couple of diary entries on Hillsborough – appear quite a bit when people are citing cases of Scousephobia. They are less likely to quote the words that followed, when he rebuked himself, and noted that, watching the news coverage, he was 'brought up short by seeing footage of a child brought out dead, women waiting blank-faced at Lime Street and a father meeting his two sons off the train, his relief turned to anger at the sight of their smiling faces, cuffing and hustling them away from the cameras'.

This second part is important, because so many of us, if we're honest, in response to a tragedy that has yet again struck a certain group of people, find ourselves silently raging that it *would* be them, and don't they milk it, and isn't it infuriating that you can't say anything because then *you're* the bigot? But then it's never long until we see or hear something that floods us with shame.

It's revealing that even – and perhaps especially – people who are capable of sensitivity and empathy still had this instinctive reaction to Hillsborough.

It's strange just how much of the criticism of Liverpool is not about the fact that terrible things happen there, but that our response is unbecoming. Two weeks after the Bulger murder, the left-wing journalist Ian Jack reported of the public grief and trauma in the city that, 'as we have come to expect over the past decade, it is a city of amazing scenes'.

In the article, Jack used the Bulger murder as an opportunity for a broader diatribe against the city, arguing that Liverpool had 'lost everything' and was 'dying'. He claimed the town had wilfully separated itself from the rest of the country, and that providing 'theatre' was its 'last function in British life'.

While he conceded that children were no more likely to be murdered on Merseyside than anywhere else, Jack noted that 'only Liverpool, it seems, has the capacity to turn a deep but very particular and personal tragedy into a communal wake. At Liverpool football club the crowd and the players observed a minute's silence last Saturday. At the New Strand shopping centre the banks of flowers grew daily. And everywhere people talked of the offence and the shame to their city, their community.'

Referencing a remark by then Knowsley MP George Howarth that the disturbance at the court appearance of the accused killers 'does not help the cause of Merseyside', Jack interpreted this as yet another insinuation that 'fate had unfairly picked on them once again'.

What does it say that such a common reaction to tragedy affecting the city is to complain that we mourn distastefully? Why, in response to horrific events, do people risk their reputation by writing in national newspapers that the grieving is a bit gauche? Or, more pertinently, why are they confident that there would be no such risk to their reputations, and they could write it freely, because it was, after all, only what many people were secretly thinking?

Probably all of this is some kind of displacement activity, to avoid thinking of horrible things and our own mortality. In his autobiography, the novelist Graham Greene recalled how as a much younger man he had lain in a hospital bed with appendicitis, and a ten-year-old boy in the next bed had suddenly died. When the child's parents arrived, screens were put up around his bed and the other young patients distracted themselves, apart from Greene, who watched and listened to the boy's mother 'uttering the banalities she must have remembered from some woman's magazine, a genuine grief that could communicate only in clichés'.

I still remember the shock of recognition from reading that quote, because it's how I personally always assumed that people respond to grief, saying the things that bereaved people on telly and films say. I thought I was the only one who'd had this thought – and I didn't realise that someone else would have actually committed it to print.

But I think this quote by Greene sums up why so many people hate Scousers: their detractors have an instinctive aversion to gaucheness, to public grief, to overt expressions of emotion. But of course, just as it was Greene who should have been ashamed of himself, not the grieving mother looking down on her ten-year-old's cooling corpse, so too should purveyors of anti-Scouse hatred; there is a darkness and a sadness within them that they need to come to terms with.

Ironically, the word 'victim' is a fairly common Liverpudlian insult.

Although heard less frequently in recent years – like other traditional slurs such as 'grass', it seems to be losing ground to the all-conquering 'Tory' – it is usually levelled at someone who is pathetic, weak and unable to stand up for themselves.

Piss-taking, sometimes of the cruellest kind, is absolutely central to Liverpudlian humour. A ruthless, take-no-prisoners attitude commonly found in schoolkids and teenagers is maintained on Merseyside well into middle age and beyond.

In the 1850s, some of the more notorious wretches on the Liverpool streets had their own cruel nicknames: one person who had one leg twisted over the other was popularly known as 'Number 4'; another person whose arms and legs didn't work and was forced to squirm along the floor was called the 'Serpent'; and 'the Seal' was the name given to a woman with stunted arms and legs.

Will Sergeant recalls when one girl in his class requested to leave the lesson to go to the toilet, the teacher refused, and the girl eventually fainted and pissed herself on the floor. For the rest of her time in the school, over the next few years, any comment she made was greeted with 'piss off' or the like.

This constant, never-ending piss taking (no pun intended) is not unique to Liverpool, but it has an unusually important place in the character of the city.

Although victimhood and vulnerability can themselves bring about hate, what really provokes venom is when someone does not act like a victim, but instead keeps their head high and maintains their pride. If they accept defeat and ask for help, it's easier to forgive and harder to hate. Refusing to do so provokes open season.

When people are roundly despised, and yet do not take any 'lessons' from that, much less respond with meek acquiescence, then they are hated even more.

There are a surprising number of similarities between Scousers and Israelis: both are loud, emotional and family oriented. Both have a bookish, poetic minority which is massively overrepresented in portrayals by outsiders. Both sets of women have a preference for long garish nails, hair extensions and lip fillers. (Although it has to be said that Israeli women wear a lot less make-up than Liverpool women; my wife said that when she met my cousins for the first time she kept expecting Ru Paul to appear and tell one of them to sashay away.) Both sets of men are proudly philistine, valuing football, sports, physical strength and shagging prowess.

But perhaps the greatest similarity is that the more they are roundly despised by outsiders, the more they grow in confidence that they must be doing something right. Criticisms by outsiders do not cut deeply; in a way that is difficult for outsiders to understand, their criticisms and opinions mean less than nothing.

Perhaps this is why the animosity towards Liverpool increased just as the city's fortunes declined, and why people were especially keen to put the boot in when they were increasingly given the opportunity from the 1980s onwards.

And it has to be said that some of this is our own fault. With the success of various Scouse comedians, footballers, singers, actors and so on over the past fifty or sixty years, and the fact that we tend to be very noticeably from Liverpool, it makes it seem as though we're everywhere.

Back in the 1990s, Alan Bennett complained that Scousers 'had the insolence of the artist's model', that we 'have figured in too many plays and have a cockiness that comes from being told too often that they and their city are special'. 'They all have the chat,' Bennett continued, 'and it laces every casual encounter . . . They are more like Cockneys than Lancashire people and it gets me down . . . Every Liverpudlian seems a comedian, fitted out with smart answers, ready with the chat and anxious to do his little verbal dance.'

As well as this, there is a deliberate 'leaning into' certain stereotypes. If people are going to assume certain offensive things about you, sometimes the best payback is to live up to these assumptions.

As this book has shown, there are some stereotypes around people from Liverpool that have more than a little basis in fact. But there are some accusations thrown at the city that are unfair and wildly inaccurate.

First among these is the idea of enjoying 'wallowing' in victimhood. In fact, Liverpool, despite its recently acquired socialist politics, is somewhere where weakness is ruthlessly punished, where it is very important not to be seen as a victim.

And despite the trope about us not being able to take a joke, people from Liverpool are ready to criticise the city, even if they do it in a hushed voice. Even Tony Nelson – former docker, trade union activist and now manager of the Casa – conceded to the journalist Simon Hughes that being from Liverpool could be 'a bit insular' and even 'a bit of a cult to be honest with you'.

And plenty of people from Liverpool are more than happy to live up to Scouse stereotypes and brag about doing so. As the former football hooligan Andy Nicholls wrote of one European away to Amsterdam:

> We travelled on the Monday night and it was the usual Scousers on Tour: card schools, ale, rob the duty free, smoke the odd spliff and round the night off with a scuffle with your best mates, great days. It sounds like stereotyping at its worse but that is how it was, and always will be. Harry Enfield has made a fortune out of the sketches mimicking Scousers. I bet it was the easiest money he ever made, as the research into it could have been done in one night away with Everton or Liverpool.

Easy for him to say, you might think: he's never been told by some obnoxious twat to 'calm down, calm down' due to the fact that his interactions with non-Scousers have generally been as part of a mob of football hooligans wielding Stanley knives.

But as well as people like Nicholls, there are lots of people who both take part in stereotypical 'Scouse' behaviour *and* still take umbrage when people from Liverpool are characterised as acting in this way (which is in some ways the most Scouse thing of all).

But the real resentment comes from people who have never behaved in this way, but who are lumped together with the worst scallies anyway. The sociologist William Julius Wilson once argued that there is a big difference between the experience of the black American middle class, who encounter prejudice as part of their competition with white people for professional development, and poor or working-class black people who might experience racism in all kinds of ways, but usually not in the form of snide innuendo from their middle-class white colleagues.

If you are from a middle-class area of Newcastle or Glasgow and go to a fancy university and/or move to London to work in a professional field, you are much more sensitive to being mocked for your accent and tastes. Perhaps especially because you have the double bind of being called 'posh' or are accused of selling out when you go back home. In contrast, people from the roughest parts of those cities couldn't care less about what the middle classes think of them.

There is a similar thing with anti-Scouse prejudice. Proper scallies couldn't care less about it because they have their own set of values to try to live up to. But those who are more likely to meet people from outside Liverpool – on holiday, at university or in a professional context – understandably resent them thinking that they are ignorant thieves because of where they happen to come from.

But given that people also take the piss out of posh accents, is this any different? I think one key difference is that when people imitate and laugh at 'posh' accents, it is a sort of coping mechanism; the implicit understanding is that class privilege and advantage will never change, hence it is only fair enough to take the piss out of their accents and mannerisms – a kind of modern version of the medieval festivals of misrule, when traditional hierarchies could be briefly upturned.

Powerless prejudice is disagreeable, but ultimately harmless – the 'sigh of an oppressed creature'; prejudice combined with power, however, or a prejudice that has some real effect on someone, is a different matter.

But at the same time, it is not the case that anyone making such an impersonation – of a Geordie, or Glaswegian, or Scouser, or of a black south London accent – is inherently malevolent, classist and racist. When people take the piss out of 'working-class' accents, be it Scouse or

Geordie or Multicultural London English or whatever, while they might be theoretically doing this from a position of power, they do not see it like this.

In fact, they implicitly believe they are doing it from a position of weakness; they feel threatened, by the other persons physical potency, or their cultural cachet, or the fact that 'you can't say anything any more', and this is their revenge.

Of course, being from Liverpool and having spent most of the past fifteen years living in London or Cambridge, I am no stranger to hearing my own accent impersonated, albeit usually in a friendly way. But what is going on here?

When someone says to me, usually drunk and their face brimming with hatred, 'I'm Stevie Gerrard! Calm down, calm down!', it is manifestly obvious that this is a person out of control, disgracing themselves in front of a crowd of people. It is equally clear that they deserve sympathy.

I was once with a mate outside the Coach and Horses pub in Soho. A woman I was talking to, professional-looking, late thirties to early forties, with what appeared to be work colleagues, started doing exactly this. I have no idea what set her off. But the hatred in her face really shocked and confused me.

She seemed to me like someone worn out by life, showing their depression and desperation through outdated class references that no longer exist. With these people, it's not as though they are genuinely bigoted or seriously believe they are somehow superior, more that they are ground down and desperate, like everyone else, and this is how it is communicated, in the same way someone else might do it through crime, or drugs, or online abuse, or self-harm, or suicide.

Even more than prejudice and bigotry in general, anti-Scouse hatred says a lot about the people behind it. If overt emotion infuriates you, if the worse you can say about people is that their grieving is overly gauche, then you need to take a hard look at yourself.

It could be that the period of anti-Scouse prejudice, which only really got going in the 1980s, reflects an important part in the history of the UK, in its transition from the imperial pomp of the 1940s and '50s, through the neoliberalism and privatisation of the 1980s, to whatever we become in the future.

The negative concepts around 'the Scouser' started to develop shortly after the idea that white Britons were not innately superior to anyone else became commonplace. Those English people who hate Scousers and invoke lazy clichés, would do well to find another basis for their self-esteem and sense of self. Because, to paraphrase Richard Nixon, one day they won't have Scousers to kick around any more.

INTERLUDE 11

The Scouse Diaspora

As with Irish pubs, there are few cities in the world where you cannot find at least one Scouser – in fact, you can usually find them in an Irish pub. There are plenty of pretty obvious reasons why there should be such a widespread Scouse diaspora, notably the city's seafaring history, the long-established tradition of moving around to find work and the economic decline of the second half of the twentieth century. At the same time, Liverpudlians abroad often remain distinct from their hosts, like earlier diasporic groups such as Armenians, Lebanese and Jews.

The 'marketability' of being a Liverpudlian, much like the distinctiveness of the city, is a recent phenomenon, which paradoxically arose around the same time as the city's economic decline.

Much of this is to do with the Beatles, who presented the country with a new type of Liverpudlian. The legendary DJ John Peel, although a Wirralite, remembers that going to America during the 1960s: 'Any American who had heard of Liverpool,' he wrote, 'assumed that if I wasn't related to the Beatles, then I must be a good pal of theirs at least. I never told them I was, but I never told them I wasn't either ... As soon as I started to speak ... in what they thought quite wrongly was a Liverpool accent, they just went mad, girls shouting "Touch me, touch me" and being sick and everything.'

The ambiguity of Peel, of being Scouse enough to have the cultural cachet, while having enough in the way of middle-class capital and resources to get himself into certain positions, is something that has been exploited by many middle-class ex-pat Scousers over the past few decades. We are authentic-sounding enough to fool those that can't tell the difference, but without as many of the disadvantages of a truly working-class Scouser.

Before the Beatles, there was a rich history of entertainers emerging from the city, but they all toned down or deliberately lost their accents. The actor Rex Harrison, who played Professor Henry Higgins in *My Fair Lady*, was originally from Huyton – surely the only example of someone from Huyton teaching elocution, fictionally or otherwise. For him and other actors of this era, such as Derek Nimmo, Glenda Jackson, Rita Tushingham or Leonard Rossiter, being from Liverpool was incidental – it was not part of their package or appeal. Ken Dodd is a prime example of this: when the Beatles supported him in 1961, he tried to get them thrown off the bill, as they clashed with his conservative values and aesthetic.

Since the '60s, however, many people from the city, from Cilla Black to Paul O'Grady, have been able to use their 'Liverpudlianess' to carve out careers in the entertainment industry.

Notably, many of these post-war Scouse celebrities were Tories, such as Cilla Black, Jimmy Tarbuck and Kenny Everett (who once spoke at the Conservative party conference). Not shire Tories of the old school, but instead typical of the developing 'New Right', who spoke about the virtues of hard graft and pulling yourself up by your bootstraps, while sneering at the liberalism of the 1960s.

(Having said that, Tarbuck did not necessarily practise what he preached – the actor Terry Thomas was friends with Bessy Braddock and once did a benefit gig in the city; he lost his trademark cigarette holder, and found that a young Tarbuck had swiped it.)

The likes of Tarbuck and Everett were also performing for a new kind of Middle England that did not have the rigid class hierarchy of the pre-war world, but despite (or perhaps because of) this, was even more given to snobbery.

If the first wave of post-war Scouse celebrities deployed traditional snobbery, and boosted Thatcher, by the 1980s this had been reversed, with students, squatters and Trustafarians embracing Scousers as some kind of 'Magic Proles'. In the 1980s you could buy Yosser Hughes T-shirts in Carnaby Street, and groups called the Black Stuff Boys and Yosser's Gang both released novelty singles.

This idea of the Scouser as a 'Magic Prole' was popularised by film and television, and especially in the films of Ken Loach. Many of Loach's pictures focus explicitly on the exploits of the Liverpool working class, such as his 1968 documentary *The Golden Vision*, which follows Everton supporters as they attend matches across the country, and the following year's *The Big Flame*, which told the story of 10,000 dockers occupying the Liverpool docks in a 'work-in'.

When his films are not explicitly about Scousers, a common motif across various Loach movies is the working-class socialist from Liverpool with a heart of gold sorting everything out. In *Riff-Raff* (1991), set on a building site in London, Ricky Tomlinson's character provides regular diatribes against Margaret Thatcher and capitalism, and in *Land and Freedom* (1995) the protagonist David Carr is an unemployed Liverpudlian and member of the Communist Party who decides to enlist in the International Brigades to fight for the Republicans in the Spanish Civil War.

Although there's no shortage of fictional Scousers in film and TV over the last few decades, real-life Liverpudlians have to take a more circuitous route to build careers in the media. Winifred Robinson, currently host of BBC Radio 4's *You and Yours* programme, was the daughter of a docker and grew up in Norris Green as one of six children. When I spoke to her in December 2023, she remembers that her and her eldest sister Mary were the only two of the siblings to go to university. She reckons this is explained in Mary's case by her being the eldest, and therefore getting more attention. Her grandparents were very 'bookish' and her grandfather on her mother's side had a bookcase full of classics by Dickens and Austen, and when her parents were young they would look after Mary.

When Winifred was born, her parents didn't have another child for five years – probably due to medical reasons rather than a sudden acceptance of contraception. For working-class Catholics of that generation, contraception was not an option, and you'd have to accept however many children you were given – or not as it turns out. On my mum's side, my nan was one of thirteen children, and my grandad one of twelve; on my dad's side my granddad had twelve brothers and sisters and my nan eleven. And yet whereas my maternal grandparents had six children, my dad was an only child. This was highly unusual at the time and definitely not through choice – my grandparents were unable to have any more children and were probably lucky to have my dad. Nonetheless, a lot of their neighbours were quite sniffy about this, assuming that they were choosing not to have any more.

Because there was such a long gap between Winifred and her younger siblings, she was able to get more attention than otherwise would have been possible, which she credits with getting her into university. Her parents were both in trade unions and her mum was a shop steward at Littlewood's pools in Walton Hall Road. 'Originally women weren't allowed to be the pension scheme. 'She got them in,' she remembers proudly.

At the University of Liverpool, Robinson first became aware of class differences; at her grammar school it was not so explicit. (This contrasts with the memories of my grandad's sister and my mum, both of whom went to grammar schools and met people who owned horses, among other outlandish symbols of wealth.)

Robinson tells me that although there were some other people from Liverpool at university (her sister had gone to Leeds and was very homesick, so she felt Liverpool was a safer bet), there were not many. On the other hand, there were lots of people from private school who talked a lot but didn't know much; she remembers feeling sorry for them if that's what private education provided.

She made friends with a girl from an affluent London family and was invited on holiday with them to the south of France. The family had never met someone with a regional accent before, and 'treated me like a curiosity' which was 'really hurtful'.

In terms of how she ended up in journalism, Robinson says that she didn't really understand what career options were open to her: '[Like advantage], disadvantage is multilayered too. That's the problem for working-class kids: they don't know about any other professions other than doctors or teachers . . . working-class people on the telly are behind the microphone as presenters, and they are the jobs you see and know you can aspire to. You never see anyone behind the scenes', such as producers and editors and so on. (This will be familiar to many working-class kids who go to university to do non-vocational degrees (i.e. not medicine or law) and are constantly asked by family members if they want to be an English/history/philosophy teacher. After someone mentioned that she'd make a good journalist, she decided to try her hand in that profession, reasoning that if it didn't work out, she'd become a teacher.

She made a slow start in her career, mostly due to a lack of knowledge of the industry: 'If I'd had better background knowledge or better contacts, I would have got on. As it was it took a while.' The *Catholic Pictorial* gave her six months, and then the *Ormskirk Advertiser* put her on their in-house training scheme: 'It was called an apprenticeship even though you're a graduate,' she recalls. 'You come out with a qualification . . . the industry paid back then. Now students pay for their own through postgrad courses.'

Apparently, social mobility was at its peak for children born in 1958, and Robinson was born in 1957. At this point, commercial radio was expanding and there were plenty of jobs for aspiring journalists – as with teachers, civil servants and other professional careers. After a job at Red Rose radio in Preston, local radio in Birmingham and regional television in the north-west, she reached Radio 4's *Today* programme.

She recalls having been ribbed in her life: 'Are you going to steal my hubcaps, etc, but not much really. At the *Ormskirk Advertiser*, regional radio and telly there were lots of people not unlike me. More like people from grammar school, their parents may have been teachers or whatever.'

Around her there were working-class people in positions of power, like Rod Liddle and Roger Mosley, but she was told at the start of her career that 'you'll never work outside of the north with an accent like that' and was advised to 'to get rid of it from your whole life. Otherwise, when you're stressed it'll come out.' While Robinson had long lost her scouse accent by the time she was working on the *Today* programme, she kept her 'flat Northern vowels' – a conscious decision.

Adrian Chiles was the first journalist she remembers hearing on the BBC with a regional accent. She thinks that to this day, having an accent of any kind is associated with being uneducated.

When she started on Radio 4, she was sent abusive letters in the post. One told her that 'your accent is an affront to educated people everywhere', that it was 'OK for a comic turn' but not suitable for serious broadcasting. There was, she says, 'completely naked class prejudice', reflecting the idea that 'certain jobs belong to the elite, and if you can get one, the job is worth less'. But overall, you 'had to accept this if you wanted to get on, otherwise you wouldn't have'.

She covered issues such as gangs in Liverpool, HIV in Edinburgh, riots in Drumcree and drug dealing in Moss Side, Manchester. She thinks her background helped her with these types of stories, as too often with middle-class journalists:

> all the poor people have to be good. People in trouble financially – it always has to be through no fault of their own. I'm not afraid of asking disadvantaged people difficult questions because I know they can answer them.
>
> Those stories always attracted me: what happened to those people at the bottom? Why did they become lawless? ... In Northern Ireland, journalists would go out to the suburbs. The war was going on in these collections of little streets – little streets like Breck Road. Exactly like Breck Road. [And] everyone knew someone who'd been murdered in a horrible way. If you don't recruit working-class people, you don't have people who feel comfortable going to these places, or even think of going in the first place.

Likewise, Paul Du Noyer thinks being from the city definitely helped his career: 'Liverpool has the cachet of Memphis ... being a music journalist from Liverpool was not a handicap but a benefit.' His first boss at the *NME* told him how jealous he was, 'to have roots like that, to have that music heritage'.

He has lived in London for many years, and when I ask him what he makes of being back in Liverpool, and what his impressions are of how it's changed, he tells me that a lot of the way he thinks about the two places

> is binary, [of the] contrast between here and London. In fact, I get into a deep depression when I arrive back from one or the other; I always need a few days to get used to either place and stop missing the other one ... In many ways, they feel like outposts

of two different countries, and correspond with two different parts of the brain. I associate London with thin people, generally younger, moving quickly, expensively dressed, whereas I associate Liverpool with older people moving slowly, overweight.

He also speaks of the dual identity of people like him (and me): 'In London I'm *Boys from the Blackstuff*; in Liverpool I'm *Brideshead Revisited*.' There were some awkward adjustments when he went to university at the London School of Economics:

> My accent was much stronger then, I'd just turned eighteen. It was a wood-panelled room, booklined, an elderly tweedy old tutor. Five or six long-haired students. Talking about whatever we'd read that week, I referred to the *book*, and I said it the way I'd always said, the way everyone around me said it [rhyming with 'puke'], and there was this awkward pause. The old tutor, he wasn't even taking the piss, he genuinely didn't know what I meant, and he said "I'm sorry, Paul, what was that?" Everyone else was supressing a giggle. I must have gone bright red.

Like a lot of other Scouse emigrants into the world of the middle class, Du Noyer 'consciously adapted' with certain words. If you listen to Wayne Rooney's earliest interviews, he sounds exactly what all other teenagers from Croxteth sounded like in the mid-2000s; listen to him now and you'd be hard pressed to say that he was definitely from Liverpool. Others might not have to make such conscious choices but do it instinctively, depending on the occasion.

And yet others, from more middle-class backgrounds, went the other way. John Lennon famously put on an accent he didn't really have to burnish his prole made good self-image. Maybe something like this is still happening; when I watched the early series of *The Great British Bake*

Off around ten years ago, I had no idea that Paul Hollywood was from Liverpool – but I can certainly hear it now. Comparing Hollywood's accent from 2013 and 2023 makes me wonder if at the earlier stage in his career it was better for him to tone down his accent, and then he could relax back into it, just like the Beatles before him.

In a different way from the first generations of Scouse ex-pats elsewhere in the UK, there has been a recent rise in 'professional ex-Scousers': people who deliberately discard certain aspects of that heritage (and emphasise others) to advance their career.

Perhaps surprisingly, these are increasingly found in the ranks of the Conservative party. Back in September 2023, during a scandal over many British schools being constructed with dodgy concrete that at any moment might collapse on the heads of their students, the then Education Secretary Gillian Keegan was caught on a hot mic complaining: 'Does anyone ever say, you know what? You've done a fucking good job because everyone else has sat on their arse and done nothing. Any sign of that, no?'

The media focus on this incident briefly distracted attention from the scandal itself; in a debate in the House of Commons, Labour's Diana Johnson joked that 'if she is really short of cash in her department, perhaps one option might be to bring in a swear box to raise a few bob?' Standing up at the dispatch box, Keegan responded that 'as a Scouser I have a bit of a higher bar' when it comes to swearing.

If we exclude prime ministers, then since 2010 there have been as many people from Liverpool (Esther McVey, Nadine Dorries, Thérèse Coffey, Kit Malthouse and Gillian Keegan) in the Cabinet as Old Etonians. Another Scouser, Jake Berry, served as chair of the Conservative party and held various frontbench roles.

In these cases, they've used their city's reputation to further their careers in Conservative politics, by stressing their working-class routes or using humour to deflect criticism.

CONCLUSION

What Can We Learn from Liverpool?

During the time I was writing this book, Keir Starmer's Labour won a landslide victory that made recent concerns about the Labour party's alienation from the 'working class' seem moot.

But since many voters were motivated more by a hatred for the Conservatives than love for Labour, and since the base of the party will remain the educated middle classes, the Labour party – just like the political left across the globe – still has a job to do to win back the support of non-graduates, manual workers and more socially conservative voters.

Since Liverpool features plenty of all three, and yet has the safest Labour seats in the whole country, it's worth asking whether the success of the left in Liverpool can be replicated in other places with similar demographics.

But there is a defined role for 'the Scouser' in politics, just as in football, music and other areas, and it's hard to see how its unusual political culture might be transplanted to other British cities.

Labour's success in Liverpool means that the broader left can project all kinds of things on the city but, in reality, it is doubtful whether people in Liverpool are any more welcoming to immigrants or supportive of trans rights or freedom for Palestine than their demographic equivalents elsewhere in the UK. Labour's success in the city is not exactly despite its turn towards identity issues and its move to become the party of graduates and urban progressives over the past two decades, but it is certainly not because of it; Labour's dominance on Merseyside owes much more to class and material issues, civic solidarity and anti-Toryism. But despite the peculiar local conditions, the party's success here can still offer some lessons for its fight to win back working-class votes elsewhere in the UK.

And the politics, attitude and sense of solidarity in Liverpool provides some important lessons that are particularly applicable to people today: pride comes before a fall; no one is an island.

So much of modern life and the modern economy encourages us to think of ourselves as autonomous agents, masters of our own destiny; listening to music on our headphones, sequestered from the world, face in our phone, ignoring those around us.

People save (or try to save), hire personal trainers, start 'side hustles', build their personal 'brand'. Sometimes, if you are doing well, you feel like a superhero. All it takes is one slip, one misfortune, and you realise how vulnerable you are, how dependent on other people.

Although this book has chronicled decline, violence and criminality, it is full of positive lessons that we can learn from the city of Liverpool: its sense of humour and optimism, its rich and varied culture, its ambition and enterprise, and its sense of solidarity.

Although there are many problems with its economy and still a great deal of mismanagement, there are lessons for similar cities in how to use tourism, culture, education and the private sector to fuel regeneration. (The conversion of the Tate sugar refineries to Tate art galleries serving as a metaphor for the transformation of the Liverpool and broader UK economy.)

If the between-two-places Scouser is such a well-established type, and seeing that this is the case for more and more people – immigrants, ex-pats, digital nomads, etc – could the professional Scouser be an archetype?

Du Noyer once wrote of John Lennon that he 'was among the first Englishmen to join the long flight from middle-class manners that would epitomise the age. As one of the Beatles, he would hasten that process.'

A generation later, the Scouse comedian Alexei Sayle was one of the few (maybe only) working-class voices among the new comedians of the 1980s, but he knew his audience was not northern working-men's clubs; he was one of many upwardly mobile young people, distanced from their parents and childhood homes, yet still not comfortable in the middle class. Eventually, through sheer weight of numbers, the teachers, social workers, media types and sundry professionals in that generation would transform the British middle-class into something like its own image.

Today, by contrast, we have a downwardly mobile middle class that will not have the same levels of affluence as their parents; who have university degrees that do not give the boost in incomes they once did but saddle them with debt; and who struggle to buy a home of their own.

I was born during probably the nadir of Liverpool's fortunes, in 1987. Since then, the British economy has been transformed, and the city's too; while there has been a great deal of economic growth since the late '80s, much of this is based on insecure, casualised labour.

If this is the future for many in the UK economy, then Liverpool provides a good example of what to expect, both in terms of the city's past, its present and its future.

John Belchem is *the* historian of Liverpool. I remember encountering his work over a decade ago and feeling a thrill of reading serious academic treatment of the history of my city. Moving to Liverpool in the 1980s, he has now become as close to an honorary Scouser as it's possible to be for a non-footballer.

Now Professor Emeritus at the University of Liverpool, when I spoke to him in November 2023, I was keen to get his non-academic opinions on what has changed in the almost forty years he's lived in the city.

There was a 'genuine feeling of depression in the eighties,' he tells me, 'that's gone completely now. I've been retired ten years and wouldn't think of going anywhere else. It's got itself back . . . it's still a proper city' in terms of its distinct and idiosyncratic ways, but it's now doing better in terms of economic growth and investment, in fact it's 'done better than many other cities' in that respect.

One reasons for this is that Liverpool is 'lucky it didn't knock down so much [in terms of its Victorian and Georgian architecture]. It was so bloody poor in the second half of the twentieth century it couldn't afford to.'

This means that the city is lucky in that it still has so much of its tangible heritage and built environment intact – unlike Manchester or Birmingham, for example, where so much of the city centre was knocked down and hardly any remains.

Liverpool by contrast has such a surfeit of classic architecture that it has appeared as Russian cities in *Red October* and *Yentl*, Hitler's Berlin in *Indiana Jones and the Last Crusade*, 1920s Paris in *Chariots of Fire*, and Gotham City and 1970s New York in various films.

'And then the intangible thing came in,' continues Belchem, 'the idea of the Scouser and all the rest of it'. But it 'used to be without', now it has more. Ultimately though 'it is a port city. Always more risky, dirty, unhealthy but more fun.'

This impression is confirmed by Robinson. When I asked her the same question about changes in the past decades, she mentions the 'waterfront, the money pouring in. It's been a massive transformation'. She remembers that all 'those places at the back of Bold Street used to be abandoned warehouses. Now there's been amazing gentrification. And they put the council housing right in among it on Parliament Street, so there has not been the kind of social segregation you get with other urban regeneration. Same with tourism: I used to think as a young woman, "Why are there not tourists around here?"; there are now.'

Du Noyer takes a similar line but is perhaps a bit more sceptical. There are 'probably more bar stools than there ever have been,' he points out, but 'bars in an American sense. Places where you can buy a beer. Places to buy coffee' – that's the kind of globalisation you can experience anywhere. 'Liverpool pubs – as I understood them – are dying out, especially in the suburbs.'

This is similar to the port: it is more profitable than ever through container shipping, but employing far fewer people. The numbers and growth are saying one thing, but this does not necessarily transfer into how people feel.

'It does seem more multicultural now,' Du Noyer adds:

> Growing up, I was not conscious of racial difference. I was pure north Liverpool. My family background and schooling were in Bootle, Everton, Anfield, etc. You never got anyone that wasn't white; never got anyone who wasn't Irish, to be honest. I had never met a black person, never met a Jewish person, till I went to London. One of the things I learned as a teenager in the seventies was that there were black lads on the hill [Upper Parliament Street] who didn't come into town unless they were willing to risk it. Now I notice women in headscarves in Walton. And a lot more students.

Traditionally, Liverpool found it hard to hang on to students once they had graduated, but with house prices in London and the south-east unaffordable for many, combined with an increase in remote working, this is starting to change.

In this heavily mobile future, the experience of Liverpool and Liverpudlians can also offer lessons. Nearly all of my friends' partners are from outside the UK. Maybe that's because we were all a little too weird for local women, but foreigners can't tell the difference. Many friends live outside the city: Dubai, London, Barcelona, Toronto, Neston. My brother lives in Texas.

The long history of people moving for work and the experience of casualised labour means that young Liverpudlians today are well adapted for the new economy.

Amid the optimism, there are many reasons for gloom. When twenty-one Chinese people died picking cockles on Morecambe beach in 2004, they and seventy others were found to be living in squalor in four houses in Kensington. This is a reminder of another parallel between Liverpool's past and the current and future economy: forced labour.

If there is one overriding lesson of the story of Liverpool, it is that wealth should not come at any price. From the slave trade to cocaine, some in the city have grown rich on the suffering of others. A city that has survived so much tells us of the importance of solidarity and working together.

ACKNOWLEDGEMENTS

Special thanks to my agent Matthew Hamilton and Andreas Campomar, Holly Blood and everyone at Little Brown UK. Many thanks to all the people I spoke to in connection with the book, including but not limited to John Belchem, David Jeffery, Winifred Robinson, Ean Flanders and Michael McDonough. Thanks in particular to Paul Du Noyer and Andrew Lees, the authors of probably the two best single-volume histories of the city (until now!) And thanks to Michael Macilwee, whose book, *The Liverpool Underworld*, has been used extensively throughout, and is highly recommended to anyone who wants to read up more on the city.

BIBLIOGRAPHY AND
FURTHER READING

Gary Armstrong and Richard Giulianotti, *Football Cultures and Identities*, Macmillan, 1999

Diana E. Ascott, Fiona Lewis and Michael Power, *Liverpool 1660–1750: People, Prosperity and Power*, Liverpool University Press, 2006

Tony Barnes, Richard Elias and Peter Walsh, *Cocky: The Rise and Fall of Curtis Warren, Britain's Biggest Drug Baron*, Milo Press, 2000

Brad Beaven, '"One of the Toughest Streets in the World": Exploring Male Violence, Class and Ethnicity in London's Sailortown, c.1850–1880', *Social History*, no. 46, 2021, pp. 1–21

John Belchem, *Merseypride: Essays in Liverpool Exceptionalism*, Liverpool University Press, 2000

—, *Irish, Catholic and Scouse: the history of the Liverpool-Irish, 1800-1939*, Liverpool University Press, 2007

—, *Before the Windrush: Race Relations in 20th-century Liverpool*, Liverpool University Press, 2014

John Belchem (ed), *Liverpool 800: culture, character, and history*, Liverpool University Press, 2006

John Belchem and Neville Kirk (eds), *Languages of Labour*, Ashgate, 1997

Lucy Bland, 'White Women and Men of Colour: Miscegenation Fears in Britain after the Great War' in *Gender & History*, no. 17, 2005, pp. 29–61

Adam Brown (ed), *Fanatics!: Power, Identity and Fandom in Football*, Routledge, 1998

Tim Burrows, *The Invention of Essex: The Making of an English County*, Profile Books, 2023

Marcus Collins, '"The Age of the Beatles": Parliament and Popular Music in the 1960s', *Contemporary British History*, no. 27, 2013, pp. 85–107

Sam Davies, *Liverpool Labour: Social and Political Influences on the Development of the Labour Party in Liverpool, 1900–1939*, Keele University Press, 1996

Christine Dawe, *Liverpool's Own*, The History Press, 2008

Paul Du Noyer, *Liverpool – Wondrous Place: From the Cavern to the Capital of Culture*, Virgin Books, 2002

Tony Evans, '"The Truth", Hillsborough, the betrayal of a nation and the catalyst for letting the powerful off the hook', *Independent*, 19 April 2020

Christopher Fevre, '"Race" and Resistance to Policing Before the "Windrush Years": The Colonial Defence Committee and the Liverpool "Race Riots" of 1948', *Twentieth Century British History*, 2020, pp. 1–23

Tom Goulding, 'The rise of football hipsterism', *Cherwell*, 11 June 2012

Brian Groom, *Northerners: A History*, HarperNorth, 2022

Sheryllynne Haggerty, Anthony Webster and Nicholas J. White, *The Empire in One City?: Liverpool's Inconvenient Imperial Past*, Manchester University Press, 2008

Simon Hughes, *There She Goes: Liverpool, A City on its Own. The Long Decade: 1979–1993*, deCoubertin Books, 2019

Dan Jackson, *The Northumbrians: North-East England and Its People*, Hurst, 2019

David Jeffery, *Whatever happened to Tory Liverpool? Success, decline and irrelevance since 1945*, Liverpool University Press, 2023

Graham Johnson, *Powder Wars: The Supergrass who Brought Down Britain's Biggest Drug Dealers*, Mainstream Publishing, 2005

Lamont, R., Moss, E. & Wildman, C. 'Who Cares? Welfare and Consent to Child Emigration from England to Canada, 1870–1918', *Liverpool Law Review*, no. 41, 2020, pp. 45–65

Andrew Lees, *The Hurricane Port: A Social History of Liverpool,* Mainstream Publishing, 2011

Michael Macilwee, *The Liverpool Underworld: Crime in the City 1750–1900*, Liverpool University Press, 2011

Stuart Maconie, *Pies and Prejudice: In Search of the North*, Ebury Press, 2007

Roger Matthews, 'Regulating Street Prostitution and Kerb-Crawling: A Reply to John Lowman', *The British Journal of Criminology*, no. 32, 1992, pp. 18–22

Frank Neal, *Sectarian Violence: The Liverpool Experience, 1819–1914*, Manchester University Press, 1988

Andy Nicholls, *Scally: The Shocking Confessions of a Category C Football Hooligan*, Milo Books, 2002

Anthony Quinn, *Klopp: My Liverpool Romance*, Faber & Faber, 2020

Keith Daniel Roberts, *Liverpool Sectarianism: The Rise and Demise*, Liverpool University Press, 2017

Sonya O. Rose, 'Sex, Citizenship, and the Nation in World War II Britain', *The American Historical Review*, no. 103, 1998, pp. 1147–76

Kevin Sampson, *Awaydays*, Vintage, 1998

Will Sergeant, *Bunnyman: A Memoir*, Constable, 2021

Frank Shaw, *My Liverpool*, Wolfe Publishing, 1971

Becky Taylor, 'Immigration, Statecraft and Public Health: The 1920 Aliens Order, Medical Examinations and the Limitations of the State in England', *Social History of Medicine*, no. 29, 2016, pp. 512–533

Michael Taylor, *The Interest: How the British Establishment Resisted the Abolition of Slavery*, Vintage, 2020

Simon Warner, '"You only sing when you're winning": football factions and rock rivalries in Manchester and Liverpool', *Soccer & Society*, no. 12, 2011, pp. 58–73

INDEX

INDEX

INDEX

Misuse of Drugs Act, 227
Mitchell, John, 257
Moby, 145
Mohan, Dominic, 111
Mokaev, Muhammad, 81
monarchy, 50, 119, 180
Monroe, Marilyn, 129
Moores, David, 114
Morales, David, 145
Morecambe Bay cockle-pickers, 296
Morecroft, Sylvester, 9
Morley, Paul, 142
Morris, James, 61
Morris, John, 258
Morrissey, 269
Mosley, Roger, 286
Moss, John, 167
Mothers' Welfare Clinic, 186
Mount Pleasant, 56
Muir, Ramsay, 41, 175
Mullen, Mary, 264
Municipal Corporations Act, 213
Murray, Tony, 245

National Line, 170
National Transport Workers' Federation, 67
Nayak, Anoop, 155
Nelson, Tony, 276
Neville, Gary, 26
New Brighton, 40, 197
New Cabaret Artists' Club, 132
New Strand shopping centre, 223, 272
New York, 11–13, 40, 86, 176, 178, 192, 294
Newcastle, 8, 38, 42, 44, 57, 87, 109, 266, 270, 277
Newcastle United FC, 95, 100, 121
Newton, John, 163
Nicholls, Andy, 81, 97, 122–3, 152, 192, 208–9, 261
Nimmo, Derek, 282
Nixon, Richard, 279
NME, 139, 287
nonconformists, 55, 60, 64, 179
Norris, Steve, 54
Norris Green, 79, 100, 155, 226, 284
Nottingham Forest FC, 104–5, 115, 121
Nugent, Father James, 224, 233, 259

Oakenfold, Paul, 144
Oasis, 142, 145
Oats, Shuannah, 198
O'Brien, Catherine, 265
O'Connor, T. P., 62, 183

O'Grady, Paul, 282
Old Swan, 249–50
Oldham, 200, 270
O'Mara, Pat, 180
Operation Crayfish, 228, 234–5, 247
Orange Order, 68, 97, 177, 179–80, 182
Orchestral Manoeuvres in the Dark, 136, 138–9
Ormskirk, 34–5
Overhead Railway, 14, 87
Oxford, Ken, 191–2, 214, 261

Page, Jimmy, 135
Paisley, Bob, 96
Paisley, Captain James, 198
Palestine, 204, 292
Paradise Street, 262
Park Lane, 201
Parliament Street, 294
Parnell, Charles, 185
Parry, Rick, 114
Parry, Tim, 97
patriotism, 48–50, 69
Pattinson, Les, 152
Peacock, Elizan, 256
Pearce, Edward, 106–7
Peel, John, 106, 138, 141, 281–2
Pennefather, De Fonblanque, 62
Penny, James, 165
Peter and Gordon, 130
Peterson, Frank, 103
Phelan, Jim, 148
Philips, Johnny, 249
Pickering, Fred, 98
Picton, Sir James, 36, 41, 218
Pier Head, 1–2, 54, 148, 198, 268
Pink Floyd, 140–1
Pioneer Women's Group, 78
police
    corruption, 214, 248
    introduction of, 213–14
    racism, 190–1, 202–6, 261
Poor Law, 172–3
Pop, Iggy, 137
Popham, Peter, 268
population, 14, 17, 23, 30, 165, 167, 177–8, 192, 219–20
    black population, 203–4, 208
    density, 10, 17–18
Poulsen, Christian, 114
Power, John, 141, 143, 153, 261
Power, Michael, 44, 150, 169
Pratt-Korbel, Olivia, 119, 225

INDEX

Sex Pistols, 137
Sexton, James, 46, 70, 186–7
Shack, 141–3, 145–6
Shackleton, David, 183
Shankly, Bill, 49, 93–6, 116, 192
Sharpe, Greville, 159
Shearer, Robert, 224
Sheeran, Ed, 139
Sheffield, 96, 145, 166, 196, 226
Sheffield Wednesday FC, 98, 104–5, 109, 111
Shimmin, Hugh, 263
shipwrecks, 45, 85–6
Showers, Delroy, 246
Simpson, Paul, 152
Skelmersdale, 34
Slater, Mary, 240
Slave Compensation Act, 55
slavery and slave trade, 3, 5–6, 11, 44, 53,
    55–6, 158–67, 198–200, 210, 218, 296
Smith, Adam, 5
Smith, Alan, 91
Smith, Joan, 64–5
Smith, Mary, 198
Smith, Peter, 198
Smith, Tommy, 93, 102
Smiths, the, 142
Smithwhite, Stephanie, 251
Smyrden, Ma, 164
Society of Lovers of Old Liverpool, 4–5, 187
Somerset vs Stewart case, 199
South Sea Bubble, 161
South Yorkshire Police, 107, 110–11
Southall Neville, 97
Southampton, 51, 89, 226, 231, 263
Southampton FC, 89, 104
Southport, 2–3, 80, 99
Spanish Civil War, 70, 283
Specials, the, 137
Speke, 187, 189, 265
Spellow Hub library, 3
Stanley Dock, 224
Starmer, Keir, 83, 291
Starr, Ringo, 47, 132, 134
Steele, Murray, 61
Stock, Dr, 174
Stone Roses, 34, 141–2
Storm, Rory, 136
Strand, The, 210
Stranglers, the, 137
strike-breakers, 206–7
strikes, 23, 34, 112, 249
    Birds Eye strike (1972), 76
    dock lockout (1995–8), 70–2, 79–80

miners' strike (1984–5), 115
police strike (1918), 187
transport strike (1911), 65, 67–70, 77,
    183
Strowe, Jeff, 139
Suárez, Luis, 114–15
Suede, 142
sugar refineries, 56–7, 292
sugar trade, 157–8, 160, 166
Sun, The, 106–8, 111–13, 152
Sunday People, 36
Sutch, Screaming Lord, 74
Sutcliffe, John, 68
Syrian Arabs, 172

Taine, Hippolyte, 234
Talking Heads, 137
Tamla Motown, 135–7, 145
Tapscott, William, 172
Tarbuck, Jimmy, 282–3
Tarleton, Banastre, 60
Tarleton, John, 166
Tarleton Street, 210
Tate, Henry, 56–7
Tate & Lyle, 202
Tate galleries, 292
Taylor Report, 124
Teardrop Explodes, 136–9, 152
Teeling, William, 133
Terry, John, 115
Terry Thomas, 282
Thatcher, Margaret, 5, 23–4, 27, 71, 76, 116,
    118, 120, 140, 219, 283
Thatto Heath, 34
Theatre Royal, 147–8
Thomas, S. G., 182
Thompson, Eliza, 240
Thompson, Phil, 101, 214
Thompson, Robert, 223–5
Thomson, Basil, 240
Tilett, Ben, 67
Timpson's, 223
tobacco trade, 56, 157–8, 160, 166
Tomlinson, Ricky, 29n, 37, 128, 283
Topuria, Ilia, 81
Torside Limited, 71
Toschack, John, 95
Tottenham Hotspur FC, 100, 104–5, 208
Toxteth, 62, 72, 102, 128, 170, 180, 189–92,
    236, 244
Toxteth Park, 56, 198, 200, 233, 258
Toxteth riots, 23, 53, 86, 108, 189–92, 208,
    229, 268

311